Feature Writing for Journalists

Feature Writing for Journalists is a lively and accessible guide to all aspects of writing features for newspapers, magazines and websites. It uses copious examples from a wide range of papers, specialist and trade magazines and 'alternative' publications, as well as interviews with practitioners and case studies of journalists from the UK, Ireland and America.

Feature Writing for Journalists covers:

- What is a feature
- Knowing your market
- Developing an idea
- Writing different sorts of features, including news features, profiles, colour pieces, columns and reviews.

Sharon Wheeler is Course Leader in Print Journalism at the University of Gloucestershire. She is co-editor of *The Journalistic Imagination* (with Richard Keeble, 2007), and has contributed to *Print Journalism: A Critical Introduction* (2005) and *Questions of Identity in Detective Fiction* (2007). Sharon is editor-in-chief of http://www.reviewingtheevidence.com and is part of the blogging team at http://heydeadguy.typepad.com/heydeadguy/.

Media Skills

Edited by Richard Keeble, Lincoln University
Series Advisers: Wynford Hicks and Jenny McKay

The *Media Skills* series provides a concise and thorough introduction to a rapidly changing media landscape. Each book is written by media and journalism lecturers or experienced professionals and is a key resource for a particular industry. Offering helpful advice and information and using practical examples from print, broadcast and digital media, as well as discussing ethical and regulatory issues, *Media Skills* books are essential guides for students and media professionals.

English for Journalists
3rd edition
Wynford Hicks

Writing for Journalists
2nd edition
Wynford Hicks with Sally
Adams, Harriett Gilbert and
Tim Holmes

Interviewing for Radio
Jim Beaman

*Web Production for Writers
and Journalists*
2nd edition
Jason Whittaker

Ethics for Journalists
2nd edition
Richard Keeble

Scriptwriting for the Screen
2nd edition
Charlie Moritz

Interviewing for Journalists
2nd edition
Sally Adams, with Wynford Hicks

Researching for Television and Radio
Adèle Emm

Reporting for Journalists
Chris Frost

Subediting for Journalists
Wynford Hicks and Tim Holmes

*Designing for Newspapers and
Magazines*
Chris Frost

Writing for Broadcast Journalists
Rick Thompson

Freelancing for Television and Radio
Leslie Mitchell

Programme Making for Radio
Jim Beaman

Magazine Production
Jason Whittaker

Production Management for Television
Leslie Mitchell

Feature Writing for Journalists
Sharon Wheeler

Find more details of current *Media
Skills* books and forthcoming titles at
www.producing.routledge.com

Feature Writing for Journalists

Sharon Wheeler

 Routledge
Taylor & Francis Group

LONDON AND NEW YORK

First published 2009
by Routledge
2 Park Square, Milton Park, Abingdon, Oxon OX14 4RN

Simultaneously published in the USA and Canada
by Routledge
270 Madison Ave, New York, NY 10016

Routledge is an imprint of the Taylor & Francis Group, an informa business.

Typeset in Goudy by Keystroke, 28 High Street, Tettenhall, Wolverhampton
Printed and bound in Great Britain by TJ International, Padstow, Cornwall

British Library Cataloguing in Publication Data
A catalogue record for this book is available from the British Library

Library of Congress Cataloging in Publication Data
Wheeler, Sharon, 1963–
Feature writing for journalists / Sharon Wheeler.
p. cm. – (Media skills)
Includes bibliographical references and index.
1. Feature writing. I. Title.
PN4784.F37W44 2009
070.4′4–dc22
2008041674

ISBN10: 0–415–33634–1 (hbk)
ISBN10: 0–415–33635–x (pbk)

ISBN13: 978–0–415–33634–5 (hbk)
ISBN13: 978–0–415–33635–2 (pbk)

Contents

Acknowledgements

'Powell and the glory: he's 91 but Ivor still loves running the Bath' by Alan Hubbard. Published in the *Independent on Sunday*, 12 August 2007, pp. 74–75 © *Independent on Sunday*. Reproduced by kind permission of Independent News and Media Limited

'Over-valued properties, fake offers and aggressive sales tricks' written by Sarah Duguid, photos by Ian Brodie. Published in *Glamour*, August 2005, pp. 11–16. Sarah Duguid/Glamour © The Condé Nast Publications Ltd. Ian Brodie/Glamour © The Condé Nast Publications Ltd.

'He shouted, he cried, he begged for mercy' (lead story) by Eddie Barnes. Published in *Scotland on Sunday*, 6 August 2006, pp. 12–13. Reproduced by kind permission of The Scotsman Publications Limited.

A lot of people have helped me hugely during the preparation of this book. I'm grateful to all the busy journalists who made time to answer my questions. And special thanks (in no particular order) go to Peter Widdowson, Peter Childs, Claire Simmons, Eamon Carr, Wayne Gunn, Penny Richards, Helen Wright, postcard queen Lora Lee Templeton, Cleland Thom, the LJ crew for all those late-night chats, and the Sad Anoraks (Cornelia Read, Andi Shechter and Louise Ure) – the best virtual band in the world. And huge thanks to Aileen Storry for her endless patience. The book is dedicated to the memory of Joan Martin, the best mentor a woman could wish for.

1
Setting out your features stall

Long ago and far away when I was a cub reporter, I used to watch the features desk with ill-disguised envy. The writers all looked terribly sophisticated in their little annexe, surrounded by review copies of books and all manner of other intriguing freebies. I wanted to be a features writer so I could recline in my seat, chewing the end of my pen (yes, this was pre-computers) and spend as long as I wanted pondering well-turned phrases, hob-nobbing with celebrities and testing swanky new moisturisers.

Naturally my dreams were shattered once I discovered the deadlines were just as fierce and that a worrying number of famous people were the sort you would cross a busy motorway in rush hour to avoid – particularly when you were the twelfth journalist they'd been forced to talk to that day. Celebrities could be dull and rude, just like anyone else, and crawling around the floor of a deserted office at Lord's cricket ground looking for a phone point to file a colour piece twenty minutes past deadline with a sports editor screaming in your ear proved this feature writing lark wasn't all it was cracked up to be.

But then there were the high spots – attending big sports fixtures, having endless books and CDs to review, and discovering one of your favourite Irish musicians was an absolute delight in person. A colleague summed it up to perfection when he said: 'Beats working for a living!'

The newspaper supplement market exploded in the late 1980s and 1990s when virtually every publication, local and national, seemed to decide that bigger was most definitely better. Colour magazines, tabloid supplements, A5 listings guides, arts, sport, travel, books, style, motoring, media, business, personal finance – the list appeared endless, and provided a significant and expanded platform for features. Whereas previously writers were constrained by the fairly strict boundaries of a newspaper, the supplements provided ample opportunity to specialise and to produce features on weird and wonderful topics. The proliferation of lifestyle programmes on TV, such as *Changing Rooms* and *Ground Force*, was reflected in the print media, as we were treated to countless features on how to transform your home and garden. The desktop publishing revolution, meanwhile, helped the magazine market along, as it became possible for people to produce magazines relatively cheaply and easily, creating opportunities for writers wishing to specialise. And, as we shall see, publications are now adapting to the fast-moving online market.

WHAT IS A FEATURE?

The quick and dirty answer to this question is anything that isn't news. But that's a very limited definition when you start flicking through newspapers and magazines. Does the crossword count? And how about the TV reviews? What about the racecards on the sport pages? And can a heavyweight, authoritative feature on terrorism really come under the same category as a no-holds-barred comment piece on safe sex for gay men?

So what do we want from a feature? We want to be transported to places we'll never visit. We want to savour the atmosphere of a big occasion. We want to be given an insight into a famous person's life and what makes them tick. We want to be outraged when a miscarriage of justice is revealed. We want a complicated issue broken down into layperson's terms for us by an expert writer. We want an armchair view of the gig we couldn't attend.

It might help to think back to what news is:

- **Topical** – we want news, not history.
- **Highly factual** – as the chap in the old cop show *Dragnet* used to say: 'Just the facts, ma'am!'
- **Stylised** – news generally conforms to an accepted formula, that of a pyramid (see below).
- **Impersonally written** – the reporter's view isn't required; opinion is provided by the people quoted in the story.
- **Crisp** – news stories are generally short and sharp. Look at how much information is packed into a tabloid news item.

By comparison, the list of what characterises a feature is significantly longer:

- **Varied approach** – there's no one correct way to structure a feature.
- **Individual voice from writer** – a good feature writer will develop their own distinctive writing style; it may be amusing, deadpan or sarcastic, for example.
- **Can involve personal thoughts, colour, description** – the journalist may become part of the feature if they try out a new sport, or want to draw attention to an interviewee's strange behaviour. They can describe a big event, and comment on what they see.
- **Longer than news** – features have room to breathe. Some of those in magazines or weekend newspaper supplements may run to several thousand words.
- **Involve narrative background** – there is far more space in a feature for the journalist to ink in background information; in a news story this may be restricted to one or two brief paragraphs.
- **Wide use of quotes and dialogue** – news stories will, of course, include quotes, but there are usually fewer of them. A feature writer has the luxury of more space for quotes, and even including snatches of dialogue where two or more people may be talking.
- **May have a more distant deadline** – news stories are generally written to tight deadlines. Features pages in newspapers may be prepared a day or more in advance; magazine deadlines may be three months hence.

There is no one correct way to write a feature. Trainee journalists are advised that the inverted pyramid (or a right way up pyramid, depending on who you listen to) is the textbook way to write a news story, with the juicy facts up top, and the less interesting padding at the bottom, where it can be cut easily if necessary. But when it comes to features, you will find that almost anything goes, ranging from first-person, eyewitness accounts, through the old faithful question-and-answer (Q&A) format, to a formal 'he said, she said' style.

And there is no one spot in the paper where you are guaranteed to find features, although the growth of supplements has meant they proliferate in those sections. They may be sprinkled throughout the paper, or have regular slots (women's issues, sport, lifestyle, arts). You are guaranteed to find a cluster of comment pieces around the editorial and op ed (opposite editorial) pages in papers, or significant review sections in music magazines.

By reading a range of papers and magazines, you will get a good idea of what kinds of features interest editors and in what style the pieces are written. Being familiar with a range of publications gives you a clue as to what sorts of writers they welcome. Newspapers cultivate their big-name feature writers, but even though a lot of high-quality writing appears in magazines, most people would be hard pressed to name any magazine feature writers – it's a land where the designer often seems to be king!

SPOTTING FEATURES

The following list isn't necessarily exhaustive, and you may find that terminology differs depending on who you deal with and where you work (for instance, profiles are sometimes known as personality pieces). But it will start to give you a feel for the vast range of features out there – and also kick-start your ideas bank.

- **News features**: an in-depth look at a story in the news.
- **Backgrounders**: digs deeper into a current news story, sometimes including historical information.
- **Retrospectives**: a look at a story from way back, often with an anniversary angle.
- **Investigative features**: uncovering information that isn't known, or that someone wants to keep hidden.
- **Specialist features**: these will be based on a particular area, be it education, arts, science, sport, travel or environment, for example.
- **Profiles**: an in-depth interview with a person. Sometimes known as personality pieces. You'll also see mini-profiles used as case studies alongside news stories.
- **Colour pieces**: an atmosphere piece where a journalist gives a first-hand, eyewitness account of a story.
- **Triumph over adversity (TOAs)**: features based on someone's fightback from the brink of disaster. Much beloved of women's magazines and tabloid Sunday magazines. Also known as TOT (triumph over tragedy).
- **Formulaic features**: these appear every day/week/month and follow a formula such as 'Sixty Seconds with', 'Day in the Life of', 'Relative Values', 'A Room of My Own'.
- **Think pieces**: sometimes known as opinion pieces. They may be written by someone with a specialist knowledge of a topic rather than by a journalist.

- **Personal columns**: again, these will appear weekly/monthly and generally with a picture byline for the reporter who writes the column.
- **Reviews**: a critical look at a new play, film, book, gig, CD, computer game, and so on.

This list includes the main features you'll come across regularly in newspapers and magazines. Naturally, not every publication will house every type of feature – the *Financial Times* won't go a bundle on the formulaic sort, while you won't find heavyweight think pieces in *Nuts* or *Bizarre*. And while the *Guardian* will include profiles of gay couples taking part in civil partnerships, the *Daily Mail* is likely to be more interested in finding people to speak out against such partnerships.

FEATURES SCHEDULE

The best way to get a feel for who uses what is to take a look at which features are used in a range of publications. I've taken three UK newspapers from the same day (Friday, 15 August 2008) and listed the features that appeared in each. The comments in brackets are my explanations of what sort of feature the piece is and further clarification, if needed, of the context of the article.

The *Sun*

p. 7: We haven't the heart to tell Pito he will never see mummy and daddy again (news story/news feature on a seven-year-old Georgian boy orphaned by a Russian bomb)

pp. 12–13: Swimply the best (news story/news feature on the Olympics, with the focus on swimmer Becky Adlington and her family – accompanied by four shorts on other athletes/news)

p. 22–23: Bling, booze, groupie sex and an early death. Sound modern? No it's the Life of Byron (feature on the poet Lord Byron and how never-before-published letters about his female following have come to light)

pp. 34–35: Madonna was a middle-class girl pretending to be tough, a religious girl pretending to be irreligious, a prude pretending to be a pervert (Germaine Greer – described in the standfirst as the most outspoken feminist of her generation – looks at the singer Madonna, who is just about to turn fifty) pp. 48–49: We've gone from 2nd gear to 5th in one movement (interview with Glasgow band Glasvegas as part of the 'Something for the Weekend' review section)

p. 50: I admit I'm retro . . . not a lot of emo going on (Q&A interview with musician Teddy Thompson, son of folk-rock legends Richard and Linda)

pp. 66–67 Heartbroken (interview with badminton star Gail Emms, whose Olympic gold-medal dream had just been dashed)

Daily Mail

p. 15: Kiss me quick! I'm retiring (after 118 years, Margate's beach donkeys are being put out to grass because the owner is giving up to look after his sick mother)

pp. 22–23: Eye massagers, moustache protectors and other must-have gadgets (double-page picture spread showing some of the more unusual artefacts from a new exhibition at the British Library of Victorian and Edwardian inventions)

pp. 36–37: When *do* you start losing your looks? (a new poll of 4,000 women claims women start to worry about losing their looks at the age of twenty-eight. Eight writers aged between thirty-one and seventy-three give their views)

pp. 42–43: When my little girl was born with Down's, I felt like I'd given birth to an alien and just wanted to get rid of her (a first-person piece by a mother about her baby)

pp. 46, 51, 54, 55: It's the joy of X (feature on the return of TV show *The X Factor* – the main item in the 'It's Friday!' section)

pp. 54–55: Dogs behaving badly (profile of actor Martin Clunes, focusing on his new TV show *A Man and His Dogs* – part of the 'It's Friday!' section)

pp. 56–57: Fame? It can eat you up (profile of the soul singer Alicia Keys – part of the 'It's Friday!' section)

p. 57: Teddy's ready to bare his soul (profile of musician Teddy Thompson – part of the 'It's Friday!' section)

p. 72: Great leaps of faith (feature in the 'Property Mail' section about churches being converted into houses, plus 'On the Market' box at the bottom with three other properties – a chapel, a watermill and a pub – which have been converted and are for sale)

p. 75: Spread your wing (feature in 'Overseas Property' about Britons moving abroad in search of new business ventures, plus 'On the Market' box at the bottom has two overseas B&Bs for sale)

p. 83: Trouble at the heart of Europe (feature in the 'City & Finance' section about inflation and recession in five other European countries)

p. 87: I used to earn £80 a match . . . it's all a bit different now (profile of Hull City footballer Dean Windass, still playing Premiership football at the age of thirty-nine)

p. 91: Keatings gives Brits a leg-up (feature on Daniel Keatings and British gymnastics at the Olympics)

Independent

pp. 16–17: From the ashes of Omagh rises a vision of hope (ten years on from the Omagh bomb attack that killed twenty-nine people – main feature accompanied by a sidebar: 'Ten years on, and nobody has been brought to justice')

pp. 26–27: Villagers caught in front line become victims of atrocities (double-page spread on the war in Georgia with reports and analysis from three correspondents)

pp. 30–31: A bridge too far? (feature on the exclusive Ile de Ré, one of France's exclusive summer retreats, where regulars fear they will be swamped after the abolition of tolls on the bridge)

p. 40: What does it mean for the US if whites are no longer in the majority? (analysis Q&A news feature on one of the day's issues)

pp. 48–49: How Wall Street's watchdog may be muzzled (business feature on how the credit crunch may hit Wall Street's regulator)

pp. 60–61: You need drive and desire, and I don't have time for people who don't have that (profile of Bolton Wanderers manager Gary Megson)

pp. 66–67: Du glistens as tears of joy mark golden redemption (feature on how Du Li, China's world champion at the ten metres air rifle, staged a comeback to win Olympic gold)

Extra pull-out section

pp. 2–5: A shot at stardom (Ben Welch, a twenty-six-year-old writer and Sunday amateur footballer, has a shot at football stardom by playing for Swindon Town on their pre-season tour of Austria – accompanied by a panel containing facts and figures on Sunday league football in the UK)

pp. 6–7: Is Turkey the new Tuscany? (feature on why Turkey is the new trendy place for the chattering classes to go on holiday

Arts and books review section

pp. 2–4: The science of comedy (a feature on what makes a good joke, plus the fifty top gags from this year's Edinburgh Fringe Festival)

pp. 10–11: An Irishman in New York (profile of the actor Liam Neeson, who has been appearing on stage in New York and also has a new film out)

pp. 12–13: Hot buttered soul (a look at the influence of singer and songwriter Isaac Hayes on Stax Records after his recent death)

pp. 14–15: An actor who rocks (feature on actor Rhys Ifans, who has formed a rock band – plus panel on 'The ones who should have stuck to acting')

p. 16: When five tribes get it on (feature on music in Kinshasa and the Congotronics sound)

p. 18: Wacky pop for now people (profile of musician Mica Levi – also known as Mikachu)

pp. 20–21: Ever thine. Ever mine (feature on writers and love letters – including eight modern writers sharing their own moments of passion)

It's possible from these lists to start to draw some conclusions as to what sorts of features interest the three papers, purposely chosen across the spectrum of the UK nationals – a compact renowned for being a 'viewspaper' as much as a 'newspaper' and with its highly (*ahem*) independent take on the news; a mid-market tabloid with a right-wing agenda; and a downmarket tabloid or 'red top' which, over the years, has shifted its allegiance between the two main political parties.

The *Sun* is not a features-heavy paper, and what there is tends to be celebrity or human-interest based. Often what looks like a feature in the *Sun* or another tabloid is in fact an extract from an upcoming book. The *Daily Mail* has a significant female readership and a focus on lifestyle, health and beauty – often with an alternative therapy angle. By comparison, the *Independent*, like the *Guardian*, is a features-heavy paper, helped by its daily 'Extra' pullout section. It's useful to note as well that spotting a feature isn't an exact science – some of the articles in the *Sun* are borderline features and in one or two cases might be categorised as lengthy news stories.

I've carried out this exercise once a year for the past ten years, and this year's schedule is twice as long as last year's – an indication of how popular supplements of different sorts are in the UK media. A number of the national papers carry Friday review-heavy supplements. All three papers examined here have their own review sections, which are a mix of features and reviews. 'Something for the Weekend' in the *Sun* is in the main part of the paper, as is the *Daily Mail*'s 'It's Friday!' section. The *Independent*'s is a standalone section. The *Sun* also carries two pull-out supplements – 'Motors' and 'TV Biz' – but neither contains features.

Inevitably, when you have writers and musicians producing new books and albums, and actors promoting new films, you will see interviews with the same person across different publications. Here, Teddy Thompson appears in the *Sun* and the *Daily Mail*. He's not a household name, but the fact that he's a friend of media darling Rufus Wainwright, and the son of folk legends Richard and Linda Thompson, would have interested the features editors. The *Independent*, though, has gone for more unusual features, including music from the Congo, that you might usually expect to see only in specialist folk and world music magazines, such as *fRoots* and *Songlines*.

The Olympics that were in progress are evident across the papers – and not just on the sports pages. Becky Adlington, who won two swimming gold medals, was a mainstay of both news and sports pages during the Games – the former because of her love of expensive shoes and her down-to-earth manner in interviews. And Britain's success in the Beijing Games across a range of sports meant extra coverage for swimming, sailing and gymnastics, sports which don't usually feature very heavily on the sports pages of national papers.

THE MAGAZINE MARKET

The next time you go into a big city centre newsagent's, take a moment to appreciate just how varied the magazine market is. Twenty years ago, you would have found a handful of magazines covering various subject areas; now, you need fingers and toes to count how many women's magazines there are, for example, or those covering the computer market. It's a volatile market, too: magazines start up, last a handful of issues, and either attempt to reposition or die completely. Anyone starting up a magazine in the present market needs to have done extensive market research and be certain they really do have a unique selling point (USP).

A large proportion of magazines cater for a specialist market. Whereas your average newspaper reader wants a broad-brushstroke look at what's going on in the world that day and may not even read all the sections, a magazine reader will often be buying the product because they are fanatical about the subject-matter. But they also know their area – you'd be most unlikely to find a fan of rap music picking up a copy of *fRoots* or to spot an Apple Mac user buying a PC magazine. General magazines, with the exception of current affairs weeklies *New Statesman* and the *Spectator*, have never really gained a foothold in the modern UK market – for instance, several attempts to launch a magazine covering all sports have been unsuccessful. These points clearly have implications for journalists targeting features at such publications. The lesson seems to be that the magazine market favours specialists over generalists.

The magazine market was boosted by the desktop publishing explosion in the late 1980s and early 1990s. Whereas starting up a newspaper was (and still is) an expensive business, and few people had a printing press stashed away in the garage, with the advent of desktop publishing it became possible to produce and distribute reasonable-quality magazines on a fairly small scale. Getting a distribution deal to have your magazine sold in high street newsagents' might not be easy, but having a strong online presence, good advertising and a healthy subscription base help smaller magazines survive. Magazines, though, tend to be significantly more expensive than newspapers, and while most people will shell out eighty pence or so for a newspaper, they might think twice about paying five quid or more for a magazine. (However, some magazines, particularly in the style arena, have played on this exclusive cachet. *AnOther Magazine*, a sister publication to *Dazed and Confused*, appears biannually and charges twenty-five pounds to subscribe to those two issues.)

Deadlines, too, are altogether different on magazines. Whereas news-paper features editors will be rushing to get their pages done on a daily or weekly basis, the vast majority of magazines are monthly – and deadlines may be three months ahead. So models for the Christmas issue will be sweltering in the middle of August, while ideas on where to go for your summer holidays traditionally appear in the New Year.

What's inside: music magazines

The music magazine market is a busy and crowded one. At one point, until the early 1990s, the market supported three weekly newspapers, known as 'the inkies' (the newsprint came off on your hands something awful!), in the shape of *NME*, *Melody Maker* and *Sounds*. Now only the first of these survives, as *Sounds* closed in 1991 and *Melody Maker* in 2000. In the Republic of Ireland, *Hot Press* continues fortnightly with its eclectic mix of music, politics and humour.

When it comes to the monthlies, pretty much anyone will be able to find a magazine to suit their interests, whether they listen to world music (*Songlines*), classical (*Gramophone* – whose title will immediately give you some idea of the target readership!) or heavy metal (*Kerrang!*). Some general magazines do exist – namely, *The Word*, *Q* and *Mojo* – but when you flick through them, you'll see that even they have clear target audiences in mind. *Mojo* is aimed at the thirty- or forty-something bloke who likes Bob Dylan and is prepared to wade through twelve-page features on Led Zeppelin or Fairport Convention. *Q*, meanwhile, has repositioned several times, and at the time of writing covered the kind of stuff that twenty- or thirty-something lads (and yes, it *does* seem male-orientated) will listen to in the indie and rock market.

With this in mind, then, let's take a look at the features these music magazines publish. Bear in mind that the contents page of magazines will often signpost you to the features – something you don't necessarily get in newspapers.

NME (New Musical Express)

Twenty or so years ago, the weekly music press in the UK was in a healthy state, with three papers (*NME*, *Melody Maker* and *Sounds*) vying for attention. The latter two are now defunct, but *NME* continues for the late teens and twenties market, focusing on a range of bands across the rock and pop range, with occasional forays into rap and metal.

A weekly paper such as *NME* will be able to cover the summer music festivals in depth, both as previews and as reviews. The 23 August 2008 issue devoted fifteen pages of features to the Reading and Leeds festivals. Here's what they went for, including the paper's blurbs:

- The Killers: The gold suit is gone. Meet moody Brandon
- Rage Against the Machine: *Still* the angriest band on the planet
- Slipknot: The masked maurauders are back back back
- 10 Other Things: Stuff to do at R&L that isn't, like, music
- New Bands: 15 essential acts you must see
- Metallica: Lars Ulrich's 10 commandments of rock
- Round Table: Indie's finest discuss thorny festival issues

The music press is always on the lookout for the next big thing, so the '15 essential acts you must see' feature is predictable. Metallica are among the big names, if not typically to the tastes of *NME*'s target audience – but people want to know who the headliners and famous bands are at festivals. Much more geared towards the target audience's musical taste is the Round Table feature (headlined 'Summit for the Weekend'), featuring musicians from twelve bands to whom the *NME* readership are very likely to listen. They tackle a weird and wonderful range of questions, from the straightforward 'What have you got planned for your set?' to the more offbeat 'What's your favourite Slipknot mask?' to the typical summing-up question, 'Who are your new band tips?'

Q

Q is aimed at an older market than *NME*, although you would expect to see some crossover in the bands mentioned, particularly in the review section. The September 2008 issue of the magazine goes for a range of general features (some of them monthly regulars) and forty-one pages based on the theme 'On the road'.

The main 'Q Interview' is with 1980s star Boy George, accompanied by a full-page colour pic of the singer made up in what looks like clown face paint. And there's a five-page feature on eccentric Welsh actor Rhys Ifans, who has formed a band with the drummer from Super Furry Animals.

The following are regular features:

- Cash for Questions: This month TV soccer pundit Andy Gray answers questions from readers.
- New: The Metros, Beth Rowley and White Lies are showcased in the up-and-coming new faces slot.
- My Brilliant Career: Spiritualized's Jason Pierce is the focus of the feature which also analyses albums he's made.
- Where Are They Now?: The 1990s rap trio House of Pain are tracked down.
- At Home With: This features Dan Gillespie Sells of The Feeling. The article is accompanied by big pictures of his house, with unusual belongings highlighted.
- The Q List: Psychic Uri Geller – best known for bending spoons – gives his views on 'ten musos who've had close encounters'.
- A Round With: A question-and-answer interview in a Devon pub with hunky folk musician Seth Lakeman.

The 'On the Road' section is made up of six features:

- Our old friends Metallica, who are apparently one of the highest-earning live bands around.
- Comedy duo Bret McKenzie and Jermaine Clement – described as New Zealand's biggest export since 'that Hobbit film' – appear as part-spoof, part-tribute band Flight of the Conchords.
- Confessions of a Tour Manager: Four of them have stories to tell.
- Q Roadies for the Pigeon Detectives: Reporter Ben Wilson samples life as a roadie for this colour piece.
- The Raconteurs: A look at Jack White's new band, accompanied by a panel on other supergroups under the heading 'The billion dollar bands'.
- Tour Heroes: Interviews with the unsung heroes behind the scenes on tour. Featured are a pyrotechnician, a sound engineer, a merchandise manager, a physiotherapist, a caterer, a stage designer, a tour manager, a tour bus driver, a guitar tech, a lighting designer and a security guard. All the first-person pieces include the same information at the top – clients, hours and pay.

fRoots

Formerly known as *Folk Roots*, the monthly magazine advertises itself as 'the essential worldwide roots music guide'. It's clearly aimed at a highly specialist market, and its readership is certainly older than that of *NME* and *Q*. The August/September double issue lives up to that worldwide tag, with the following features:

- Root Salad: A selection of one-page features on Norwegian trio Valkyrien Allstars, Max Pashm Band (who play Greek/Jewish music), Tibetan chanting monks appearing at a central London record store, East London multicultural band Grand Union Orchestra (who've been going for twenty-five years), English composer Ralph Vaughan Williams (who drew on folk music in his compositions), ballad singer Brian Peters, and a radical dance and techno reworking of folk legend Ewan MacColl's *Radio Ballads*.
- Les Amazones de Guinée: A feature on a female army orchestra from Guinea who have just produced their second album more than forty years after their first.
- In Foster Care: A feature on British folk veteran Chris Foster, who is now based in Iceland and has just produced a new album.

- Careful Now: An interview with Very Be Careful, who play old school Colombian 'cumbia' (dance) music – despite coming from Los Angeles.
- A Lounge Too Far: A look at fifty years of Brazilian bossa nova music.
- Nomad's Land: Reporter Nick Hobbs travels to Anatolia (which comprises most of modern Turkey) to hear how local music is kept alive in remote villages.
- Slack Key Ladies: A feature on how the art of Hawaiian slack key guitar is no longer a male preserve.
- Rights and Wrongs: A look at how proposed changes to European copyright laws on sound recordings may rob folk and roots music fans of access to fifty years of vital cultural resources.
- Chicago Now: Reporter Garth Cartwright visits Chicago fifty years after the heyday of classic Chicago blues to see what's happening now.

It's worth remembering that all three magazines have sizable review sections – one of the reasons why many readers buy them in the first place is to find out about new releases and to read what happened at live gigs. Those review sections in specialist publications are big draws for readers who want to find out about all the new books, albums and DVDs in their area of interest.

Other magazines

The women's magazine market is highly competitive and equally eclectic, covering everything from soap opera gossip to eye-wateringly expensive designer dresses and handbags. There's a world of difference between the likes of *Take a Break*, with its real-life stories, and the high-society publication *Tatler*; and between Muslim women's magazine *emel* and lesbian magazine *Diva*, although both are loosely aimed at the lifestyle market.

As with much of the magazine market, publications start up and reposition themselves fairly often. *New Woman*, for example, changed focus several times (and its name to *NW*) over the course of twenty years, moving from a fairly standard features and fashion magazine for twenty- or thirty-something women to one focused predominantly on shopping, before publishers Bauer finally axed it in early 2008.

The breadth of the market means that there are magazines covering almost every minority interest. These may not be freely available in newsagents', though, and often depend on subscriptions and/or a strong web presence to get themselves noticed.

A significant, but often ignored, part of the magazine market – particularly if you are a freelance journalist – is the trade press or business-to-business (B2B) publications. You won't necessarily find them on newsagents' shelves, as they are targeted at people in industry. But they have a clearly delineated readership, and provide journalists with a chance to specialise in an area. They may also offer journalists the chance to see their work in a much wider context than just the print medium. Susan Love, publisher and executive editor of *Ceramic Industry* magazine, and publisher of *Adhesives & Sealants* in the US, says: 'As electronic media gains prevalence, the print magazines have become part of an integrated media package with products such as digital ezines, enewsletters, webinars – online web seminars – and website products (tile ads, banners, rich media, sponsorships, videos, podcasts and more) also supporting the titles.'

THE ONLINE MARKET

Many existing print publications are still feeling their way in the online world. For every *Guardian*, which has an outstanding site and now runs a twenty-four-hour news operation, there are still those who use a site as a vague dumping ground for exactly what's in that day's or month's issue. And website designers are all too aware that a lot of people find reading on screen difficult, which can make the format user-unfriendly for longer features.

The rise of online magazines such as iGizmo (http://www.igizmomag.co.uk/) and Monkey (http://www.monkeymag.co.uk) shows that interactivity is the way forward – although, ironically, both have been produced to look like traditional magazines, so a reader must click to turn the page. Within each page, though, there are hot links to other stories, websites, video clips or adverts (the reader can't always tell in advance which of these a link will be). Rolling a mouse over the page also brings up more information. iGizmo allows the reader to download a pdf version to their computer to read at their leisure.

Features must be adapted or rethought for the online market, and the emphasis is very much on short, sharp sections, as we shall see later.

Websites can react quickly and update often with topical features. After American swimmer Michael Phelps broke the record at the 2008 Beijing Olympics for the number of gold medals won by an individual in a single Games, the BBC site was quick off the mark with a backgrounder where they asked a nutritionist to analyse Phelps's phenomenal diet of 10,000 calories a day (http://news.bbc.co.uk/1/hi/world/asia-pacific/7562840.stm; accessed 15 August 2008).

And take, for example, *Pink News*, a website for the gay, lesbian, bisexual and transgendered (GLBT) community. A print version is available monthly in the south of England, but the online site is updated daily. Here's the start of a feature with an unusual angle on Gay Pride marches. Reporter Katherine Knowles interviews David Gwinnutt, the man responsible for designing the eye-catching pink flags that have appeared at the various marches:

> First there was the flag. Pink and cheerful and vibrant, spilling silkily out of the envelope, bringing a smile to the bleary eyed 9 am workers in the PinkNews.co.uk office, then gracing the lectern at our paper launch party, where it drew admiring glances from MPs and members of the gay choir alike.
>
> Then there was the artist, David Gwinnutt, 'You like it? Oh my god that's fantastic! You thought it was cheerful? Fantastic! Being gay is fantastic! I wanted to celebrate it. Really, there's such a lot of drama, but I think it's fabulous!'
>
> Straight off my interview list and onto my fantasy dinner party guest list. Full of fascinating nuggets of gossip; 'I remember driving up to Blitz one time, and I saw Boy George chatting outside. He was wearing an Elvis jacket, a Mohican and bondage trousers! Oh, and this other time, I was over at his squat with all the crowd, and suddenly this huge fight broke out when Jeremy Healy accused Boy George of stealing his hairspray. Honestly, it was terrifying!'
>
> http://www.pinknews.co.uk/news/articles/2005–2030.html (accessed 22 July 2006)

Some rather rocky grammar and punctuation aside in that third paragraph, the reporter takes the correct approach in letting an interviewee like this speak for himself – the quotes show him to be chatty, exuberant and with plenty of good stories to tell. And who can ask for more than that in a feature?

CASE STUDY – RICHARD DREDGE, FREELANCE MOTORING WRITER

How did you get into feature writing?

I started writing for various car magazines and a few of them began asking me to write different types of features for them. While many of the features I write are fairly dry consumer-related ones, I've also been asked to do various drive stories, colour pieces, interviews and reviews. Because the motoring journalism world is a small one (much like most other specialist areas), it doesn't take long for word to spread, and for new outlets to open up – as long as you look after your customers. By not being too choosy about the commissions I initially accepted, I found myself getting asked increasingly to write different (and usually more interesting) types of feature.

Which features are you most proud of?

The consumer ones which are entertaining to read – because most factual writing is very hard going for the reader. It's very easy to assume that this type of feature is only read by those who will plough through it regardless, because they stand to gain an insight into something and will benefit in some way (usually financially). But it doesn't have to be that way; consumer features can (and should) be an enjoyable read. I recently had to do a 5,000-word article on motorhome insurance, with the assumption being that the audience wouldn't recognise humour if it was handed to them on a plate. Having taken over this annual feature, the feedback was incredibly positive because I approached things from a different angle.

What's your approach to feature writing, from thinking up an idea to delivering the finished product?

The bare bones of the feature are normally dictated as part of the brief. There are certain key pieces of information that have to be there, although the structure is often left fairly open for the writer to sort out. As a result, I'll make a series of notes then work out a very basic structure for the piece before I start to write it. However, I do relatively little plan-ning before diving into the writing; I find it easier constantly to revise the structure as I go along. I don't tend to write a piece from start to finish then hand it in; instead, I'll do a rough first draft and constantly refine it. It may be that I rearrange things once it's under way (usually as I have new ideas), or I may just think of different pieces of information along the way. However I tackle it, I tend to go back to an article several times over before it's handed in. That way I can constantly hone it to ensure it's as sharp as possible.

What are the top tips you'd give a young feature writer?

The number-one priority when accepting a commission is to get a decent brief – and make sure you stick completely to it. If there's anything you're unsure about, ask questions. Don't deviate from the brief because you think your ideas are better than those of the person who commissioned you; they won't thank you for it! Don't hand in a feature until you've gone over the brief once more, just to make sure you've done exactly what you were asked to do. And whatever you do, don't ever miss a deadline.

Don't turn your nose up at any commissions at first – or at least not if you can help it. If you can carve out a niche for being able to produce a certain type of feature, you'll probably be offered opportunities elsewhere. Ultimately you should be able to do a bit of cherry picking; if you're too choosy at first, you may find that the commissions dry up before your career has even got going.

Learn your markets; find out who likes which types of feature and how you can muscle in on the market. Don't be afraid to use this information to approach editors; offer a few really good ideas and say you'd like to have the chance to come up with the goods. Don't ever talk about rates until the work is done; your priority at this stage is to ensure the customer is satisfied, so don't give the impression that you're only interested in the money. You'll invariably find it's worth your while; freelance magazine rates are usually pretty good. Besides, if you think it's not worth your while afterwards, you can just walk away if you're approached by the same outlet.

Make sure you can spell and that your grammar is excellent too; it's amazing how few writers possess these basic skills. Sub-editors are not there to make up for your shortcomings! Also ask for a style sheet, so you don't commit any fundamental errors when it comes to terminology used.

Know the subject you're writing about – especially if it's a specialist one where your audience should be learning from you. If you don't know what you're talking about, you'll be ripped to shreds by the knowledgeable audiences which usually read the specialist press.

Once you've handed a piece of work in, follow things up with a phone call or at least an email. I prefer to use the phone because emails are impersonal and it's hard to have a two-way conversation. If your work is criticised, don't take it personally – and don't argue or make excuses. You're the newcomer, so you have to accept that you don't know best. And never be precious about your work.

How do you adapt to writing for different markets?

Most car magazines tend to have a broadly similar editorial style. One or two are slightly different, but not enough to cause a problem when it comes to adapting my writing style. However, where I have to change significantly is when I'm writing for different media. Although newspaper features are much the same as magazine ones, those written for the web are quite different. Many web writers fall into the trap of assuming there's unlimited space available, so they can be as verbose as they like. Nothing could be further from the truth: writing for the web is about reducing to the minimum and saying something in far fewer words than you would compared with print media. There are whole books on this subject, but suffice to say that web writing is a skill that's frequently undervalued – except by web editors.

Who do you write for?

I started out as a staff member on *What Car* before being appointed website editor of *BBC Top Gear*. Since going freelance I've started writing for various motoring magazines such as *Auto Express, Practical Classics, Octane, AutoTrader* and *What Diesel*, and I'm also editor of *First Car*, a magazine aimed at young drivers. More specialist outlets include *Auto Italia*, the British Council and *Classic Cars for Sale* as well as *Classic Car Mart*. I also contribute to motoring websites such as *NewCarNet, CarKeys* and *MSN Cars*. Besides this I've written a variety of books for Haynes Publishing and Amber Books.

2
Developing an idea

Writing features can be both a lucrative and a rewarding area for staff journalists and for freelances. Magazines in particular, with their small staff teams, use a lot of freelances – but if you want to write for the likes of *NME* or *Cosmopolitan*, it can be a difficult area to break into. Nevertheless, the explosion in the magazine market over the past fifteen or twenty years means that whatever your interest, there's at least one magazine catering for it.

What's important, though, is to be realistic. You may want your features gracing the pages of the *Guardian* or *Cosmopolitan* or *NME*, but then so do most other freelances! So think widely – and never underestimate the B2B (business-to-business) or trade press. Magazines such as the *Grocer* have circulation figures that many editors would give their right arm for!

And bear in mind that a good feature should not just be a one-shot. While it's bad form to offer the same feature around lots of places, there's nothing to stop you, once it's been used somewhere, refining it for different markets, be they print, TV, radio or online. Also make sure you keep a note of when you completed a feature, as revisiting the subject area to see what's happened six months or a year down the line will often guarantee a follow-up article.

WHAT MAKES A GOOD FEATURE?

Before you set about trying to develop or sell your idea, it's worth mulling over what makes a good feature. Bear in mind, though, that what you think is a must-write feature may not appeal to a features editor. Although knowing your market is essential, the likes and dislikes of the person commissioning the work from you are also crucial. So your

2,000-word profile of the comedian Billy Connolly, written in fluent Glaswegian, may not be a Welsh features editor's cup of tea! The following points will get you thinking about whether your idea has legs or whether it should be left in the back of your notebook.

Topicality

Features needn't always be topical. In fact, features editors like to stockpile a stash of timeless features for quiet times of the year (the 'silly season' over the summer and the Christmas/New Year break). But there always needs to be some sort of peg to hang the feature on so that the reader isn't left scratching their head and muttering, 'So what?' under their breath.

Human interest

People make news. They also make features. Very few features can run satisfactorily without people being interviewed in them – and that includes colour pieces. So if you're sent to cover the biggest car-boot sale in Europe, wandering around and writing about what you see isn't the full story. Talk to people – find out why they're there, what they have bought and whether they have found any bargains in the past. You might discover that the middle-aged woman slopping about in a tracksuit is a high-flying corporate lawyer who could afford to buy any number of designer items new, but prefers to search out a bargain.

Intriguing/unusual angle and approach

If it's a big story, you can virtually guarantee that every other media outlet will be running it too. So you should look to put an unusual spin on to the story or find an angle that no one else has come up with. For instance, the sports pages covered Wayne Rooney's sending-off against Portugal in the 2006 Football World Cup. But the story also found its way into other parts of several papers, including some of the features and specialist pages. The *Independent* used it as a peg on which to hang a feature about anger management in its health section ('Tame your anger', 4 July 2006), complete with interviews with an anger management consultant, two psychologists and a man whose life had been turned around by undertaking an anger management programme.

Any writer who can 'think outside of the box' and come up with unusual feature spin-offs is a valuable asset. Simon Mills wrote an entertaining feature in the *Guardian* about cream teas in London's posh hotels ('Everything stops for tea', 5 July 2006). The prompt for this was being sent to interview American TV personality Joan Rivers, and not being able to find anywhere to have tea without booking months in advance.

The same paper came up with an equally entertaining angle after pop star George Michael was found cruising on Hampstead Heath. The writer, Jaq Bayles, decided to ask lesbians if they went cruising. In the feature 'Cruising in style' (31 July 2006), Bayles discovered the answer was yes, but not as gay men would recognise it!

> A few years ago, in the interests of securing easier access to some leg-over action, a bunch of women tried to get a lesbian cruising scene started up on Hampstead Heath. With active female sexuality no longer regarded as entirely deviant, it seemed logical that lesbians should be able to enjoy the same freedom that some gay men had long been pursuing. But dykes weren't quite so hot as, say, George Michael, at grabbing strangers, having sex with them, and moving on to the next bush. They wanted to know the shaggee's first name. Also, preferably, her second. Then, well, it would be quite nice to know what she did for a living and whether she had one cat or two. And perhaps the cats' names as well . . .
>
> All of which rather undermined the whole cruising idea. Erica Jong's 'zipless f**k', a no-strings sexual encounter, just wasn't ready to take hold in the lesbian community. After this abortive experiment, the old joke – 'What does a lesbian take on her second date? Her furniture' – seemed more appropriate than ever.
>
> Although dykes may have drawn the line at frolicking in the bushes, it's hard right now to escape the sense that other forms of cruising and casual sex among lesbians are on the rise. Late-night saunas, pole dancing, stripping and online dating are all being marketed zealously to the lesbian community, offering us just as much incitement to get laid as our gay male peers. Despite all this opportunity, though, the question remains: are lesbians any better at cruising now than when they were haplessly roaming Hampstead Heath?
>
> Some of the women I spoke to had no notion of what 'cruising' means. When I explained the idea of a casual hook-up, they acknowledged that this sometimes happened but said that it was very different to male cruising.

Lively people interviewed

Find people with a story to tell. They needn't necessarily be famous – a single mother surviving on the breadline in a Glasgow housing scheme or a postman who has done the same round for forty years won't be household names, but they will have a story to tell. The *Independent on Sunday* found a good talker in the shape of eighty-three-year-old Bill Nankeville as part of its 'London 1948 to London 2012' Olympic series ('Rags to riches for the "high-class Del Boy" who dreamt of gold, not money', 17 February 2008). He just happened to be the father of entertainer Bobby Davro, but sixty years previously he had been a star name in British athletics and finished sixth in the 1,500 metres. The interview contrasts the British team for Beijing preparing in a five-star resort in Macau with the 1948 athletes who were housed in RAF Nissen huts in Uxbridge:

> 'Mind you, the grub was quite good,' Nankeville says. 'It was supplemented by food parcels from Canada. My wife's cousin had a butcher's shop, and as there was no weighing machine I used to go down there and weigh myself by hanging like a carcass. Then he slipped me a nice bit of steak for my breakfast. A different world then.'

Spot-on structure and pacing

Features tend to be substantially longer than news stories and you have to ensure that your reader stays hooked to the end. So it's not enough just to have a snappy intro; you need to keep the reader with you all through the piece. They must want to read on. A good feature writer will keep you hanging in there to the end with a judicious mix of narrative, quotes and reported speech.

Knowing your market

You can have the best ideas in the world, but if they're old news or not well targeted, you're wasting your time. And, if you're a freelance, time is money. If you're a staff reporter, will the idea convince the features editor? Will your readership be interested? Will it make a series or at the very least be worth following up? If you're a freelance, who will use the piece? Can it be re-spun for different markets at a later date?

The only way to get yourself familiar with markets is to read every newspaper and magazine you can lay your hands on. Unfortunately, not many jobs pay you to lounge around reading in the name of research! The chances are that if you're a music fan, you already buy the main music magazines, or those covering your particular interest. But break outside of that box. What I know about science can be written on the back of a postage stamp, but I still buy *New Scientist* once a month. And I'm often tempted by history magazines, despite the fact that my A-level history course was a fair while ago and no one ever commissions me to write history-related features! But I can appreciate the reader-friendly approach to science in *New Scientist* – which they achieve without the slightest hint of dumbing down features. And flicking through *History Today* has given me ideas for sports features with historical angles. The more you know about publications across the spectrum, the better prepared you will be when it comes to submitting features to them, or for thinking of new angles for other publications. And you are less likely to be met with the 'we ran an article on that a month ago' response, which is guaranteed to make you feel stupid and unprofessional.

How a feature is approached depends very much on the publication. The *Sun* used a highly visual angle when reporting on a study from the British College of Osteopathy which found that some push-up and plunge bras hampered women's breathing and exerted pressure on the spine. The one-page feature ('Girls are literally killing themselves to look great', 8 August 1998) showed a woman looking straight at the camera, with seven text boxes, each containing half a dozen paragraphs, pointing to the areas of the body where women were putting themselves at risk through smoking, tight cut clothes, tattoos, push-up bras, body piercing, suntans and high heels. The feature contained quotes from *Sun* doctor Rosemary Leonard and Sky fashion correspondent Karen Kay (oddly enough, there was no quote from Charlotte Wright, who had carried out the original study).

Knowing your market – a quick quiz

Look at the following feature ideas and speculate on which publications would use them:

1   The porn film 'Oscars'
2   The rise of Cajun music
3   Career women who take drugs
4   Where are all the Asian football pros?
5   How feng shui changed my life

6   Why Welsh devolution spells disaster for the West

7   Why I gave up my husband for my dogs

1   **The porn film 'Oscars':** This is in contrast to the wall-to-wall coverage of the conventional Oscars that fills acres of newsprint each February. This kind of story is likely to interest the men's magazines, such as *FHM* and *Maxim*, or one of the new breed of weekly downmarket magazines, such as *Nuts* or *Zoo*. It's possible that the very downmarket 'newspaper' the *Sunday Sport* would cover it too. As an outside bet, one or two of the women's glossies might go for the feature, if only for the head-shaking 'look what they're doing now' approach!

2   **The rise of Cajun music:** Cajun music comes from Louisiana in the United States, and gained popularity in the UK from the 1990s onwards. It has never become huge here, although you're likely to encounter Cajun bands if you attend world music or roots music festivals. Given it's not the sort of music you'd hear on Radio 1, the market for a feature is likely to be music magazines aimed at the thirty- or forty-something market, specialist music magazines, or daily newspapers with a music supplement. I wrote a feature on this topic for the music magazine *Rock 'n' Reel*, and other features on the same subject subsequently appeared in the *Guardian*'s Friday music pages and in *Q* magazine, a monthly publication.

3   **Career women who take drugs:** There are likely to be plenty of markets for this one, depending on the quality of your case studies – a feature like this stands or falls by who you interview for it. Someone who has had serious problems will be a more compelling case study than someone who dabbled with the occasional spliff before giving it up in favour of clean living. A number of the women's magazines – *Cosmopolitan, eve, Red, Marie Claire* – would probably be interested in the feature, as would newspapers such as the *Daily Mail*, whose features pages have a strong female bias.

4   **Where are all the Asian football pros:** This feature was written by a former student of mine and appeared in Birmingham's *Sunday Mercury* newspaper. She used West Midlands contacts, but clearly it could be adapted to wider markets, such as the sports pages of papers like the *Guardian* and the *Independent* or magazines such as *Four Four Two* and *When Saturday Comes*.

5   **How feng shui changed my life:** At one point a few years ago, feng shui was the new trendy passion, as people bought wind chimes for their front rooms and rearranged their furniture to create positive

vibes. Lifestyle sections in newspapers – particularly the upmarket Sundays – went to town on the subject. There was also a small explosion of alternative therapy magazines, most of which didn't stay the course. Now you'd be looking for an angle that has not been done to death – or, more likely, for the latest new fad to replace feng shui.

6   **Why Welsh devolution spells disaster for the West:** Prior to home rule for Wales, devolution stories were featured in most of the then broadsheet nationals, but also in regional papers such as the *Western Daily Press* in Bristol and the *Western Mail* in Cardiff. Now the Welsh Parliament is up and running, the new angle is whether the regions of England will ever get self-government. Local papers often have stories or features on the possible merging of regional police forces, or emergency services covering several counties being joined under one roof.

7   **Why I gave up my husband for my dogs:** These real-life stories are the staple diet of those downmarket weekly women's magazines such as *Bella* and *Take a Break*, and the *News of the World*'s Sunday colour magazine. The magazines are designed for easy reading – the sort you flick through during your coffee break or while waiting your turn in the doctor's surgery.

Developing your idea

All the best feature writers have countless ideas percolating through their mind at any one time. Not all of them will make, as journalists say, but you should never be short of ideas to bounce off demanding editors. Bear in mind, though, that most features can't be done on the fly. They require a lot of research, careful planning and thorough interviewing of people involved. There's no right or wrong number of interviewees for a feature, but given the fact you have more words to play with than in a news story, expect to talk to upwards of half a dozen people.

The *Guardian* took this idea to extremes when it decided to track down all the musicians who had ever been in the pop group the Fall ('Excuse me, weren't you in the Fall?', 5 January 2006). Lead singer Mark E. Smith has a reputation for being difficult and for sacking people seemingly on a whim. So reporter Dave Simpson started phone-bashing:

It's a Tuesday morning in December, and I'm ringing people called Brown in Rotherham. 'Hello,' I begin again. 'I'm trying to trace

Jonnie Brown who used to play in the Fall. He came from Rotherham and I wondered if you might be a relative.' 'The Who?' asks the latest Mr Brown. 'No. The Fall – the band from Salford. He played bass for three weeks in 1978.' 'Is this some kind of joke?'

This has been my life for weeks. I've become an internet stalker and a telephone pest, all because of an obsessive drive to track down everyone who has ever played in the Fall. That's 40-odd people, including drummers abandoned at motorway services, guitarists left in foreign hotels and various wives and girlfriends of the band's provocateur-ringmaster, Mark E. Smith.

As Simpson explains later in the feature, tracking down forty-three musicians required a lot of luck, persistence and hard work. Incredibly, he found all bar one.

I started with Smith, who sank pints of lager in a Manchester hotel as he explained his policy of successively 'freshening up' the band. 'It's a bit like a football team,' he said. 'Every so often you have to get rid of the centre-forward.' Smith has based his career on looking forward, so he was unlikely to give me numbers for clarinet players who left in 1981. The numerous record companies the Fall have had over the years had only ever dealt with Smith. The Musicians Union claimed to have 'no information relating to anybody who was ever in the Fall'.

I did have another lead, however. Sixteen years ago I interviewed a man called Grant Showbiz, and remembered that he sometimes produced the Fall. He gave me some numbers, though sadly, most of them were dead – the numbers, not the ex-members.

Ambitious features such as this one look tremendous when they're finished and dressed up for the pages. The *Observer*'s health editor, Jo Revill, put together an epic feature, 'Miracle workers who rebuilt Danny's life' (29 January 2006). The piece was a tribute to staff at St Mary's Hospital in London who saved the life of Danny Biddle, who was badly injured in the Edgware Road Tube bombing on 7 July 2005:

Danny Biddle has run out of words. On 7 July 2005, the 26-year-old building projects manager took the full force of the terrorist bomb which was detonated on a Tube carriage at Edgware Road. Barely recognisable as a human being, he was stretchered into St Mary's Hospital in west London. He is now trying to express his gratitude towards an extraordinary group of people who have painstakingly rebuilt him over the past six months.

Last week Danny returned to the hospital for the first time to meet the staff who contributed towards his fast and, frankly, unexpected recovery. The Observer brought together people from 20 different professions for this meeting and a remarkable photograph. Afterwards they were keen to talk about their memories with their former patient. He couldn't have known some of them because he was unconscious for much of the time he was in hospital, but it was important that he could tell them what they meant to him, and above all show them that he was whole and ready to begin living once more. But the right phrases to express that overwhelming sense of gratitude just wouldn't come.

'Thank you is just two little words,' he said over coffee as they all recalled the terrible events of that July. 'How do those two words begin to express what everyone here did for me, and what they did for all the others, too? I wouldn't be alive if they hadn't given me this extraordinary level of care. I just wish others could see the support I've had.'

As the nurses, therapists and doctors came up to shake his hand, they told him of their involvement. From the first paramedic who found him to the physiotherapist who is now teaching him to walk on prosthetic legs, a chain of care was constructed around Danny. 'I don't consider myself unlucky, you know,' he said. 'My bad luck ended on the day that bomb went off. Everything that's happened to me since then has been very good – and it was my great fortune to end up here.'

The feature took up two broadsheet pages of the Sunday newspaper. Across the top of the spread is a photo that includes all the staff who treated Danny. Getting them together at the same time was a challenge far beyond what could be realistically expected, so the newspaper set up a studio in the hospital, and busy staff popped in when they could to be photographed. A uniform backdrop allowed the newspaper's imaging department to blend the portraits together to create the line-up of people. Also included in a separate box, headed 'The saving of a life', are the timelines, beginning with the bombing and moving through Danny's treatment to November 2005, when he began to learn to walk again using prosthetic legs that had been specially made for him.

While aiming high is often a good thing to do, don't think that all features have to be as dramatic as these two. A one-to-one profile with a person with a great story to tell can still pack an emotional punch. Or find someone with an off-beat story to tell. *Washington Post* reporter Gene Weingarten came up with an amusing feature (16 February 2003) based on what the headline called 'The worst novel ever written'. The novel in question, *Great American Parade*, was by Robert Burrows, a retired university professor, had sold the grand total of 400 copies and had been slated in the few publications that had bothered to review it. Weingarten puts himself in the intro on the grounds that Burrows was gobsmacked to be contacted by a journalist from such a big newspaper – and because he has a trenchant view of the quality of this book:

> I am on the phone with Robert Burrows, author of the recently published political novel *Great American Parade*. This book has sold only 400 copies nationwide, and Burrows seems flabbergasted to be hearing from me.
>
> The most prestigious newspaper to have shown any interest so far is the *Daily Student* at Indiana University.
>
> I tell Burrows that if he is willing to submit to an interview, I am willing to review his book at length in the *Washington Post*. The only catch, I said, is that I am going to say that it is, in my professional judgment, the worst novel ever published in the English language.
>
> Silence.
>
> 'My review will reach 2 million people,' I said.
>
> 'Okay,' he said
>
> I have said this before, and I'll say it again. I really love my job.

The interview takes place over the phone, and Weingarten – who realises that understatement tends to work far better than overstatement – reproduces the bulk of the feature in question-and-answer format. This turns out to be a sensible move, as it showcases some of the interviewee's more bizarre answers:

> Me: You have people speaking in paragraphs, using words like 'indeed' in casual conversation. After your protagonist, Joan Milton, watches the planes hitting the World Trade Center, she turns away in horror and says to her friends: 'What an almost unbelievable tragedy! It will take a great resolve to overcome this terrible blow.' My question is, have you ever heard real human beings speak?
>
> Burrows: This is the way I speak. In my circle, I am regarded as a fascinating conversationalist. I have a dinner group that has been meeting for maybe 30 years. I admit that may be a little limiting.

In this instance the often hackneyed Q&A format is perfect, as narrative and reported speech would have taken the focus away from Burrows's unintentionally droll answers.

GETTING GOING WITH FEATURES

1   **Jot down ideas as they occur to you, even if they are half-formed**. The time might not be right for the feature at the moment, but you can return to it, or work on it at quiet times. Keep a notebook with you at all times, or one of those digital recorders where you can record odd words or sentences to jog your memory later. You might find it useful to start your own writing journal, where you can formulate ideas and plan stories.

2   **Think fast for topical features, but have timeless ones on the go**. You may be turning out regular features reflecting what's in the news at the moment, but don't neglect the less urgent ones. You don't have to write immediately the feature on the man who has every Aston Villa football programme since the First World War or about the bloke who collects aeroplane sick bags (unused, I hasten to add – and this strange creature does exist!), but they are useful to be working on for quiet times or when someone asks you what you have that's ready to roll.

3   **Keep cuttings that might help you**. Get used to trawling through publications and keeping an eye open for useful articles. You should save your own cuttings as a matter of course, but you need to know what the opposition is doing too. You're not going to copy them, as that's both unethical and legally dodgy, but they'll provide you with useful background information and will also spark off ideas, particularly if you reckon you've got a better angle.

4   **Research the area**. You can't busk features – they require far more preparation and research than most news stories. You'll need to look through your own publication's cuttings library (generally accessible online now) and search websites, as well as checking other media, relevant books and chatting to useful contacts who may know the people and/or the issues involved.

5   **Read widely to see who would use your article**. We've already established that you need an encyclopedic knowledge of the print media. Also get used to having the main media guides at your fingertips to check on possible markets. *The Guardian Media Guide* is updated annually and is affordable. *Benn's* and *Willing's*, the big two, are invaluable for both home and overseas contacts, but are also outside of most journalists' pockets. Find a library that stocks them.

6   **Talk to people for background information**. Make use of contacts and mutual acquaintances when you are researching features. You don't necessarily need to quote them in the finished piece, but they

can often provide you with useful background information about people or issues that you couldn't obtain elsewhere. They might not necessarily want to be quoted anyway, but could be willing to chat to you off the record. And they can often point you towards people who *are* happy to be interviewed on the record. It goes without saying that you must respect people's confidences. If they tell you that a conversation is off the record, you should respect that, unless you want to gain a reputation for stitching people up – or unless this is the investigative feature of a lifetime which will expose all manner of wrong-doings!

7   **Decide who you *have* to interview**. When you set out on a feature, you'll have in mind a wish list of interviewees – and there's a point at which you have to be realistic about who you can and can't talk to. You might well want to be the first person to interview Michael Jackson after his court case, but if you work on a small weekly paper in the back of beyond, that's not likely to be possible. You might be able to put a local spin on a national or international story, though. The *Gloucestershire Echo* found an excellent angle on the Michael Jackson saga through Cheltenham resident Mark Lester (the child actor star of *Oliver!* and now a physiotherapist in the town), who is a close friend of Jackson and was willing to be interviewed for several articles.

8   **Prepare a reserve list if your A list is no-go**. So what do you do when the person you really *have* to talk to is in the Caribbean for three months? You either knock the feature on the head or, more probably, with a features editor breathing down your neck, find someone else to interview. If you can't reach your main person by email or phone, start looking around to see who could take their place. There are very few features where you can't find someone else equally important to talk to.

9   **Be prepared to take your idea in another direction**. David Templeton was faced with a challenge for his column in *North Bay Bohemian*, an alternative weekly that is part of the Metro newspaper chain in northern California. He explains: 'For 14 years, I have been writing a column called Talking Pix, in which I take someone to a movie or arrange for them to see it wherever they are, and then we discuss it in what we sometimes call my "quest for the ultimate post-film conversation". My guests are often authors or other celebrities. Over the years, I have seen *Shampoo* with Heidi Fleiss, *Everyone Says I Love You* with Larry King, *Paradise Road* with Joan Baez, *The Winter's Guest* with David Malouf, that sort of thing.'

All well and good, and David was looking forward to a lively discussion of Oliver Stone's *World Trade Center*. Except no one would see the film with him. He says: 'I made a total of eight inquiries, some of which received no response at all (not unusual for me at all; the whole "let me take you to a movie" thing throws people off on a regular basis, and then I'll find someone who instantly "gets" what I'm doing). That list included firefighters in my town and one firefighting author from Portland whom I once did take to a movie, and it included a couple of mayors from large cities, whom I thought might have something interesting to say. Those who declined all said they wouldn't see it because they either disapproved of the movie being made, or because it was too painful.'

After these knockbacks, David was wondering how he was going to fill his column. Then he began to realise that his story was the refusals. His sister-in-law Lee, who runs an online radio show, came up with a contact in New York which sent the piece spinning in another direction. (Family can often be a useful source of contacts, but you might want to exercise caution in interviewing them to avoid possible rifts.)

The focus of his column then became author, musician and playwright Larry Kirwan, leader of Irish/American rock band Black 47. Kirwan and his band's Manhattan gigs were always well attended by New York firefighters. After September 11, they started playing weekly at a Manhattan pub, to an audience of police, firefighters and rescue crews. A forty-five-minute early-morning coast-to-coast call on deadline day produced a powerful human interest feature for David where the outspoken Kirwan made it clear why he had no wish to see the film (http://www.bohemian.com/bohemian/08.16.06/talk-pix-0633.html, accessed 18 August 2006).

10   **Store up potential other angles**. Or do what the *Guardian* did and find an off-beat angle. They ran a feature ('Professionally yours', 31 March 1997) on the return to British television of 1970s cult cop show *The Professionals*. This was an occasion where talking to the three main actors was going to be problematic – Gordon Jackson was dead, Lewis Collins had moved to the United States, and Martin Shaw had a reputation for being grumpy about the show. So feature writer Charlotte Eagar made it a light-hearted nostalgia piece and spoke to friends, fans, psychologists and those behind the successful advertising campaign for Almera cars that parodied *The Professionals*. Sadly, rather too many of them didn't want to be

named, which took the edge off a sparky feature, particularly for those of us of a certain age who were at school when the show was originally broadcast.

> There is a whole generation of women, aged 27–35, who giggle when you say 'Come in, Four-Five.' A 29-year-old psychologist, who won't reveal her name, gasped when I left a message about *The Professionals* for her colleague, an expert on teen idols. 'I had all the magazines and the big poster you could buy at Smiths. I wonder if I've still got my scrap book.'

> Her colleague was useless. But he's a man, so I don't think he gets it. You see, despite their dangerous image, for teenager girls, *The Professionals* were 'safe' to fancy. 'They were the first bits of rough trade,' says a staid mother of two – another Bodie fan. 'Before that, we had The Saint, who you suspected might be gay.'

It's obvious from the feature that the writer went on to the internet and did a search for Bodie and Doyle – she tells us there are 4,882 references. This was also a useful way of tracking down some fans to interview – Alexandra MacKenzie from Washington, DC, and Dave Matthews, who set up a *Professionals* website.

11   **Fix up interviews – and do your homework.** As with any article, be it news or features, it's generally best to fix up interviews with people. This gives the arrangement a feeling of formality, and also allows the interviewee some time to collect their thoughts and maybe sort out material that might be relevant. Of course, you should keep that appointment, unless an emergency crops up. Arranging interviews in advance focuses your mind too, as you can mull over possible angles (without going in with a preconceived idea) and spend some time researching around the topic and/or the people you'll be interviewing.

12   **Bear in mind follow-ups, spin-offs and series.** When you're developing an idea for a feature, try to see the broader picture. Can you ensure the idea lives on beyond one appearance in print? Follow-ups can keep a story running for months or even years – just think how many articles there have been about Louise Brown, the world's first test-tube baby, over the past twenty-five or so years. Her life has been revisited every time she has passed a landmark birthday, when she got married – and when she gave birth to her own baby. The *Daily Mail* produced a lengthy feature on her new arrival ('Britain's first test-tube baby on having a baby of her own', 13 January 2007).

Keep an eye open, too, for possible series, which go down well during quiet times of the year. Some years ago, the *Guardian* and the *Independent* ran off-beat series during the silly season. One that particularly stuck in my mind was entitled 'Great British eccentrics', which included profiles of a seaside bed-and-breakfast landlady, a Hampstead liberal, and Irate of Tunbridge Wells (supposedly a regular letter-writer to *The Times*).

SELLING YOURSELF

OK, so you have this wonderful feature idea that leaps out of your notebook and on to the computer screen. So how are you going to get it used? If you're a staff member of a newspaper, you have the features editor at a nearby desk to persuade. But for freelances, particularly those starting out, it can be a struggle. Many magazines rely on freelances, but you need to get your name known – and it's that Catch-22 of how to get published when they don't know you or your work.

If you've done your homework and are familiar with a range of publications, you should have a fairly shrewd idea of who will be interested in your piece. There's no point trying to sell a feature on a folk singer to a magazine specialising in garage or urban music. But *fRoots* or the *Guardian*'s Friday supplement might be interested. If you've worked with a publication on other occasions and have built up a good relationship with them, you should perhaps approach them first with new ideas.

There is another Catch-22 in the early stages of writing a feature: do you write it first and then try to sell it, or do you attempt to sell the idea, then write the piece? Realistically, once you're an established journalist, you always do the latter, as time is money and it would be pointless writing a feature that no one wanted. But when you're starting out, you may find you have to do it the other way round.

APPROACHING AN EDITOR

Find out the features editor's name by phoning the publication's switchboard, checking one of the media guides, or scanning the staff list in the front of the magazine. Phone up to introduce yourself and ask how they would like the story idea submitted. Most editors are happy with email; a few still prefer to see a hard copy. If you don't get a response within a few days, follow up politely – but take a hint if they are obviously not interested. You could follow up by email rather than phone, but emails are easier to ignore than phone calls (assuming you get to speak to the right person), and you may also fall foul of the publication's spam detector.

If you're starting out, or haven't worked for the publication before, it might make sense to send a copy of your CV and samples of your work to show them how good you are. Never send the original cuttings – if they're not returned, you will lose your life's work. If you have a blog and/or a website, make sure it's mentioned on the CV (and appears in your signature on your email).

Be prepared to get published lower down the scale at the beginning of your career – it will at least give you some cuttings. For instance, in areas such as music and sport, fanzines have provided would-be journalists with forums to get their names known. And with the advent of the internet, it's possible to build up a profile by writing for websites. If you're a professional or would-be journalist and not blogging, you should be asking yourself why you're not.

Editors like specialists, so it's worthwhile building up an area of expertise. Over the past twenty years I've covered sport, music and education, which has led to some interesting and challenging assignments – just how do you make an article about school budgets readable? The answer is to find talkative people. An articulate and thoughtful school governor was able to make the topic accessible and absorbing. And I earned the easiest seventy-five pounds of my life (this was the early 1990s) by sitting in a room and captioning photographs taken at the Glastonbury Festival. The photographers had shot off rolls of film, developed them and presented the deputy editor with the prints without knowing who most of the musicians were.

Most importantly, ensure you deliver the goods. Word gets around very fast if you prove unreliable and can't hit a deadline to save your life . . .

A GOOD IDEA

If someone wants your idea, you're then racing against the clock. It's not unusual to be asked to file the feature within hours or by the next day. If you are working on a topical piece, the deadline becomes even more pressing – particularly if you have an unusual angle that no one else has found. The *Guardian* (13 July 2005) settled on a fascinating angle when it came to the terrorist attacks in London on 7 July 2005. Marie Fatayi-Williams, mother of one of the victims, made a moving appeal for news of her missing son in London's Tavistock Square, scene of the bus bombing. The paper asked Colonel Tim Collins, renowned for his stirring speeches to his troops during the war in Iraq, to analyse what she said. The feature, headlined 'Straight from the heart', was not textbook feature writing by a professional journalist, but it was a memorable account by someone who was not an obvious choice to comment on the story. The feature was made even more powerful by the inclusion of Mrs Fatayi-Williams's speech itself, headlined by a pull quote – 'We cannot live in fear because we are surrounded by hate'.

It makes sense to ensure you're properly briefed by the features editor before embarking on writing up – that way you know how many words they want and whether they have a preferred angle. Some publications will tell you to give it what you think the piece is worth and to go on what you think works best; others will have a much clearer idea of what the shape of the finished piece should be.

Be realistic, too, as to whether an idea will genuinely pan out. Your timeless feature, for example, might be a classic case of 'so what?' Do we really care about the traffic warden who spends her off-duty time collecting ceramic frogs? We might do if she has thousands of them and her husband is threatening to move out, but if she has only a couple of dozen, probably not. There's a saying in fiction-writing circles: you may have to murder your darlings – that is, scrap the part of the story you've slaved over and think is word-perfect. The chances are it's gumming up the action. In feature-writing terms, you can get too close to a piece and fail to realise that it really isn't worth the attention you're lavishing on it. Learn to let go of an idea that's not panning out. You might always be able to come back to it later with a fresh angle. I remember, as a trainee, spending hours interviewing people from an obscure charity that was celebrating its seventy-fifth anniversary. I handed the feature to my tutor, who read it and said simply: 'Who cares?' And he was right.

THREE FEATURES THAT WORKED

Tim Coulson: the angel of Edgware Road (*Sunday Telegraph*, 6 July 2008)

This is the sort of immensely moving feature that sticks in your mind for hours after you read it. There were any number of powerful human interest stories following the 7 July 2005 Tube and bus bombings in London. Three years after the event, reporter Rowena Mason talked to one of the survivors, Tim Coulson. She allows him to tell his story, but intersperses the memories with her own observations to help round out the picture, while never letting us forget who the subject of the feature is:

> In the reflection of the television screen, I can see that tears are rolling down Tim Coulson's cheeks. We are sitting side-by-side in a sunny conservatory at Tim's home, near Henley-on-Thames, watching a documentary about the bomb that killed seven people at Edgware Road Tube station on July 7, 2005.
>
> In this Channel 4 film, due to be broadcast for the third anniversary of the London bombings, Tim gives his first detailed account of the day when middle-aged businessman Stan Brewster died in his arms and he saved the life of a young Australian office worker, Alison Sayer.
>
> 'I went back along the same Tube route three months after it happened,' Tim says calmly. 'It was very difficult, but it wouldn't have been right to stay away. I couldn't bear to let the bombers win.'
>
> He is a kindly-looking, bespectacled man dressed in loose summer clothing, who is able to draw the occasional smile as he talks about helping wounded passengers, several of whom are now his close friends.

When people are retelling traumatic stories, the journalist often has to coax them along with questions to draw out what happened. Mason closes the piece – which works as both a three-years-on feature and as a TV tie-in – by asking Tim Coulson for his thoughts on the bomber and also to assess what happened to him. This allows the feature to end on a very powerful quote:

> Does he feel resentful towards the bomber, who has not only taken people's lives and limbs, but wreaked havoc with the mental health of so many survivors?
>
> 'I saw the bomber's body, so I can't feel angry towards him. He is dead. It would be a bit like feeling angry towards a chair or a table.'
>
> So how does he rationalise what happened? 'I just can't believe that people, the bombers, would choose to spend their lives doing such things. It is a feeling of disbelief, not anger.
>
> 'There are deep mental scars,' he continues. 'Just like physical ones, that are never going to heal completely. I have come to accept that I won't be the person that I was, but that's fine with me.'

4 Games in one day but don't call us anoraks
(*Sun*, 2 September 2000)

This feature was fun – reporter Dave Kidd 'on a magical mystery tour' where he followed seventy non-league 'ground-hoppers' round the Home Counties on a Bank Holiday Monday as they watched four matches in ten and a half hours. We're not talking Chelsea, Manchester United and Aston Villa here – this whistle-stop tour took in the delights of Penn and Tylers Green v. Chalfont Wasps, Kidlington v. Headington Amateurs, Carterton Town v. North Leigh and Didcot Town v. Abingdon United in the Cherry Red Records Hellenic League.

Kidd pitches the feature just right – a judicious mix of colour, human interest and keeping half an eye on what happens on the pitch. And his relaxed style allows him to weave together narrative, anecdotes and direct and indirect quotes as he chats to a semi-retired Yorkshireman called Derek Sidebottom:

> He said: 'I used to follow Leeds until the 70s when the violence got really bad. Then I gave up on the professional game and started ground hopping. There's no aggro and you just meet people and make friends. This is my 2,254th ground.'
>
> Surely this mind-boggling figure is the all-time record?
>
> 'Nah,' said Sidebottom, 'the real big boys aren't even here today, they have already "done" the Hellenic League.'
>
> The godfather of all ground-hoppers is a man named Graham 'Hoddy' Hodson, a 30st giant from Crewe, who is reckoned to have visited more than 3,000 grounds, including many in South America. And the most eccentric hopper is a legend known as Bob the Tram, a former Blackpool tram conductor and another member of the 3,000 club.
>
> The Tram insists on touching the crossbars of each ground and refuses to count 0–0 draws. He went to three successive matches at one Scottish club after the first two ended 0–0.

Anecdotes such as these don't need embellishing or any commentary from the writer – they work just fine told straight, as they are here. Kidd captures the faint sense of the absurd of these grown men careering round Middle England to watch obscure football matches, but he avoids going OTT on the anoraks angle.

Sleighed (Merry Christmas everybody, *Loaded*, January 1999)

Men's magazine *Loaded* is known for its irreverent attitude to life. So John Perry's colour piece of a ride in a four-man bobsleigh is suitably in-your-face:

> Halfway down the mountain, I start to cry. My spine is bent like a coat hanger, my nose flattened against my chin and my cowardly face is streaked with tears and snot. In a bobsleigh, no one can hear you scream. My snowy Norwegian sleigh ride wasn't at all how I had imagined. I had pictured myself as David Niven, my knees draped in a tartan blanket, an Alpine trilby hat tipped at a rakish angle, waving at rosy-cheeked children as I glided sedately past. After all, Lillehammer's dazzling chocolate box scenery: shimmering snow-capped peaks, pointy gingerbread houses and quaint shops selling rotting reindeer meat, looked every inch the sort of place Dave would take his missus – Doris Day perhaps – for a sturdily romantic honeymoon. Unfortunately, gazing lovingly over the fjords isn't really an option when you're having your face squidged into your ears.

The reporter gets to chat to Britain's Olympic bobsleigh team, who had won bronze at the last Winter Olympics. Amid the chatty, slangy style, he also makes the necessary facts about funding and the mechanics of the bobsleigh accessible. This feature is a classic example of starting at the end, and then recapping, as Perry does the interviews before undergoing the bobsleigh run, which he compares to 'jumping into an upturned phone box and having your head bashed in with a spade'. In keeping with the tone of the piece, he ends with some sparky quotes, courtesy of bobsleigh driver Sean Olsson:

> 'Congratulations,' grins Sean, shaking my shaking hand. 'Now you're a bobsledder, one of the elite!'
>
> 'Cheers,' I stutter. 'So why do I feel like someone has hit me in the back with a cricket bat?'
>
> Sean roars with laughter and slaps me squarely between the shoulder blades. 'Want a lift to the bottom?' he asks.
>
> 'No thanks,' I say. 'I think I'll walk.'

THREE FEATURES THAT DIDN'T QUITE PAN OUT

Crime Time magazine (available online at: http://www.crime-time.co.uk/make_page.php?id=526; accessed 20 April 2006)

You can have too much information and not know what to do with it, or feel you have to be terribly even-handed when it comes to dealing with interviewees, or simply be unable to deliver what was a good idea. *Crime Time* magazine, which focuses on crime fiction, had a good feature idea which involved talking to the translators working on the sudden avalanche of European crime fiction being translated into English. They managed to get most of the main translators on board, but then merely put exactly the same questions to each of them and reproduced their answers verbatim. There was no attempt to weave the quotes into a narrative feature or to follow up on promising leads.

There were eleven questions and ten interviewees, making the feature very long and rather a plod. One of the questions was: 'Have you been able to establish any kind of professional relationship with your authors? If not, do you consider such contact desirable and why?' Here are two of the answers:

> Elfreda Powell: I have exchanged letters, phone calls and e-mails with some of the authors, where their texts are ambivalent or they have referred to something very obscure, or words are actually missing, but on the whole life is much simpler if there is little contact. It is not a question, as I have said, of translating the text literally (that is only the first draft): it has to be recreated into an acceptable English idiom, and this is something some of them find difficult to accept. This is less of a problem with Italian and Spanish authors than it is with the French, who very often consider they have a better knowledge of English than the English them-selves. On two separate occasions I have been told that I should translate 'flic' as 'bobby'!

> Laurie Thompson: I have translated crime novels by three Swedish authors. One wants no input whatsoever, but is willing to answer questions, if I really need to ask any. Another is keen to read the English version and answer questions, but will leave details and final wording to me, only pointing out errors or misunderstand-ings. The third, who is a former English teacher, is keen to point out stylistic subtleties he is rather proud of which I might have missed. This is very useful. I think it is always useful – even essen-tial – to contact the author and form a working relationship. We translators are playing around with their babies, after all. In my

experience almost all authors have been most co-operative and helpful, acknowledging that their English is pretty good but not good enough to make detailed judgements on style and subtleties, which they leave to me. It can get awkward if an author is convinced that his English is better than the translator's. Luckily, in my experience at least, this rarely happens. It has done, but not in connection with a crime novel.

There are some potentially interesting angles here, which would have been better followed up in conventional feature form, such as the problems of dealing with difficult authors who think they speak the language better than the translator, or how the translator approaches their work. The piece would also have benefited from some specific examples of the writers involved – naming names is always desirable.

The longest weekend (*Observer Magazine*, 26 March 2000)

This is one of those features that seemed like a good idea at the time, no doubt. But even the standfirst would fill the poor reader with a certain amount of trepidation: 'Few can resist a two-for-one offer. But who wants to spend more than a night in a service station? Michael Bywater checks into Clacket Lane Road Chef for an unwelcome break.' Sadly, the intro and second paragraph are no more enticing:

> It's not the Dome. Nothing is the Dome. Nor is it the Ayling Wheel, British Airways London Eye, going nowhere slowly and annoying the Queen. It's Clacket Lane.

> More than a motorway service area, Clacket Lane is the epitome of Mr Tony's New Britain. You can tell from the name itself, quivering with resonance. Clacket Lane. Say it. Clacket Lane. Hear the tappet-click of an aged slackjaw in NHS dentures munching through a microwaved service-station pie: adipocere pastry, centrifuged meat slurry, cloacal hogo, 'Good enough for the likes of us, can't be bothered with that mucked-about foreign stuff.'

Twenty-one rather hefty paragraphs later, we discover that there were not an awful lot of laughs to be had there, but really, do we care? A colour piece such as this needs a light touch which it didn't get here. Adipocere? Cloacal? Not many readers are prepared to go searching through their dictionaries just to read their Sunday newspaper!

Speed kills, there's no getting away from it
(*Gloucestershire Echo*, 24 August 2001)

This feature ignores one very useful rule of feature writing – personalise where possible. Here are the first two paragraphs:

> Road accidents happen every day, most of us stop and stare when we see one but we never think it will happen to us.
>
> This is the attitude which road safety campaigners are trying to change during August – National Road Victim Month.

The intro states the bleeding obvious! It would be much better to focus on someone who has either been in a serious accident or has lost a loved one in a crash. But in this feature that doesn't come along until paragraph nine, when we finally meet Jan Wildman, whose thirteen-year-old daughter was knocked down by a car in 1996. Then it turns out that in a thirty-five-paragraph feature, Mrs Wildman is the only human interest angle. Just two other people are interviewed: Gloucestershire County Council's road safety officer and a trustee from a charity called RoadPeace, which gives support to people injured or bereaved by road accidents. With a feature of this length (almost all of a tabloid page), you really need several people to act as case studies. Road safety contacts and appropriate pressure groups and charities should have been able to help with finding them.

PITCHING FOR WORK

Some features editors will prefer to deal with your ideas over the phone. Others will want an outline of what you are proposing by email. This can work to your advantage and give you something in writing in case there is a dispute later about what was agreed. If you are using email, make sure you have an appropriate and professional-sounding email address – sending pitches from something like sexysadie@emailaddress.com or superstud@thisismyemail.com send out entirely the wrong message! It's worth considering setting up a separate email address from your personal one so that you can channel all your work-related messages into that. If you have bought a related domain name with the intention of starting your own website, you can generally have a linked email address to that.

Press Gazette, the industry trade paper, has carried a regular 'how to pitch' column, where features editors and commissioning editors say what they are looking for. Gilly Sinclair, editor of *Chat*, the women's real-life weekly, gives us a lively rundown on what she wants:

- **Pitch to**: Me, the features editor: devinder_bains@ipcmedia.com or deputy features editor: ben_gelblum@ipcmedia.com.
- **Type of article**: Real-life, real-life and more real-life! Once and for all, we don't do celebs! Give us stories that will make us laugh, cry or leave us shocked. Give us pictures that will make us throw up or well up.
- **Topics**: Murder cases, miracle babies, juicy love rats, one-tonne boyfriends, psychic pussies, aliens stealing body parts and, of course, anything to do with Elvis.
- **How to pitch**: Email us with 200-word tasters that are short and sweet. Add bizarre, jaw-dropping headlines and pictures, and always make sure that all the legals are checked out.
- **Post-pitch**: If we like the story we'll get back to you pretty quickly with some questions or offers of wealth. If we haven't but you're sure the story's a winner, pick up the phone and call us.
- **What will impress**: A psychic hedgehog would make our day.
- **What won't impress**: People who don't read the magazine . . . I repeat, we don't do celeb stories! We don't take very kindly to 2,000-word tasters either.
- **Rates**: We discuss each story individually and it's fair to say that we offer very competitive rates. If it's a really great story we'll send you pizza too.
- **Images**: No, but it helps if they can advise us if collects [photos provided by the interviewee] and court pictures are available.
- **Any other info?**: It's believed that freelances who pitch to *Chat* before offering this stuff to other mags live at least ten years longer than those who don't. (http://www.pressgazette.co.uk/story.asp?sectioncode=7&storycode=41875&c=1, 13 August 2008; accessed 14 August 2008)

The outline works like a sales pitch, selling your idea to the features editor. It's a chance to be positive and to convince them what a great idea you've had and how their publication simply *has* to carry your feature. It's not an excuse to waffle on in excessive detail, though; you need to make the outline sharp, focused and positive in tone. Bear in mind that features editors receive countless press releases and proposals for features, so they don't want to have to wade through yours to find your story angle. Put it in the intro, then expand on it. Spend time making sure the outline looks professional – email is no excuse for sloppiness or informality – and that you have targeted it appropriately. If you've done your homework, you'll know who the features editor is and whether the publication is likely to be interested in your stunning proposal. Make sure you keep a copy of all your outlines. If you're a busy freelance submitting numerous ideas to a small number of magazines, you need to know which one has been accepted when someone contacts you to give you the go-ahead.

Do bear in mind, though, that you need to strike a balance between providing a commissioning editor with enough information and giving them too much, so that they might be tempted to take the idea and ask a staff journalist to write it up.

A pitch to the mythical Muddy Waters, editor of the equally mythical *Music World* magazine, might look something like this:

> Dear Mr Waters
>
> Would you be interested in a 1,000-word feature on the rise of Cajun music in Britain? What was once confined to dingy bars in the Deep South of America now has thousands jiving in clubs across the UK.
>
> The British phenomenon started in deepest Derby, and I'll be visiting the Swamp Club there to talk to the punters and to soak up the atmosphere.
>
> I'll also talk to Chris Hall, leader of Britain's top Cajun band, R Cajun and the Zydeco Brothers, who has set up his own industry devoted to the music. If you want to sample Cajun food, learn how to dance properly to the music, find a rare record, or book a band from the States, he's the man to approach.
>
> Also included in the piece will be some background on Cajun music, which originates in Louisiana. I'll also be asking British festival organisers why they're queuing up to book the authentic American bands.
>
> As an experienced music journalist, I have excellent contacts which will allow me to talk to the above people. I hope you will be interested in the finished article and I look forward to hearing from you soon.
>
> Yours sincerely
>
> Sharon Wheeler

A few points to bear in mind with pitch letters

- If you don't know who the features editor is, phone up the publication's switchboard and ask, or check in the front of the magazine or on the website.
- Don't send the pitch as an email attachment, unless you're specifically asked to. People often mistrust attachments because of viruses, or their word-processing package might not be compatible with yours. Paste the pitch into the body of the email.
- Note the use of Mr (or Ms, if appropriate). 'Dear Muddy Waters' sounds like you're trying to sell the poor man a *Reader's Digest* subscription or double-glazing. Only use 'Dear Muddy' if you know the features editor well.
- Be friendly without being overfamiliar, particularly if you don't know the person you are writing to.
- Don't waffle – and don't give too much away.

WORKING TO A BRIEF

Not all editors and features editors work in the same way once they have commissioned you to write a feature. Some will brief you verbally over the phone ('A thousand words, and make sure you interview Joe Bloggs'); others will confirm in a brief email. Others again may send you a formal brief that sets out angle, deadline, submission details and payment. This latter kind of brief is the ideal in most cases, as there can be no confusion as to what's required, and it saves wrangles over money later. There's nothing to stop you emailing your own summary of what has been agreed if you've only been briefed verbally.

It will depend very much on the degree to which you can deviate from a provided brief. But often you will carry out interviews and find much better angles. If you can put up a convincing argument, many features editors will be happy to be persuaded, especially if they have worked with you in the past and know you have a good nose for a story. If, though, they have a fixed idea in their head and will not compromise, you will have to accept that their angle is correct – after all, they're paying your wages!

MAKING CONTACTS

If you've worked as a news reporter already, you will be familiar with the concept of building up a contacts book. This particular item, be it an old-fashioned indexed address book or an electronic version (which, naturally, you have backed up to avoid disaster) should be guarded with your life, as it contains the names, phone numbers and email addresses of useful people who can help you with your story gathering. When you move into feature writing, many of these will still be useful. But there will be a range of other people you'll encounter or need to contact, and their details must be recorded assiduously. You can guarantee that if you don't note them down, you'll need them ten minutes before deadline! You will rapidly learn to be proactive when it comes to finding stories and making contacts – people do come to you, but not as often as you might like.

You will not come away immediately with screeds of copy, as it takes a while for people to get to know and trust you. When you phone or meet contacts, develop small talk and take the time to be pleasant and to chat – you will not get a story every time, but people will remember you. Be prepared to put yourself about a bit, attend relevant events and make lots of phone calls.

You might well find that as a features writer you decide to build up a specialist area. By covering sport, music and education I have a wide range of contacts stored away and a constant stream of features demanding to be written. When I started out covering music, I did so cold – and as a freelance. So I had no support to draw on for finding contacts and stories. It took a couple of years to get my face and name known in the music world. Going to gigs and festivals, and chatting to people without necessarily needing their immediate input for a story, was an excellent way of getting to know who was who as well as making myself known.

I've used music reporting as an example here for the sorts of people you should be targeting as contacts. You can adapt it easily to other areas, and to general news and feature writing:

- **Management**: agents and managers of bands; festival organisers; venue managers/bookers; record company PR people;
- **Workers**: the musicians themselves;
- **Support people**: record company or venue staff;
- **Observers**: fans (including fan clubs); and
- **Other experts**: music historians; specialist writers; university music departments.

If you want to build up a specialism, you'll need to put in some legwork to make sure the stories flow. When you're starting out – or trying to up your story rate as a fairly experienced journalist – you should consider the following.

Reference books

As a music writer, the *Rough Guide* and the *Guinness Who's Who* series have been invaluable. Even though it's several years since I covered music regularly, I still buy Irish- and world music-related books as a matter of course. If you're starting out and you're on a tight budget, check your library, and remember that they can order you almost any book. If you're determined to own the book, and it's either out of print or eye-wateringly expensive, check second-hand bookshops or online sources such as Amazon Marketplace or Abebooks.

Magazines

Buy as many as you can afford in your area of interest. You need to know what the opposition is up to, and they will provide ideas on where to sell future articles, or a new spin on a story idea. The appearance of many magazines online is a fantastic space-saver, as you can now bookmark them, although some parts of the websites may be open only to subscribers. If you save the print copies, it makes sense to cut out the articles that interest you. If you're more interested in hanging on to pristine copies of the magazines, either photocopy the useful features or make a note of the month and the page number. I have an attic full of back copies of *Q*, *Mojo*, *Vox*, *Select*, *NME*, *fRoots*, *Rock 'n' Reel* and *Hot Press* and can confirm from personal experience that it's time-consuming (and distracting, as you're bound to get side-tracked) riffling through back copies to find the one article you want urgently.

Websites

Bookmark useful websites assiduously – and back up the bookmark file in your browser. Make sure you clearly label the site rather than saving it as 'home'. As well as bookmarking publications, as suggested above, think laterally about which sites you might find useful in future. I have a folder full of websites for bands, both the official and unofficial sites. Fan sites can be particularly useful if you need to rustle up someone in a hurry to quote in a feature. Online radio stations are my latest craze, as they keep me in touch with new bands or new trends in the industry. General sites can be useful as well, such as those with a historical or survey bent to them. And thanks to the rise of social bookmarking and sharing websites, such as del.icio.us, Digg, Reddit, Facebook and Stumbleupon, you can store, tag and share links across the internet. And you can access those links from any computer, which is useful if you're at work and need the information urgently.

Discussion lists

Sign up for online discussion lists – Yahoogroups, for example, host lists on virtually every topic under the sun. These act as a giant 'copy to all' message. You send out a message and it appears in the inboxes of everyone who has subscribed to the list – which might range from single figures to thousands. But be honest about why you're there. If you're leaping into the discussion as a fan, fair enough. However, if you're there as a journalist nosing out stories, make this clear if you approach people offlist for quotes. It's unethical to use information gained on these lists without letting people know what you're doing.

Blogs, MySpace, Facebook

Unless you're a complete computer Luddite, the chances are that you will have one or more of these on the go. Every journalist – particularly freelances – should have a work-related blog, which acts as a calling card for them. You can set up a blog either for free or for just a few pounds on LiveJournal, Typepad or Blogger. Paying for an account generally means you are spared annoying adverts, and it may allow you extra functions. Using tags (keywords) wisely means your entries will show up in internet searches. Link, as well, to useful and relevant people (although it's good etiquette to check with them first). On LiveJournal this is known as 'friending'. Filling in your profile and interests on LiveJournal will ensure like-minded people can find you – although 'friend' with care, as they can read your private, locked posts. Facebook is an excellent way of maintaining a public profile as well as being able to search out useful contacts. Be cautious, though, about how much private information you give out online, and never put up anything that you wouldn't want an employer to see.

Mailing lists

In the music world, joining a mailing list is an accepted way of keeping musicians and fans in touch. At one time you scribbled your name and address down on a scrappy bit of paper at the merchandise table after the gig. Now you join online and periodically a newsletter will drop into your inbox. In the electronic age email mailing lists are now the norm across a range of areas. I subscribe to a number from crime fiction writers which keep me up to date on new books for the website I edit.

Fan clubs/societies

Make sure you know who the key contacts are for fan clubs and societies related to your area of interest. You don't have to rush out and join them all – in fact, when it comes to fan clubs, it's probably better if you don't, to avoid possible conflicts of interest later. Stay in touch with organisers, though, as you would with any other contacts.

Conferences/conventions

Keep an eye open for specialist events and attend them if you can – the chances are that lots of key people will be gathered together in the same place, and you'll think it's Christmas as you mingle with them, distributing your business card to all and sundry. Some of the events are worth stories in their own right – I always enjoyed a student's colour piece on a Dr Who convention where her intro focused on a Dalek running over her foot and the rest of the feature detailed her encounter with the actor Jon Pertwee.

Conventions often provide fantastic material for colour pieces. The *Guardian* (13 August 2005) had a field day when an event to mark the fiftieth anniversary of the full publication of *The Lord of the Rings* took place at Aston University in Birmingham. The piece was headlined 'Hordes of the rings', and accompanied by a picture of a fan dressed up as Tom Bombadil sporting a very splendid pointy hat and long beard. Reporter Patrick Barkham found plenty of people to interview – an 'official' source in the shape of Chris Crawshaw, chair of the Tolkien Society, plus half a dozen fans in various states of fancy dress (including a sixteen-year-old who had spent £4,000 on Tolkien collectables, and a dealer in hobbit paraphernalia who had travelled over from Colorado for the event). Shame about the feature's intro, though, which wins no prizes for snappy writing:

> Beyond the man in the leather waistcoat, past bears and medieval-style black jeans that are laced together where seams should be, is a vision in blue with bright yellow boots. Hey dol, merry dol, as JRR Tolkien's character would sing, it's Tom Bombadil. Wearing a blue feather in a felt hat, a blue cape and carrying a posy of lavender, Mr Bombadil – real name Firiel Tindomerel – flew from Switzerland to Birmingham as Middle Earth came to the Midlands yesterday.

BUILDING UP A SPECIALISM

Editors like specialists. They can call on them for instant background information on a story, and will rely on them to turn out a range of features on a topic. Once you have gained a reputation for knowing your area, you should find the phone rings a lot. If you flick through several newspapers and magazines, you'll soon be able to spot who the specialist writers are, beginning with the obvious ones on the sports page, and moving through the reporters covering home affairs, politics, the environment, motoring, music, the arts and so on.

Becoming a specialist

There's no one way to become a specialist reporter. Often on newspapers people will start off as news reporters, and then branch out when it becomes apparent they have a particular interest, or if a gap opens up. It will often take persistence, particularly if you want to move into popular areas such as sport and music. And depending on your specialism, you may find yourself still being required to do some news reporting, alongside covering such areas as the environment and politics. Because magazines have a different training structure, a reporter is more likely to start out as a specialist from the beginning.

A specialist reporter must be versatile, possess a contacts book to die for, have an encyclopedic knowledge of their area, and be able to turn out a variety of stories at the drop of a hat. As we'll see later, specialists come into their own when big stories hit the headlines. Aside from the usual news stories and features diet, they may well find themselves knocking out backgrounders, quotes stories and think pieces related to their area.

Finding an area

The following list is in no way exhaustive, but it will give you an idea of the specialist areas out there. Although many reporters find their niche and stay there, others are versatile and work across several. Things will change during your career as opportunities open up.

- Sport
- Women
- Health
- Fashion
- Arts/entertainment
- Music
- Media
- Computing/technology
- Science
- Business
- Finance
- Politics
- Environment/green
- Farming
- Travel
- Food
- Gardening
- Legal
- Education
- Motoring

Knowing your market

Bear in mind there will be some differences in the way you operate, depending on whether you're a staff reporter or a freelance. Many freelances opt to work on their own simply because they can make a living from covering something that interests them, rather than being sent off to cover court cases or chase fire engines.

But there are a lot of freelances out there, many struggling to make a reasonable living, and finding that they need to be versatile to ensure they can pay the mortgage every month. So while we'd all like to be able to pick and choose what we do and whom we write for, it's also a matter of spotting a gap in the market and being realistic about it. There are plenty of football reporters, but not many journalists covering, say, three-day eventing. There are several reasons for this, not least that football is substantially the more popular of the two sports and that someone covering a niche sport may find it difficult to make a living as a freelance, or would be expected as a sports desk member to carry out other writing and/or sub-editing duties. So reporters wanting to cover three-day eventing may find that they need to be versatile, by covering several equine sports, for example.

Be realistic about which markets will take your features. Make sure you are familiar with a range of newspapers, magazines and websites – and never overlook the trade press if you have the specialist knowledge that will be useful to them. You might not make a fortune, but you could ensure regular work, which helps pay the bills:

Someone working as a music freelance will have a vast market in front of them. The weekly music press is nowhere near as influential as it used to be, although NME still has a strong presence. Mojo, Word and Q are the main general monthly magazines, although each caters to a slightly different market. There are any number of specialist publications as well, including Kerrang!, Mix Mag, Rock 'n' Reel and fRoots. And on the more technical side you'll find DJ and Music Week. The style magazine market has declined in importance since The Face closed, but the likes of Dazed and Confused and i-D use music features. Most of the national papers have music pages, although many are review-based (see both the Guardian and the Independent on Fridays for features as well as reviews). And never overlook your local paper, although they may be interested only in bands from their patch. Nevertheless, if you live in a city such as Bristol or Glasgow with a lively music scene, you'll never be short of ideas.

With the internet, it's worth remembering that dealing with overseas newspapers and magazines is now much easier (although getting paid can sometimes be a challenge – to avoid bank charges, consider setting up a Paypal account).

Finding a niche in the market can make you very useful to editors. Transport expert Christian Wolmar says he got into it by accident. 'In 1992 I was transport correspondent of the Independent. It was a good time to do that job, as the railways had been privatised, there were lots of protests and accidents, and it got a lot of prominent coverage. I eventually went freelance five years later. It was a niche not many people were in.' Wolmar now writes for a wide range of media, including the specialist press, and he is also in demand as an expert – he may be asked to do several hundred TV and radio interviews each year to comment on big transport stories.

CASE STUDY – EMMA ELMS, FEATURES DIRECTOR, *EVE* MAGAZINE

What's your approach to features editing – from thinking up ideas to the finished product hitting the news stands?

Once a month the features team on *eve* have a big ideas meeting with the editor where we'll all pitch ideas for the next issue. You need to be able to 'sell' your idea to the team, so it's best to do your research first, making sure you're clued up on what makes it newsworthy or what kind of case studies you might include. Ideas can be sparked by anything, from a chat with a friend or something in your personal life, to a story you've seen in the papers, on TV or on the web.

After the features meeting, the next step is for the editor, along with her deputy and the features director, to decide on a list of features for the next issue. Each month the magazine often has a special theme and we have certain regular slots to fill to ensure a good mix, such as the 'real life' slot and the 'columnist' slot.

Next, we'll commission all the features, writing detailed briefs for any freelance writers. About half the features are written in-house by our two staff writers, the rest are commissioned to freelancers. We have a large pool of regular journalists we use, but we're also open to new writers if they come up with a great idea.

We'll have at least two picture meetings a month to discuss visual ideas to go with the copy. It's important to think of the feature as a complete package and to make it as clear and eye-catching as possible.

Once the copy comes in, I'll do a thorough edit, sending the feature back to the writer for any changes I think it needs – this could be extra quotes from an interviewee or a slight tweaking of the tone. Once I've done a final polish, the copy goes through to the editor to read, before being subbed and fact-checked, then designed on the page by the art team. It's a great feeling seeing the final feature on proof.

What sort of features interest you the most?

I'm particularly keen on dramatic or emotionally charged real life stories. Nothing beats the thrill of securing a big exclusive interview with someone who's in the news. It's a real honour when someone chooses to share their life story with you.

I also love quirky trend reports. In *eve* we've run some great LA stories such as 'The dating club for women wanting to marry a millionaire' and a report on 'The Hollywood wet nurses' – women hired by the LA elite to breastfeed their babies. I like to commission stories our readers won't have seen anywhere else.

What's your approach to editing and commissioning for the crowded women's market?

It's important to know your reader inside out – you need to put yourself in her shoes and work out what her hopes, dreams and fears are. The best way to do this is to read the letters that come into the mag or attend any reader events if possible. If you're the target audience yourself it's even easier – I tend to commission and edit pieces which I know will interest my friends and me.

The balance of features is crucial – you need the magazine to offer a range of different reads, from thought-provoking reports and compelling emotional stories, to light-hearted opinion pieces and bite-size pieces of life advice.

The tone of features is important too – the voice of the magazine needs to be consistent. As a reader, you want the magazine to feel like a 'friend', so it needs to feel on the same wavelength as you.

Which features have been particularly memorable/effective?

The powerful first-person stories are always the ones that stay with you. I'll never forget one woman's account of her miscarriage. She described the experience with such honesty and raw emotion, yet also managed to convey a sense of optimism as she'd gone on to become a mother afterwards.

Another memorable feature was a report I commissioned on China's *ernai* – women paid to be 'second wives' by wealthy businessmen. It was a tough one to pull off as I had to find a local journalist prepared to approach *ernai* and their agents in hostess bars, but it all came together perfectly. It was a fascinating read.

Another favourite was a shocking report on the rise of 'freebirthing' – women who choose to give birth alone, with no medical assistance. It was one of those features you just can't put down.

What are the top tips you'd give a young feature writer pitching to you?

Email a brief, lively synopsis of your idea to the features editor (ideally no more than three paragraphs). Add an attention-grabbing headline and mention any topical or newsworthy hook (e.g., a new survey, new research, a new TV programme/film, a celebrity angle). Give details of any potential case studies you'd aim to include.

You should also say which other magazines you write for. If you're still studying, just describe yourself as a 'freelance journalist' initially. Also, make sure you familiarise yourself with the magazine first so you don't suggest an idea which they have recently covered.

The most important thing is that your idea sounds fresh and original. If you have special access to a juicy real life interview that can be a great way to get started as you're the only journalist who can do the story.

Biography?

I have been a journalist for twelve years, working within the women's glossy magazine market. Before joining *eve* as features director, I worked on *Marie Claire* as deputy features editor, writing and commissioning everything from global reportage features to compelling real life stories. I have also worked on *Cosmopolitan* as senior writer, specialising in investigative reports and real life stories, and interviewing celebrities such as Britney Spears.

3
How to write features
Getting personal

Features are challenging articles to write. It's not simply a matter of knocking off a 250-word 'he said, she said' news story. With a feature you may have a 3,000-word space to fill and half a dozen interviews to sift through. Half the challenge – and half the fun – of feature writing is the revising and rewriting process during which, when the pieces fall into place, you gain a great deal of satisfaction from the final polished product.

Feature writing, too, is a chance to develop a 'voice'. After those straight-down-the-middle constraints of news writing, it's possible for a feature writer to elbow to the front of a piece. This, of course, depends on what your subject matter is. It's probably not going to be appropriate for the writer to make a sudden guest appearance in the middle of a serious news feature on gang warfare in Britain's inner cities – unless they get held up at gunpoint. But a colour piece in which a reporter wanting to give up smoking decides to try acupuncture is another matter. And very often with profile writing, the interviewer plays a significant part in the story.

The *Independent*'s Deborah Ross is one of the most distinctive voices in the genre. Chirpy, chatty and forthright, she is an acquired taste for some readers; you may enjoy her role in the story, or you may feel she threatens to overwhelm it and relegate the subject to a supporting role. In Ross's profile of TV gardener Charlie Dimmock ('Storm in a B-cup, 19 April 1999), the star finally appears after several hundred words. Prior to that, the writer is firmly centre stage:

> Charlie Dimmock – that great pioneer of bra-less gardening – is coming round my house! We are all very excited. I am excited, because I want to show her my own water feature, cleverly constructed from a wholly nasty B&Q barbecue left out for six winters, and now full of big, floating, rusty bits. However, my partner is even more excited. Naturally, this is not because he is especially

keen on gardening although, that said, he has, on occasion, put on old trousers and told me where to dig. No, he is excited because Charlie, he says, is pure horticultural Viagra. Charlie's bosom, he continues, is a magnificent thing, especially when she's out there with a pick-axe in one of those superbly thin T-shirts and the weather is playing ball. He has even come up with a little plan to make his fortune. He is, he says, going to set up a stall outside, offering teas, coffees and binoculars to the local males of the neighbourhood, according to the following price scale:

If the weather is mild: 50p

If there is a nip in the air: £7.95

If there's a lot of nip in the air, plus every chance of a downpour: £69.80

Your view on whether this intro works may depend on how tired you are of constant references to Charlie Dimmock not wearing a bra. I could have lived without the rather 'tee hee hee' tone, although there is no disputing Ross has a strong and entertaining voice. Also, as the feature progresses, and once the juvenile fascination with bras has run its course, there's a skilled weaving together of biographical detail about the star and the running gag about Ross's own back garden.

Lynn Barber, perhaps the best and most experienced feature writer operating in British newspapers at the time of writing, has another approach. She is often part of the story – but only in a way that helps nail another facet of her subject. Take her interview with actor Jeremy Irons, originally published in the *Sunday Express*, then reprinted in *Mostly Men* (1992), a selection of Barber's profiles. It's a classic example of letting someone stitch himself up with minimal help from the interviewer:

This is not an objective article. I don't want to give a cool appraisal of Jeremy Irons, or even to be snide. I just want to boil him in oil.

A month ago I had no strong views on Jeremy Irons. He was a tall, handsome English actor who was good in *Brideshead*. Then a nice PR asked if I'd like to see a preview of *Danny, the Champion of the World*, starring Jeremy and his ten-year-old son Sam Irons, with a view to interviewing him. I saw the film, I liked it, I said yes.

My diary thereafter has scratched-out appointments with Jeremy Irons on practically every day. I was supposed to meet him in the Groucho Club, at home, in a photographer's studio. One day I was supposed to have lunch with him but he cancelled at a few hours' notice because he 'didn't like to eat and talk at the same time'. The PR was often almost sobbing as he delivered these messages to me.

This continued for three weeks or more. Finally there came a morning when I had a 10.30am appointment with Jeremy Irons at a West End hotel and the PR didn't phone to cancel. I assumed this was mere oversight, but went along anyway. Who should be there waiting for me: not Jeremy Irons, not the PR, but Theo Cowan. Now Theo Cowan, I should explain, is the doyen of film publicists and a much-loved and respected figure on the showbiz scene. Finding him waiting to babysit a Jeremy Irons interview was a bit like going to the passport office to renew my passport and finding Sir Geoffrey Howe behind the counter.

''E's late,' said Theo Cowan. We sat and waited. At 10.50 Jeremy Irons sauntered in. He didn't apologise for his lateness, he didn't say hello or shake hands, he said: 'Well, we all know who we are and why we're here – let's get on with it.'
(Barber, 1992: 196–197)

These first few paragraphs of a thirty-two-paragraph feature do more than set the stall. The intro leaves us in absolutely no doubt as to Barber's feelings about Irons. But the slightly overstated 'I want to boil him in oil' retains a sense of humour beneath the annoyance and exasperation. At no time during the interview does Barber descend to personal insults. Instead she reports, without comment or elaboration, how Irons behaves – she shows him getting up during the interview and replacing the curtain ties on the curtains because he can't bear to see them upside down. The judicious use of italics in the direct speech focuses on the actor's inflections and allows the reader to draw their own conclusions about what sort of person Irons is.

The writing is relaxed, fluent and tinged with deadpan humour. Barber retells what happened in the style of a friend sitting with you in the pub, sharing a 'guess what happened to me today' anecdote. I particularly like the comparison between PR doyen Theo Cowan babysitting Irons and Sir Geoffrey Howe (foreign secretary when the article was first published) handing out passports. It's worth noting the final paragraph, in which Barber saves one of the most telling quotes for last:

And at the end when he still hadn't mentioned, let alone apologised for, our two dozen cancelled appointments, I raised the subject myself. 'Oh that,' he said airily. 'It was the publicity people's fault. They just can't do their jobs.'
(Barber, 1992: 202)

It's only fair to point out that hatchet jobs – no-holds barred critical attacks on subjects – aren't everyday occurrences for most reporters. But it's not unreasonable, when you are trying to portray a person to the readership, to report the negative alongside the positive when it's appropriate and deserved. And, as Barber proves in the profile, the most effective way to get the message across is through understatement.

The best feature writers are relaxed and fluent storytellers. In fact, fluency in writing is a non-negotiable requirement. Bear that in mind when trying to adopt a distinctive voice. The *Radio Times'* Andrew Duncan has adopted a faintly bizarre approach where he seems to avoid mentioning the subject's first or last name. Once you notice this affectation, it makes reading the profile an off-putting experience, as you are constantly aware of the 'he, he, he', 'she, she, she' mode of writing.

Don't get the idea, though, that profiles only work if they are about famous people. On the contrary, some of the best pieces can be about ordinary people with a good story to tell. That might be the woman infected with the HIV virus by a former boyfriend, or the man who collects airline sick bags, or the amateur rugby player still taking to the field at the age of sixty-five.

The *Observer* found a reluctant heroine in Aileen Jones, a lifeboatwoman in south Wales. In the profile, 'We save people, it's just our job' (14 August 2005), reporter Louise France finds an interesting, if rather bemused, interviewee:

> You would never guess, walking along Porthcawl's faded Victorian seafront, where couples wrestle with nothing more unpredictable than melting mint choc-chip ice creams, that this is one of the most dangerous stretches of coastline in the world. But behind the elderly volunteer manning the Royal National Lifeboat stall, robustly battling both gusts of wind and a shortage of small change, a notice states: 'This station has carried out 24 services and has saved 10 lives since January 2005. Most recent: 31 July. Speedboat in bay. Two people rescued.'
>
> To be honest, neither would you guess that Aileen Jones, the slightly built, modest woman I meet inside the two-storey lifeboat building, is a local hero (a description she would most definitely wince at). This 42-year-old teaching assistant and mother of two, as the newspapers near her home in south Wales have taken to describing her recently, is rather embarrassed about the attention she's received this past year. Almost exactly 12 months ago, on 24 August 2004, in the midst of force eight winds and 10-foot waves, she was instrumental in rescuing two fishermen. She has now become the first woman to be awarded a Royal National Lifeboat medal in 116 years.

Later in the piece, the journalist tries to find out what makes this brave woman tick:

> The idea that people would court force eight gales, four-metre swells, rain like stair rods, all for no financial gain, seems strangely old-fashioned.
>
> Why does she do it?
>
> Aileen looks baffled. Not because she can't think of an answer but she can't understand why I'm even asking.
>
> 'It's something that I want to do. It's good. We save people. It's the comradeship. It's the training. It's the lady in the shop who is in her eighties. It's the whole team. I love that. And I love the sea . . . I love the fact that when you're going into the wind, it hammers in your ears. When it's behind you, it's silent.'
>
> But doesn't she get frightened?
>
> 'If you're scared, then you're not the right person to do it.'

Including your questions in the piece can be risky, as it can often look like you're asking more questions than are being answered. But in this case, with a reticent interviewee, the writer didn't have a lot of choice. You may also want to do this sometimes if you have had a short, sharp exchange with the interviewee that will look revealing in print.

INTERVIEWING FOR FEATURES

In almost every case, the best profiles come as the result of face-to-face interviews. But there will be times when you can only chat to people on the phone or via email, and in those cases you have to make the best of the situation. Both phone and email have advantages and disadvantages to bear in mind. On the phone you get to hear the person's voice, but you will miss facial expressions and may not pick up on deadpan or sarcastic comments. And you can't guarantee that you have the interviewee's undivided attention – they may be flicking through a newspaper, channel-hopping on TV or surfing the internet while talking to you. If someone doesn't like the way an interview is going, slamming a phone down is a lot easier than being rude to someone's face. But grabbing a chat with someone on the phone is better than nothing, and may even be the difference between no feature and something that will get published.

The same goes for email interviews. I would have found it difficult to carry out some of the interviews with American journalists for this book without email – people in different time zones can deal with the questions at a convenient time to them. And asking follow-up questions was easy once I had their initial answers in front of me. Some interviewees even seem to prefer email, as they can mull over the answers and perhaps provide supplementary information that you might not get with a done-and-dusted phone interview. Email interviews make writing up the feature easier, in that you can cut and paste quotes into the piece – although note that you must still sift information sensibly. The disadvantages are a lack of urgency – you have to remind email interviewees that you have a deadline to hit and that you need their answers by a certain time. Emails also run the risk of ending up in the other person's spam filter. There's no sure-fire way of avoiding this, but not using some of the free email accounts may help. And, of course, online you can't always be sure whom you're speaking to – so obtaining email addresses by official sources (via websites, colleagues of the person, employers or trusted contacts) is preferable. After an email interview, I will often try to phone the person as well, if feasible, just for my peace of mind and for a quick summary conversation.

Phone interview tips

- Do as much preparation as you can – people will not want to give you lots of background over the phone. And if you've got only fifteen minutes with a celebrity, you'll need every second of that time to coax something new and interesting out of them.
- Ensure you're speaking to the right person – being passed between switchboards guarantees confusion all round.
- Identify yourself and your publication clearly.
- Remind the person briefly why you are interviewing them – often famous or busy people are in the press for other reasons, and they might not remember that you are doing a profile of them, rather than just asking them about their new book.
- Get essential details (full name, age, address, occupation) at the start of the conversation in case the interview is terminated abruptly for some reason.
- Double-check spellings of names – it's easy to mishear on the phone and to assume someone is called Nick when their name is actually Mick, for example.
- Keep the questions brief – complicated ones will lose the other person.

- Sound bright, friendly and alert – and don't mutter.
- Listen to the other person's tone of voice, and check if you are not sure about something they have said.
- Try to avoid long pauses – otherwise the interviewee might think you have been cut off.
- At the end of the interview, thank them for their time and check whether they will be contactable for the next twenty-four hours or so, in case you need to clarify anything with them. If appropriate, give them your phone number and/or email address in case they want to contact you.

Email interview tips

- Try to track down the person's email address through a legitimate source so that you can be fairly sure they are who they say they are.
- Outline at the top of the email what it is you want from them, and when you need a response by.
- Keep the questions sharp and focused.
- It's often best not to send a long list of questions that might look off-putting to the interviewee. Start with, say, half a dozen, and wait for the responses to those. Then you can email some more, and also ask follow-up questions based on the information they have given. If, though, you know it's a one-shot email, then you must prioritise the questions.

Preparing for the interview

You cannot busk most profiles. And, if you know you're going to be allowed limited time with the interviewee, it's in your interests to do as much homework as you can beforehand. The more preparation you can do, the less time you'll need to spend on routine biographical questions – especially if you are likely to be up against the clock. Be prepared, though, to check with the person about anything contradictory you come across in cuttings about them.

The main research areas are your newspaper or magazine's own cuttings library; the internet; and other publications. If you work on a publication of any size, previous articles will have been archived into an online library, so it's worth browsing through these to see what's been written about your subject in the past.

Thanks to the internet, you can also access other publications' back editions. Don't lift information from these – it's not good practice, and you have no way of knowing if what's been printed is 100 per cent accurate. But you should be able to see what angles have been covered elsewhere. The internet itself is a mixed blessing for journalists. If you work on the Sturgeon's Law principle – that 90 per cent of what you find is rubbish – you won't be too disappointed when a search brings up little of use. But always check to see if the person you are interviewing has their own website, or whether official websites (such as those belonging to a government body or a company) contain helpful material. You might find that fan websites contain useful snippets, but be sure to check their accuracy.

You should also aim to monitor other publications that may feature the person you will be interviewing. Again, do not try to copy what they have done, but make sure you don't miss an angle. Most newspaper offices will stock opposition papers, but you should get into the habit of keeping up to date with specialist publications. If you're a general music writer, don't miss the *Observer*'s monthly music magazine, or *Mojo*, or *Q*. If you cover more specialised areas of the music world, get the specialist magazines. It's also good practice to start building up your own library of useful books. And get friendly with your local librarian.

Chat to people who know the person you're going to interview. These might be colleagues who have interviewed them in the past, or their acquaintances. Any friends and enemies might be worth quoting in the finished article.

If you're about to interview someone who has an agent or a publicist, ask them to send you any biographical material that might be useful. Most of what they send will probably be puffery and of limited use, and bear in mind that every other publication will probably receive it too, but it might provide an insight into the person and their background. Publicity material has been known to be wrong, so check anything that looks unclear.

Map out some questions and themes that you'd like to talk about with the interviewee. You don't need to write out twenty-five questions laboriously – the danger here is that you get too attached to them and miss clues that might be dropped in your path. You may find that a small list of themes is quite enough to keep your mind focused, but be flexible – if the interview goes off in a more fruitful direction, scrap your list and go with the flow. You might want to come up with a couple of off-beat questions to be tossed in if the person is heavy going, or if you feel the need to try an ice-breaker. David Randall (2007: 88–89) suggests some short, sharp questions which, he says, often yield unexpected answers, or persuade the subject to open up about areas of their life:

- What is your first memory?
- What was your mother/father's best advice?
- Who has had the most impact on your life?
- What was your first job?
- What was your worst job?
- What was your first car?
- Who was your first love?
- What do you do when you are nervous?
- What are you compulsive about?
- Have you got a bad temper?
- What do you eat/not eat?
- Who is your best friend?
- What is your worst habit?
- What makes you angry?
- What do you study?
- How often do you read?
- How many hours a night do you sleep?
- What do you do if you wake in the night and can't get back to sleep?
- What is your ideal day off?
- When do you plan to quit?
- Who would be your favourite party guests?
- Do you like Christmas?
- What is your favourite song/book/film/singer/artist?
- Who do you admire most?
- What is your favourite drink?
- Where is your favourite vacation place?
- Where would you live if you had total freedom of choice?

I can confirm from personal experience that throwing in a slightly unexpected question *does* often work (although not always – with some interviewees such questions will not be appropriate). Some years ago I interviewed a top Cajun band whom I'd once poked fun at in a review – and their memories were longer than mine! The interview was decidedly slow to get going, but when I lobbed in a question about which ten Cajun records they would recommend to newcomers to the genre, the ice was broken and they talked and argued among themselves very happily, giving me some great quotes.

It's not sensible to go in with a preconceived angle. Some publications will want a specific focus, certainly, but you run the risk of skewing the profile, or of missing more intriguing opportunities. You're the person conducting the interview – if necessary, try to persuade the features editor that you have come back with a better take on the person. They might not go for it, but it's always worth a try.

Conducting the interview

You might not have any say in where the interview takes place – the interviewee may insist on neutral ground – at their record company, in their publicist's office, or in a pub or restaurant. If you get the chance, though, try to interview them on their own territory, be it home or work. You'll draw your own conclusions about a businessman who keeps you waiting twenty minutes, has a gigantic desk with just a phone and blotter placed minutely on it, waves you to the low chair and spends most of the interview taking calls on his mobile. Home locations can be equally revealing, as Val Hennessy discovered when she travelled to Kent to interview Bob Geldof for *you* magazine:

> I had the privilege of meeting Bob Geldof back in 1983 when he was simply a Boomtown Rat and I had seen his star in the South East and had come to worship him. A newspaper had set up my visit to the Geldofs' medieval friary home in Faversham where the dazzling Paula Yates shoved a microwaved corn cob (Geldof grown) and a potato-in-its-skin under my nose and the effervescent Bob said 'You're f*****g welcome to stay the night.' I was entranced. He was so unstar-like. Love, of a Chernobyl intensity, radiated between Bob and Paula. When each walked the other's way a thousand lead guitars began to play. In the morning I was woken by Bob's flock of sheep bleating outside his mullioned windows and by Bob himself, like Albert Schweitzer on amphetamine, crashing in with a cup of tea and perching on the end of the spare bed in his shortie dressing gown to rage about injustice, bureaucracy, Apartheid, Mrs Thatcher and the 'f*****g slime' who write nasty things about Bob and Paula in *The Melody Maker*. I hung onto his every word. No flies on Bob. Later, he cooked me some toast and, at some point, threw a telephone across the kitchen.
> (Hennessy, 1990: 48)

The mix of overstatement ('the thousand lead guitars began to play') and punchy sentences make this an admittedly long, but highly atmospheric and effective intro to a profile.

Be prepared to ask plenty of questions so you can build up as full a picture as possible of the person. If you know this is going to be a time-limited interview, prioritise what to ask. Often, if someone says they can spare only half an hour, you can scrounge a little extra time. But don't rely on it – particularly if this is a famous person with a queue of journalists waiting downstairs.

It makes sense to open up the interview with the new angle – the reason why you're there. Questioning in themes often works well, allowing you to move between career, private life, interests and any other relevant areas, while always remembering where you have been. Listen for clues as the interview progresses and be prepared to follow them. And let the subject talk – if you keep interrupting them it's disconcerting and makes it difficult to build up any fluency in the interview. If they ramble, though, nudge them back on to the topic. The 'that's very interesting, but I'd like to ask you about . . .' approach generally works. If they're monosyllabic, make sure you ask open rather than closed questions. And try to vary the pace of the interview with some of those off-beat questions Randall suggests. These can often act as ice-breakers – as long as you're not interviewing a very grand person who might not take them in the right spirit!

Sooner or later, you will have to ask an interviewee some tricky questions. Don't dodge them, but be careful when you throw them in. It makes sense to keep them until the end, so if the person storms out in a snit, you still have plenty of material. And frame them subtly: 'How do you react to claims that you sacrifice cats in your back garden?' may get more of a response than saying bluntly, 'What about all those cats that you've nailed to your garden fence?'

GETTING READY TO WRITE UP

We've already established that the best thing you can do is immerse yourself in what other people do. You'll soon start to develop a feel for which features work and which don't. Personally, I dislike those question-and-answer-style features. They're fine for short, sharp, formulaic pieces (we'll look at those in Chapter 6), but for anything over a couple of hundred words, they run the risk of becoming an unedited information dump where a reporter has set their recorder going, thrown in some questions, then simply transcribed the result.

Notebook versus recorder

Any trained reporter will tell you just how useful shorthand is. It takes you into places that recorders can't go. And it doesn't run out of batteries or get knocked on the floor in a media scrum. A good shorthand note of an interview is also vital in case of dispute. However, a recorder's hand doesn't feel like it's about to drop off at the end of a two-hour interview! Unless your shorthand is impeccable, writing for long stints is a challenge.

My own preference for longer interviews – any over half an hour – is to use a recorder, but to have a notebook alongside. The advantage of a recorder, particularly when you are doing long profiles, is that you can set it going, then more or less forget about it (except to check periodically that it's still running). This allows you to engage better with the interviewee and to maintain eye contact, something that's difficult to do when you are scribbling frantically with a pen and notebook to capture what's said.

Having a notebook alongside you, though, is very useful for jotting down impressions of the person you're interviewing, or the place where the interview is taking place. And it's also a good place to store spellings of names and places. I often also use the notebook to keep a record of when something particularly vital was said. Knowing that the perfect angle for your intro came up twenty minutes into the recording will really speed things up when you come to write up, and it will save you lots of fast-forwarding and reviewing as you search for the relevant section. If you do use a notebook for the whole interview, getting into the habit of creating a margin where you can asterisk key points or jot down observations will also help during the writing-up stage.

It's a matter of courtesy to check with interviewees that they don't mind being recorded. Most are likely to be fine about it, particularly if you persuade waverers with the thought that there won't be any doubt about what they have said. Some people positively prefer being taped – veteran politician Tony Benn sets his own recorder alongside the interviewer's at the start of each interview.

Which brings us to what you do when you have a notebook or digital recorder full of information. About the worst thing you can do is transcribe everything – and you simply won't have the time in most situations. One of the first things you learn as a journalist in a busy newspaper office is that working straight on to the computer is the only way to go. Scribbling countless handwritten drafts is a waste of time when you are up against tight deadlines and have a perfectly good cut-and-paste facility on your computer.

That doesn't mean, though, that you can't marshal your thoughts with some sort of plan before you start writing up. This often helps if you've got a complicated feature with a number of different strands to it. Jotting down a bullet-point list of what you *must* include, and in what order, is a useful aide-mémoire to have by your side as you type.

Finding an angle

Your first thought when embarking on any feature (or, indeed, almost any story for a print market) should be human interest. Readers are nosy – they want to know about other people. There are very few stories where you can't find a person to provide the focus. A good, strong, human interest angle will personalise a story and make it feel closer and more immediate to the readers.

What's often a challenge, though, is finding an angle on a big national or international story. Good feature writers think laterally, and cater to their specific market. When *Dr Who* reappeared on British TV, there were countless features on stars Christopher Eccleston and Billie Piper, retrospectives looking at the former Doctors and their assistants, and articles asking whether the Daleks were scarier than the Cybermen. Gay men's lifestyle magazine *Attitude* did a profile of actor John Barrowman, who played bisexual hero Captain Jack and is gay in real life. The cult TV magazines, meanwhile, went to town on the return of the show and published detailed interviews with most of those involved, as well as looking back to how the show had evolved over the years.

But what do you do if you've been asked to come up with a new angle on the annual ritual that is *Big Brother*? The *Guardian*'s Gareth McLean came up with a nifty profile of Marcus Bentley, the Geordie narrator from the show: 'You don't know this man – but you know his voice' (9 August 2002).

> It was, apparently, the way he said 'chickens'. Marcus Bentley says it again. 'Chickens.' It is quite a thrill. Say it again, I ask. 'Chickens.'

For some reason, this pleases me no end. As an added bonus, he continues in familiar Geordie tones: 'Day 44 in the *Big Brother* house.' I clap my hands. I am having a conversation with the voice of *Big Brother*. And I can see his lips move.

WRITING UP

Writing features can be a slow process. You may be used to knocking off news stories in twenty minutes, but things aren't so swift when it comes to 1,500-word features that include multiple interviews. As any fiction writer will tell you, revising and redrafting is the name of the game.

A feature is not like a news story with its inverted pyramid – the structure will vary, depending on what sort you're writing. There's no one correct way to write up or structure a feature. What you have to work out, though, is how to keep your reader hooked for over a thousand words.

You might find that the egg-timer approach works: ensure the most striking material is in the first third of the feature, put any secondary material in the second third, and then have a good, strong ending to reel the reader in. Or the feature might resemble an upright rectangle, where all the information is equally important. However, sub-editors can find features tricky to cut if a writer has gone for a 'running gag' approach, in which the ending may mirror the beginning. Whichever, the key is to unfold a feature logically and to have either a mental or a written check-list to ensure all the key information is included.

ASSEMBLING THE FEATURE

When you are finally slotting the feature together, think of it as a jigsaw puzzle – a variety of different-shaped components make up the whole.

Topic

- *What's your angle?* Unlike news, where there tends to be a limited number of angles, features often have several possible strong points. As a general rule, remember that people make features just as much as they make news.
- *What's so special about your topic?* Be honest with yourself – if the angle and the content are weak, then this is almost certainly a feature to rewrite or to consign to a bottom drawer. But conversely,

what's so unusual about it? There are plenty of people who collect
football programmes, but not many who have every Aston Villa
programme since the First World War. And there are any number
of women magistrates around the country, but not many who have
been on the bench for forty years.

- *Have you spoken to all the right people?* A feature can stand or fall by
whom you interview. As we saw earlier with the feature on the
return of cult TV show *The Professionals*, an inability to interview
the main protagonists did not mean the piece had to be shelved.
In fact, it became an affectionate look at the show's fans. However,
if you have been commissioned to write a profile of your constituency's new MP, it's not really going to be much of a feature
without their input. Bear in mind that friends and enemies can
provide much-needed balance to a profile, but they generally can't
compensate for the absence of the subject.

A monosyllabic interviewee can be a challenge, but you might still
get a piece out of the interview – although the likelihood is that
the feature will then focus on the interview itself, rather than the
subject. *Independent on Sunday* journalist Cole Moreton interviewed
rapper Dizzee Rascal ('I still get the bullshit that black boys get', 17
February 2008). At the end of the feature – much of which is narrative background and very short quotes from a clearly reluctant
interviewee – Moreton is clearly fed up with Dizzee, who claims he
feels 'humble' to have been invited to play at the NME Awards,
having been honoured for innovation:

> But not humble enough to have a proper conversation,
> instead of sitting hunched over the table and refusing to
> make eye contact.
>
> Unusually, I feel like giving up. One more go, though: how
> would he describe his music to someone who has never
> heard it? 'I don't think it needs too much description,' he
> says, smirking at his friend. 'Vague as it sounds. Put it on and
> if you feel it, feel it, yeah?'
>
> Yeah, Dizzee. Whatever. We're done.

- *Selecting info.* Best practice is always to write up a feature as soon as
possible after the interviews are completed. But realistically you
might have others on the go, and have to relegate the one with the
most distant deadline to the bottom of your list. Then, when you
come to write it up, it won't be fresh in your mind. Or you might

have carried out some of the interviews several weeks previously and be waiting for one final person to become available before you can start writing. In these cases, it makes sense to refresh your memory by scanning through your notes or skimming through your recordings to get an overview. If you want to jot down some bullet points to help you along, now's the time to do it.

- *Select the best quotes.* Just as you need people with a story to tell in your features, you also need juicy quotes from them. A feature with bland comments is a bore to read whereas one with well-chosen quotes guaranteed to make your audience laugh, cry, gasp or raise a quizzical eyebrow is another matter altogether. As you conduct your interview, keep a weather ear open for soundbites – often your story angle will arrive in the form of a quote, complete with bells and whistles. It's also worth keeping back a strong quote for the end of the feature. A well-balanced feature will use both direct and indirect quotes to get the story across.

- *Prioritise other information.* The thought of writing more than a thousand words might be off-putting, but if you have good material, rest assured that you're more likely to trim rather than pad out. So, as with any story you write, you need to prioritise the information you have – what *must* be used, what's second string, and then anything else that can go in if you have space.

Start by grabbing the reader

With news writing, nine times out of ten you must put the most unusual, dramatic or newest angle in the intro. The exception is the delayed drop intro, where the point of the story appears several paragraphs down and the first paragraph is more of a teaser. You'll find in feature writing that you can get away with teasers more often.

We've already established that almost any story requires human interest, so it often makes sense to lead a feature on a person – particularly when it comes to issues-based pieces. If you're writing a feature on the arrival of gay 'marriages' in the UK in the form of civil partnerships, it would be illogical not to feature in the first paragraph a couple who are registering their partnership.

A particular incident can also be a good way of opening a feature, be it something that happened to change someone's way of thinking or a physical confrontation of some sort.

There's a school of thought that you should never start a story with a quote, and generally that's advice that makes good sense. No matter how strong the quote is, it can be disorientating to be pitched straight into the story with no context – you have no idea who's speaking, why they are being quoted and what the point of it all is. That's not to say that it can never happen, of course, as rules are there to be broken, if need be. An Ed Vulliamy article for the *Guardian* (Friday, 7 August 1992), headlined 'Shame of Camp Omarska' and providing the first eyewitness account in a British newspaper of detention camps in Bosnia, proves this:

> 'I don't want to tell any lies, but I cannot tell the truth,' says the young man, emaciated, sunken-eyed, and attacking his watery bean stew like a famished dog, his spindly hands shaking.
>
> This is lunchtime in the Omarska camp or 'investigation centre' operated by the Bosnian-Serbian police for Muslim captives, near Prijedor in north-eastern Bosnia.
>
> The internees are horribly thin, raw-boned, some are almost cadaverous, with skin like parchment folded around their arms, their faces are lantern-jawed, and their eyes are haunted by the empty stare of the prisoner who does not know what will happen to him next.
>
> The prisoners, or internees, emerge from a huge rust-coloured shed, 30 at a time, into the sun and heat.
>
> They are lined up by a prison guard, a civilian policeman, and then, as part of some pathetic camp drill, they run in single file across a courtyard and into the camp canteen, under the watchful eye of a beefy policeman with a machine gun in a glass observation post. There are no barked orders: they know the drill only too well.
>
> In the well-kept kitchen they line up again and wait for their ration: a bowl of beans augmented with breadcrumbs and a piece of bread, which they wolf down in silence at the metal tables, before quickly and obediently forming another line by the door, and then running in line back across the yard, into the aluminium shed.
>
> The meal takes five minutes. It appears to be their only one of the day. If they ate even twice as much they would be only slightly less gaunt and withered. Some take their bread with them to eat later. Then the next 30 appear, and jog across the yard.
>
> Omarska is an old iron mine and ore processing plant. It is now the most notorious on a list published by the Bosnian government naming 57 of what it calls 'concentration camps'.

Naturally there's nothing to stop you using reported speech in an intro to get across what someone said. Feature intros can also be longer than their news counterparts, so you might consider a sentence of context followed by a quote in the second half of the intro.

Content

There's no definitive list of what you must include in a feature, as clearly it's going to depend on what sort you are writing and for which publication. But you are likely to need to include several of the following:

- *Personal experiences*. People make news, so ensure you have them in your features. And your readers are nosy – they want to read about an interviewee's success story or how they dragged themselves up by their bootstraps.
- *Colour and description*. Feature writers can intrude, within reason, on what they write. It's your job to get across to the person reading the article just what it feels like to be running for your life after witnessing a riot, or watching how people behaved at Princess Diana's funeral.
- *Narrative*. The nuts and bolts that keep the feature moving along. You do encounter some features told exclusively as first-person accounts, but generally you will need to intersperse narrative with the other elements mentioned in this section.
- *Background*. Never assume your reader knows everything. They might have recently arrived in the country, could have been on holiday and missed earlier stories, or simply might not be regular readers of your publication. Work on the principle that you will always need to recap briefly on an issue, as well as filling in the back story.
- *Quotes and dialogue*. We've already seen how quotes can add freshness and immediacy to a feature. In some cases, too, where you are interviewing more than one person at the same time, you might want to capture the flavour of this double act by including dialogue. This can move a feature along swiftly, but it can also be confusing, so make sure your reader knows who is speaking.
- *Comment*. News reporters are told to leave their opinions at the front door when they arrive for work each morning. But, as we'll see in Chapter 5, comment pieces form part of the features repertoire. And there may be occasions in features – although generally not

news features – when the writer's opinion is valid. Always remember, though, that the feature isn't usually about you.

Structure

Again, there's no one correct way to structure a feature. You might generally find you write a news feature in the accepted inverted pyramid style, but that will not necessarily work for a profile, where you want to exit the story as strongly as you started it. And remember that features tend to be substantially longer than news stories, so you have more chance of losing a bored reader along the way if you don't keep them hooked.

- *How can you grab readers' attention?* Feature writers can use gimmicks to keep the reader with them for the ride. *Independent* journalist Corinne Sweet took two lads in wheelchairs for a night on the town in London ('Inside I'm cursing', 16 October 2004). The peg to hang the feature on was the release of a new film, *Inside I'm Dancing*, which showed two young Irishmen in wheelchairs finding independence. Furthermore, part two of the Disability Discrimination Act had just come into force, meaning that businesses and public services had to become more user-friendly for people with disabilities. The feature presented a tiny clock at the start of each paragraph to measure the trio's progress and charted their success at finding wheelchair-friendly venues.
- *A to B may be OK in some cases, but it may also be deadly dull.* In the case of the disability feature above, a chronological approach worked fine. But generally it can be a fairly dreary way of writing a feature. Imagine you were writing a travel piece – you'd be most unlikely to begin with how you got out of bed, had your breakfast, travelled to the airport, stood in line to check in, waited two hours before you could board the plane, fell asleep for most of the journey, arrived on time, waited for your luggage and then caught a taxi to your hotel. You're much more likely to want to focus on the memorable parts of the trip – that perfect private beach overlooking blue sea; the delicious meal at a tiny restaurant; your first sight of Rome's Colosseum or bungee jumping off a crane in New Zealand.
- *Can you start in the middle, then recap and unfold?* With the above in mind, it often makes better sense to leap into the middle of a story with the best angle you can find, then recap for the reader so they know where they are before unfolding the rest of the piece.

- *Check your piece reads smoothly and logically.* If you think your finished product jumps around, has gaps and reads like a road with potholes, so will the features editor! Go back and rewrite.

Closing the feature

Unlike news stories, you can rarely get away with dumping the least important information at the end of a feature. If your loyal reader has stayed with you for 2,000 words, they're going to feel a touch shortchanged if the piece tails off. So aim to make the ending strong and get out of the feature in style. Consider the following devices for the finale:

- *A strong quote.* You don't have to use all your juicy quotes at the start of the feature. If what's said seems to sum up a situation or provide a defiant flourish, for example, then make it your final paragraph.
- *A sting in the tail.* This ending will make the reader raise their eyebrows – and often has a touch of irony to it. It can have the feel of a slightly throwaway comment that would be out of place higher up in the feature.
- *Something that sums up the situation neatly.* This might be a quote, or something that you observe as you conduct the interview. Occasionally, it might bring a feature full circle.
- *Something that looks forward.* Again, this might come in the form of a quote, or it might be a snippet of information that provides the subject with some kind of hope for the future.

AN IN-DEPTH LOOK AT A FEATURE

The best way to analyse a successful feature is to look at its component parts. The following piece, reproduced in its entirety, appeared on the sports pages of the *Independent* (12 August 2007; available at: http://news. independent.co.uk/people/profiles/article2856812.ece):

POWELL AND THE GLORY: HE'S 91 BUT IVOR STILL LOVES RUNNING THE BATH

'The Professor' is football's oldest coach and will be in the dug-out when his university team kick off the new season.

By Alan Hubbard

Ivor Powell has passed a fitness test and will be on the bench when his club, Team Bath, play a home friendly with a Cardiff City XI tomorrow night. He is still suffering a bit of a foot problem – nothing as glamorous as a Beckham-style metatarsal, just an old-fashioned bunion on his toe. Mind you, he is 91.

Dear old Ivor, you see, is a team coach, the oldest working model in the land – and something of an icon down at the University of Bath, where he is in his 35th year on the football coaching staff, and raring to go for the new season.

The bunion is why he joined Thursday's training session in carpet slippers, joshing with the university lads, who call him 'The Professor'. Powell will be on the bus, and in the dug-out as usual, when Team Bath kick off in the British Gas Business Football League Premier Division at Banbury next Saturday. A far cry from the heady days when he won 14 caps as a terrier of a half-back for Wales, captained Aston Villa and coached under Don Revie at Leeds and with the Greek side PAOK.

But the little Welshman says he has never been happier, which is why he was relieved to get the all-clear when he went to hospital for a check-up last week. He came through with flying colours, and says: 'I told them, "I've done a hell of a lot in my life, and in football, but there's still a lot more I want to do." I'll never give up my work. Never.'

A Fergie-like fervour courses through his veins in tandem with his Celtic blood. The passion is evident as the eyes flash and the words tumble forth when he recalls not only memorable moments from the 'good old days' but his commitment to the modern game.

He thumps a fist into his palm. 'Aggression, determination, the will to win. These have always been my watchwords, and they still are. That's what I try to instill into these youngsters. And they listen, they really do.'

'The lads love him,' says Team Bath's head coach, Andy Tilson, ex-Grimsby and QPR, who, at 42, is less than half the age of his venerable assistant. 'He's one of the game's great characters, brimful of fire and enthusiasm. He's indispensable. Players like continuity, a familiar face, and they have so much respect for him. In Ivor you have the most experienced football brain in the land.

The little snippets he passes on to them and to me and the other coaches are invaluable, because he's been there, done it, and got the international shirt, even if it was in a different era.

'The thing is, he's so open-minded, and even though the game has changed so much he's learned how to adapt and impart the knowledge he has. He's so keen we have to hold him back a bit, because we don't want him overdoing things.'

Clearly Powell is not just a talisman, or another old-timer with a few rheumy-eyed reminiscences of those good old days. Team Bath's manager, Ged Roddy, who is also the university's sports director, says: 'The word "legend" is overworked but Ivor is exactly that, an institution. I don't know what we'd do without him. When he walks in, he lights the place up.'

He is recognised by the *Guinness Book of Records* as the oldest working coach in football, and has also had an FA coaching badge for 56 years. 'There's no record of anyone having coached for a longer period at this level,' confirms the FA historian David Barber.

Powell was a member of the backroom team when Team Bath became the first university side in 122 years to reach the first round proper of the FA Cup five years ago, losing 4–2 at home to Mansfield. Last season they were BGB League runners-up, losing a play-off final for promotion to Blue Square South (a division down from the old Conference). Helping them to achieve promotion this season is Powell's goal.

'These boys play the game the way I like to see it played, hard but fair. When I'm in the dug-out I see little things, and they appreciate me telling them quietly. So does Andy. My way is not to shout or put my foot down, but to coax and encourage. I never curse. You can do it without effing and blinding. They understand what I am talking about, and when I demonstrate, whether it is passing or heading, they know I've done it – and I can still do it.'

Spry and alert, he was still turning out for practice games when he was in his 80s. A diminutive midfielder built on the lines of Alan Ball, he was 'aggressive but never dirty' in the days of half-backs and inside-forwards, when full-backs would have got a rollicking had they dared overlap. Strikers, sweepers and wingless wonders were still a twinkle in the eye of revolutionaries such as Ron Greenwood and Sir Alf Ramsey.

But Powell, when he became a coach, had to latch on to 'total football'. 'I couldn't have players saying I knew nothing about the way the game is played today. Then we never knew anything about 4–2–2 or 4–4–3 [*sic*]. Tactics were more adventurous, with more possession, more accurate passing, better use of the long ball.

'There wasn't all this man-to-man marking. You had spaces where you could receive the ball and run with it. We played for ourselves, but we also played for the team, and the spectators, too. What I really wish is that today's fans could see and enjoy the game as we used to play it. It would be an eye-opener.'

A grammar schoolboy who was the seventh son of a seventh son in a family of 10, Powell started working life down the mines for 12 shillings and sixpence a week with his father and brothers, but after three years was spotted by a QPR scout when playing for South Wales League side Bargoed Thursday, aged 17. 'I said to myself, "I'm never going down that bloody mine again". I never did.'

He made his first-team debut for QPR in 1937, won a Division Three (South) championship medal with them, was transferred to Aston Villa for a then record fee for a half-back of £17,500 and played for, coached or managed Port Vale, Bradford City, Leeds, Carlisle, PAOK and Bath City before joining the University of Bath coaching set-up in 1972.

In his managerial heyday, Powell was responsible for some of football's legendary malapropisms. Asked the secret of his team's success at Carlisle, where he was a successor to Bill Shankly, he put it down to 'the harmonium in the dressing room'. He was also reputed to have once remarked that the dressing room was so hot 'the compensation was running down the walls'.

Powell is probably the only man around who played both with and against the late Sir Stanley Matthews, guesting for Blackpool during the war years, when he was an RAF physical training instructor. Matthews was best man at his wedding, and Ivor's eyes still fill with tears when he speaks both of his pal's death and that of his own wife of 63 years, Joan, who passed away four years ago. 'But for football,' he says, 'I don't think I could have carried on.'

As left-half for Aston Villa and Wales, Powell often had the dreaded task of marking the doyen of the dribble. 'They say Stan couldn't have been the player he was in the modern game, but don't you believe it. What everyone forgets is his speed. We used to train with the great West Indian sprinter McDonald Bailey, and Stan was as fast as him over 10 yards. No one was better at anticipating a tackle. He could see it coming and he'd be up and over them. I'd back him against any of today's defenders. He'd have skinned them alive.'

Powell also marked other tricky forwards, including Don Revie, who made him trainer/coach at Leeds, where he worked for four years with the likes of Billy Bremner, Norman Hunter and Jackie Charlton.

Among his proudest moments was being inducted into the Welsh Sports Hall of Fame in 2004, along with other Wales sporting greats including Gareth Edwards, Dame Tanni Grey-Thompson, Ian Rush, JPR Williams and John Charles.

'When I see today's antics on the field, the jersey-pulling, the kicking and all that, I'm really proud I was never sent off, or even cautioned. Yes, I tackled hard, but I made sure I was never late. There's a hardness, a ruthlessness about the game now that didn't exist then, and of course it's all down to money.

'Our wage was £8, with a £2 win bonus and £1 for a draw. And £6 in the summer. When I was transferred I got £750. But the cheque I received was for £412 and 10 shillings. They took £337 and 10 shillings for income tax. We never had agents or accountants to take care of that sort of thing. My transfer fee was £17,500. Some Premiership players get more than that in a week. If I was getting the money these buggers are getting now they would never get the ball off me.'

No big money at Bath, though, whose team is comprised largely of youngsters released by League clubs or their academies. Here they are given a fresh start in football alongside a foundation degree course in sports performance at the country's most prolific and progressive sports university.

A year ago last July, they gave Powell a 90th birthday party, and many of the Professor's graduates came back to help him celebrate. Nick Bath was a biology student there from 1972 to 1976. He recalled: 'Ivor was passionate about the game then and he still has that same fire in his eyes. He believed in keeping it simple, and being coached by someone of his calibre made us feel good. We were pretty hopeless by comparison, but he never gave up on us.'

The Powell philosophy is equally simple: 'You've got to have a winning heart. That's everything. And as long as I get pleasure out of doing what I am now, and help others to get pleasure out of it, then I know I am doing justice to myself and my career. I could never give this up. As long as they want me, I'll be here.'

LIFE AND TIMES

IVOR VERDUN POWELL

BORN: 5 July 1916, Gilfach Bargeod, South Wales.

PLAYING CAREER: Signed by QPR at 17. Transferred to Aston Villa in 1948 for then record fee for a half-back of £17,500. Capped 14 times for Wales in 1930s, '40s and '50s.

COACH/MANAGER: Port Vale, Bradford City, Leeds, Carlisle, PAOK (Athens), Bath City. Now assistant coach and president at Team Bath.

FAMILY: Seventh son of seventh son. Wife Joan died in 2003.

OTHER ACHIEVEMENTS: *Guinness Book of Records* as oldest working football coach. Elected to Welsh Hall of Fame in 2004.

AND ANOTHER THING: Middle name given by his father, who fought in the First World War.

Further reading about Ivor Powell's achievements at www.team bath.com/?p=288

What makes this such an effective feature?

- *Relaxed tone*. The reporter adopts a pleasantly chatty style for the piece. By the end of the feature, the reader thinks they were in the room when the interview took place, as they can picture Ivor's passion as he talks about both his present role and his memories of his career. Features like this often stand or fall by whether the writer can engage our attention. In this case, the story is told with affection – even the mention of Ivor's malapropisms isn't cruel.
- *Subject matter*. To most twenty-first-century soccer fans, Ivor Powell isn't a household name, and nor is Team Bath. But that doesn't matter if there's a good story to tell – and there is here. It's a feature, as well, to appeal across the age ranges: older fans may remember Ivor from way back, while younger ones will marvel at a ninety-one-year-old still being active in the game. There's also the unusual angle of a student team playing at a higher level than is usually associated with university sport. Because the feature is on the sports pages, it will assume some knowledge among the readers, but it's certainly accessible enough for the casual browser.
- *Anecdotes*. Interviewees like Ivor are a gift, as they will provide you with a wonderful stream of stories, including marking the great Stanley Matthews, and how much he was paid.
- *Structuring the piece*. Very few features need to be written chronologically. Just think how this article would have missed the point if it had started with Ivor's early days in the game and then come to his coaching at the age of ninety-one at the end. We want the new and unusual – and rather off-beat – angle at the top, with the historical background coming later. The quotes can be woven in amid this basic structure. The feature flows beautifully, thanks to chatty links such as 'dear old Ivor' and 'mind you'. And it ends with a strong, punchy quote that gets to the heart of the subject.

- *Other people's views of the subject.* A profile of Ivor simply using his own quotes would probably have worked fine. But this feature goes the extra mile and talks to colleagues at the university, a former student and a football historian.
- *Panel at the end.* This provides a potted biography of Ivor, accompanied by some quirky little facts (he's the seventh son of a seventh son). And there's a useful link to the team's website for further information.
- *Punning headline.* Reporters don't write headlines – these are provided by sub-editors. In this case, the gentle pun in the headline gives us a clue to what the story is about (a ninety-one-year-old) and implies that it's not going to be a totally serious story. (You wouldn't use a pun for a hard news story or feature, as it would be totally inappropriate.)
- *Pictures.* To complete a good features spread, there are four main pix, plus a smaller one in the 'life and times' box. The feature takes up all of a left-hand page, with a cut-out pic of Powell leading Aston Villa onto the pitch in the 1950s surrounded by text. On the right-hand page are pix of Powell in a tracksuit and kicking a ball in a present-day Team Bath training session, of him and Sir Stanley Matthews, and of a plaque dedicated to him at the University of Bath.

WRITING PROFILES

If you're a typical journalist, you'll adore writing profiles. After all, they give you carte blanche to find out about people's lives and what makes them tick. How often do you get to pry into someone's life like that?

A profile – sometimes known as a personality piece – is a feature based on a single person, just like the one we've just read on Ivor Powell. It's often a lengthy look at them and their life, and aims to portray them vividly, including what they look like, how they act, what they say and what motivates them. The best profiles tend to be written face to face, but it's not unusual, if you're strapped for time or the person isn't easily available, to do the interview over the phone or by email. The finished product may also include information and/or quotes from friends, enemies and acquaintances.

You will sometimes find profiles done as 'cuttings jobs' – compiled with the help of previous interviews or by chatting to friends and acquaintances, but without talking to the main subject. The *Observer* traditionally runs such a profile every Sunday. If this is your publication's style, so be it, but bear in mind it's not a particularly satisfactory approach. Cuttings jobs have a tendency to feel second hand, and there may also be accuracy issues – mistakes in previous articles can be perpetrated for evermore.

Profile writing allows a journalist to develop their own distinctive voice as they attempt to portray their subject to the reader (see the extract from Deborah Ross's profile of Charlie Dimmock at the start of this chapter). It's always worth remembering, though, that the article is about the other person, not you.

Choosing your subject

You tend to be faced with two potential groups of subjects when operating as a profile writer – either celebrities or ordinary people with an unusual story to tell. When you're starting out in journalism, you assume it will all be terribly glamorous and that you will swan around interviewing celebrities who will be witty, charming and intelligent. Sadly, this is rarely the case. Most famous people have been interviewed countless times, so finding a new angle can be a challenge. Many are press-ganged into doing interviews by agents, managers or publicists, and may make it clear that they'd rather stick pins in their eyes than talk to another journalist. Some are absolutely charming, I hasten to add, and it's somehow reassuring to know that so-and-so off the telly is as nice in real life as they seem to be on the screen. But even they may be doing the interview only because they have a new book/film/play/album out and will want to spend most of the interview plugging it. Award-winning feature writer Lynn Barber has some good advice here ('How *does* Lynn Barber do it?', *Independent on Sunday*, 24 February 1991):

> Another key point at the beginning if the interview is The Plug. Most FPs [Famous People] nowadays only give interviews when they have something to sell – a new film or a book or whatever – and they are fretful until they have done it. I therefore let them do their plug at length and generously at the beginning of the interview, to get it out of the way. Merely listening to it doesn't mean that I have to include it in the written article and I use this time for familiarising myself with their voice, their turn of phrase, making mental notes on their appearance – checking that the tape recorder is working.

Interviewing famous people can be fun and rewarding, but you rapidly discover that the freshest copy often comes from unlikely or ordinary people with a good story to tell. *Guardian* reporter Randeep Ramesh found a very powerful profile subject in a fourteen-year-old schoolgirl who set fire to herself in England in support of Kurd leader Abdullah Ocalan, who was facing the death penalty ('To die for', 8 June 1999):

> There are few images that shock a nation's consciousness. One that did was a picture last February of a 14-year-old schoolgirl running with her back and neck ablaze, her arms outstretched and her face warped by pain. Plastered over the next day's newspapers was Necla Coskun, preparing to die for a man she had never met and a land she had never seen.

> Coskun was among the crowds of Kurds protesting at the arrest of Kurdish leader Abdullah Ocalan by Turkish secret agents. Ocalan is on trial on a prison island south of Istanbul, charged with treason. The verdict is expected this week; if found guilty, he faces the death penalty.

> 'If he dies, there will be war in Europe,' Coskun says. 'I would do it again. Dying is not important. I can do it if it helps my people.'

During the piece, Ramesh mentions Necla's teddy bear collection, her Calvin Klein baseball cap and how her headteacher described her as a model student. 'The question was, how could she be so normal, so ordinary, yet be prepared to throw away so much for an alien ideal?'

Topical profiles

The most obvious topical profile features someone who is in the news at the time. With these, you need to react quickly – and bear in mind that finding a different angle from your competitors can be a challenge. An actor with a new film to promote or a musician with a CD coming out can become very focused on this and it can be tricky to prise much else out of them. Some years ago I interviewed a gold medal-winning Olympian. He was absolutely charming, but had a new business venture to promote. Every question I asked him relating to his sporting career and what he'd done in the past was met with 'Oh, that's past history and in all the cuttings files!' True, but it was also why people knew him and what had put him in the position to launch his new enterprise. There's no need to make a profile a history lesson, but readers will want to hear about the interviewee's great achievements. And, of course, there might well be a new angle you've discovered, or areas of their life where they have previously been coy. So aim to balance past and present when you write a profile (see the Ivor Powell profile earlier in this chapter for an excellent example of this).

The other sort of topical profile you may be asked to write is one to illustrate a story in the news at the moment. These are often more like mini-profiles or case studies, but they add that essential human interest slant to a current story. So it's vital that the person chosen is relevant and illustrates the piece well. The news stories on the UK's new civil partnerships for gay couples were accompanied by numerous profiles of interesting people – the first couples to sign the partnerships in each part of the UK; people in their sixties and seventies who had seen a lot of changes in society's attitudes to homosexuals; and those in their twenties who have grown up during a period of liberalisation, in terms of both legislation and people's views.

A mini-profile of 300 or 400 words can be almost as tricky to write as a 1,500-word piece. You won't have a lot of space to play with, and the article must be focused and to the point – there simply won't be enough words for colour, teasers or excessive description. Forget the surroundings and concentrate on providing a snapshot of the person with some strong quotes, their personal details and why they are relevant to the story.

Most mini-profiles or case studies work best if you get the person's name into the first paragraph and ensure that there are several well-chosen quotes alongside the rationale for the story and some brief biographical details.

A slightly different slant on a topical profile may be of someone who isn't necessarily famous but has a key behind-the-scenes role to play. There were countless examples of this in all manner of publications after the Tube and bus bombings in London on 7 July 2005, when people from the emergency services found themselves thrust into the limelight. And *The Times* came up with an unusual angle during the Rugby Union World Cup in France in 2007 – sports writer Matt Dickinson interviewed Nigel Owens, the first openly gay international referee ('Gay referee takes pride of place in the tolerant world of "macho" rugby', 11 September 2007).

Timeless profiles

Timeless profiles can be stockpiled and slotted in when there's a gap in the paper or magazine. You'll often come across interesting people when you're out researching other stories, so it's useful to make a note of their details and come back to them when there's a quiet moment.

As we've already established, you will earn yourself brownie points from features editors if you can build up a small stash of profiles to be used in these quiet times. The classic people to look out for here are those who may be eccentric or off-beat, or have an unusual story to tell. West Country journalist David Foot seems to have an endless supply of people who make good profile subjects – and they're rarely household names. His profile 'Fiddler on the hoof' in the *Western Daily Press* (17 March 2000) introduces the reader to Gerry Parker: 'He's a dyslexic journalist, a top racing tipster who stays at home and watches Cheltenham on the box, a bookie who hardly ever places a bet on himself.' That sort of intro guarantees that the reader will be intrigued enough to read on, and to discover that Gerry is better known to horseracing fans as Bob Watts, a tipster for the *Western Daily Press* who has been known to go through the card (that is, predict the winner of every race at a meeting). Because Gerry has had such a varied life, he provided Foot with an off-beat profile that could be run at virtually any time.

People like Gerry Parker make good profile subjects because they are influential in a specific area, be it a geographical area or an area of expertise. Again, you may find that someone behind the scenes who doesn't usually receive any publicity has a good story to tell. One of my favourites appeared in the *Guardian* and featured the two women who wash and iron the Manchester City footballers' kit. Both were an absolute gift to interview, as they were good talkers, and they had a stock of anecdotes about the players and the club. It made a refreshing change from bland profiles of footballers who either can't or won't say anything of interest.

Writing up the profile

You may want to use the following checklist when you come to write up your piece:

- **Potential intro angles:**
    - The way a person looks or behaves.
    - Something they said.
    - Something that was said about them (this is where friends and acquaintances come in useful).
    - Something about the surroundings.
    - An incident or an anecdote (either from them or from someone who knows them).

- **Weave quotes in fluently:**

  - Avoid starting with a quote.
  - A quote can be useful for closing the piece – especially if it's funny, hard-hitting or defiant.

- **You should balance in the feature:**

  - Quotes.
  - Reported speech.
  - Anecdotes from elsewhere (if used).
  - Your impressions of the person.
  - Narrative (including background).

WRITING COLOUR PIECES

These can often be the most enjoyable and entertaining features to write. After all, you're being paid to attend a big or unusual event and to transmit what happened to the reader at home in their armchair. At their most basic, colour pieces are atmosphere pieces. They aim to provide a vivid description of an event and to paint a scene for the reader of what happened. There is often a sense of drama, particularly with topical colour pieces, and the reporter may try to play on the reader's emotions and make them laugh or cry. Even though it was a TV piece, Michael Buerk's famous 1984 reportage from Ethiopa beginning with those unforgettable words 'Dawn, and a famine of biblical proportions . . .' was the classic colour piece, spawning Bob Geldof's Live Aid efforts.

Big events lay themselves open to colour piece writing. You may recall a number of memorable aspects of Princess Diana's funeral – male members of the royal family walking behind the coffin; the crowds outside Westminster Abbey and in Hyde Park; Elton John's rendition of 'Candle in the Wind'; Earl Spencer's controversial speech criticising the royal family; the funeral cortège's journey to Northamptonshire. All of this provided feature writers with unrivalled material to fill the newspapers the next day.

Big sporting events are also ripe for colour pieces. Many newspapers send more than one reporter to these – one person will write the match report, while one or more will cover what's happening off the pitch.

Don't assume, though, that all colour pieces have to be about big, grand events. Seemingly ordinary occasions can provide fascinating pieces: a night spent in a hospital casualty unit seeing what staff put up with on a daily basis, perhaps, or a day out with an RAC man who may have excellent stories to tell about rescuing stranded motorists.

Colour pieces can be timeless and stashed away in the computer's hard drive until there's a quiet moment. However, they can also reflect what's in the news – many papers carried colour pieces during the Fred and Rose West case in Gloucester when police discovered ten bodies buried at 25 Cromwell Street. Most focused on the police investigation; others included what was going on around, including enterprising residents selling coffee and tea to thirsty reporters, or producing Cromwell Street Tee-shirts. And you can guarantee that every year at the time of the Oscars ceremony in Los Angeles, there will be a plethora of colour pieces in newspapers and magazines as reporters watch the big names arriving, soak up the atmosphere of the glamorous ceremony, then go schmoozing at the after-show parties.

Timeless pieces, on the other hand, don't date, so features editors are always glad to stockpile a few for those notoriously quiet times during the summer or over Christmas and new year. So that piece you've always fancied arranging with your police contact to spend a day with the motor-way patrol, or having a go at kick-boxing for the first time, or joining a hippy retreat in the north of Scotland can be written whenever you have the chance, then used when there's a lull. The *Bristol Evening Post* sent journalist Tom Henry to a 1970s themed break at Butlin's in Minehead – dressed up in appropriate garb, he boogied to bands of the period. Tom's experiences ('Camping it up', 17 February 2001) were accompanied by one serious and one light-hearted panel – 'How Butlins has evolved since the 70s' and '10 things you'll need', respectively.

What to watch out for

Half the fun of writing a colour piece is being able to wander around and soak up the atmosphere of a big event. Try not to panic about finding an angle – just concentrate on people-watching. Listen in shamelessly on conversations; chat to those around you; watch what people are getting up to. Unless it's a totally dire event, you'll soon be in possession of more story angles than you have a hope of using. If you want some pointers on what to watch out for, keep an eye – or an ear – open for the following:

- A *striking incident*. This might be funny, sad, unusual, off-beat, or simply helps sum up the occasion. I remember struggling for an angle on a Pilkington Cup Final colour piece in the 1980s when Gloucester had been beaten out of sight. My colleague who was writing the match report was looking smug, as a sending-off and an avalanche of tries had given him plenty of material. I trawled around Twickenham countless times, interviewed anyone who didn't run away from me, and noted down anything that looked out of the ordinary. (Why was a jazz band playing at a rugby final? Because the Rugby Football Union had booked them to entertain the crowds in the car park. Oh. Damn!) In the end, as I was walking to Twickenham railway station at about 7 p.m., despairing of ever finding an angle, I saw the bloke in front of me rip his Gloucester rosette off his jacket, tear it in half and throw it into the gutter. It certainly summed up his day – and gave me an angle for my story.

- *What people say.* This might come from things you overhear or from snippets or anecdotes you pick up when you're talking to people. Some years ago, the psychologist Geoffrey Beattie used to write colour pieces for the *Guardian* based on his observations of people in bars or at events such as boxing matches. The articles themselves tended to be quite hard going, as they were pretty much all reported speech (and you generally need variation for a good feature), but the things he overheard people saying were the focus for these pieces.

- *What people do.* This is where you are the observer and can people-watch to your heart's content. You can focus on what individuals do – the woman crying her eyes out at Princess Diana's funeral – or how the group behaves. If you can chat to the people as well, so much the better, but just their actions will often provide you with good copy.

- *What people are wearing.* Who would have thought that the scruffy woman in a baggy tracksuit and grubby trainers haggling over a cheap item at a car-boot sale is a high-flying city lawyer? And what about all those famous sports stars, looking uncomfortable in their smart suits, celebrating when London was awarded the 2012 Olympics? And how was a reporter treated when she spent the day going around London dressed in a chador? Lynn Barber created a memorable image of the singer Shane MacGowan in her interview with him in the *Observer* (11 March 2001). She'd been waiting two hours for him to show up:

  > So on the one hand I am relieved to see Shane at last. On the other hand, I quite want to bundle him back in the lift

and forget him. I was prepared for the teeth, the famous blackened stumps, but the suit is an unanticipated horror show, with its thickening patina of stains down the trousers culminating in big blobby spatters on the shoes. If he has not been sick down his trousers several dozen times, he must have a very good stylist. His skin has the shiny pallor of someone who has never seen daylight. He lurches towards the bar. The photographer tries to head him off, saying he wants to do photographs outside before the daylight fades. Shane says, 'Ginantonic' and plonks himself in a chair. I chatter brightly about James Joyce; Shane mumbles unintelligibly; the photographer tears his hair.

- *Sounds, sights and smells.* I can never think of covering music festivals without imagining the distinctive smells of suncream, beer and, more often than not, dodgy substances. The changing rooms at sports grounds smell of sweat, overlaid with too much aftershave. Schools smell of floor polish, too many little feet in training shoes and, yes, school dinners. Let your nose loose on events. What do you hear as well? And what do you see?

Compiling the colour piece

You are at this event and the reader probably is not, so your job is to provide them with a flavour of what is going on. Watch and listen, and don't obsess about getting everything down in your notebook to start with – get a feel for what's happening first.

A good colour piece needs people, just as any feature does. Mingle with the public and chat to everyone you can. You don't have to quote them all, but if you've put yourself about a bit, you'll be spoiled for choice when you come to write up. You'll often find that Joe and Josephine Public's take is better than the official line. That's not to say that you don't need to speak to those in charge or organising an event – of course you will, if you want numbers who are attending and so on. But the person in the street will add that much-needed human interest angle. Ensure you get their full details – name, age, address and occupation – so you can present well-rounded figures to your readers.

Most importantly, push yourself forward because your impressions matter, although you do need to beware of swamping a story. It's fine if the colour piece is about you trying acupuncture to give up smoking, or taking part in rock climbing for the first time. But if it's an event, balance your comments with those of others.

Structuring the piece

Writing a colour piece differs slightly from how you would approach other features, such as profiles, simply because you may well include a larger proportion of description. Resist the temptation to write up the piece chronologically. If you're looking for an intro to grab the reader, go for the unusual incident, someone's peculiar behaviour, or their off-beat appearance.

A colour piece must always have context, so you need to explain why you're at the car-boot sale, which may be the biggest in Europe, or why you are lying on an acupuncturist's couch with needles stuck in your head. Weave in the background information amid the other narrative and the quotes. And, as always, spend as much time as you can selecting the best quotes.

Make sure that the piece ends as strongly as it starts. If you can keep back a sharp quote, all well and good. If there was a particularly poignant or funny moment that you observed, go for that. Or maybe an incident that sums up the occasion will get you out of the piece with a bang.

CASE STUDY – JEFF COHEN, FEATURES WRITER

How did you get into feature writing?

I quit my job at a trade magazine because I was tired of commuting into Manhattan every day, a distance of less than ten miles that quite often took more than two hours to navigate. And I was young, and stupid, and unencumbered by spouse or family, so all I had to worry about was paying the rent on my rent-controlled apartment. I thought I'd freelance for a few months, until my next 'real job' came along. It's been more than twenty years now. I've been writing features because I was tired of covering only one beat, and wanted to write about whatever struck my fancy. So I started sending out query letters, and got some assignments.

Which features are you most proud of?

My favourite, without question, is a *New York Times* article I wrote on lawn tips from the head groundskeeper at Yankee Stadium. As a lifelong baseball fan, and a Yankees fan to boot, there was nothing better. I got to walk on the field with the man who keeps it looking perfect (it was a

---

cold March morning, and there was no one else in the stadium, as far as I know). I got to visit the players' clubhouse – granted, with no players in it. I toured the facility, and was treated like a visiting dignitary. You have to be a student of the game to appreciate it. And I think the piece came out pretty well, too.

I'm also proud of a *Premiere* magazine piece I did on letterboxing, in 1989, the week my son was born. That was fun.

I think, though, that I'm proudest of a feature on Asperger syndrome I wrote for *USA Weekend* [a Sunday supplement for *USA Today*] in 1999. It was among the first pieces to discuss this neurological disorder, which my son has had all his life, and it landed on thirty-four million doorsteps one Sunday morning. My son was very brave in letting me tell his story when he knew he'd be teased about it; and, indirectly, it led to his getting a free trip to Disney World, when Disney and McDonald's sponsored a contest for 'Millennium Dreamers' for 2,000 young people who had done something to contribute to their communities. I'm pretty proud of that one.

What's your approach to feature writing – from thinking up an idea to delivering the finished product?

I don't know if I have an approach. When I get an idea, it can be either something I brainstorm about in order to come up with something for a specific publication, or an idea I get for which I have to find a publication which will be interested. I think the latter is the better way to go, because it indicates it's something I want to write about on my own. So I write a query letter, something I've gotten *very* good at over the years, and send it via email or snail mail, after checking the publication's writer's guide-lines. If the assignment comes through, I start researching, interviewing and gathering information, and then, when I can't push the deadline back any farther, I'll write it. Writing is the least time-consuming part of the process: I'm pretty fast. Then I send it out, and wait very patiently for the cheque to arrive. Well, I wait, anyway.

What sort of features do you enjoy writing the most?

What I like about freelancing is that there isn't one type of thing I'm writing all the time; I like the variety. But I guess I'm best at profiles of specific people. I like asking questions and getting answers. For a few years, I was the designated interviewer for a magazine about screen-writing, so I got to ask questions of top screenwriters and directors like William Goldman, Budd Schulberg, Garry Marshall and Barry Levinson. That was a lot of fun.

How do you adapt to writing for different markets?

It's extremely important to read the publication carefully beforehand, and to adapt your style to what the editor is likely to want. That doesn't mean you have to stop being yourself, but a ponderous, in-depth think piece for *People* magazine would probably be a bad idea, as would a snarky celebrity profile for the *New Yorker* (and I choose those two publications because I've never written for either – although the *New Yorker* would be pretty cool).

Who do you write for?

Anybody who calls up and asks, with very, *very* few exceptions. I've turned down work twice, maybe, over twenty-one years, based on ethical disagreements – not that an editor wanted me to be unethical, but that the subject matter was something with which I disagreed so intensely that I couldn't see myself doing the job to their satisfaction, or living with myself if I did. But aside from that, if you want to pay somebody to write something, feel free to call.

What are the top tips you'd give a young feature writer?

Try to think of something else you could do for a living. Because if this isn't what you want beyond all other things, you shouldn't be involved. You should find something that provides a steady pay cheque. If this *is* all you want out of a career, I'd say be organised and let no opportunity go by. Write query letters every week, and follow up on them. Write as much as you can about things you care about, because you'll do a better job on those. And if I had it to do over again, I probably would concentrate – not exclusively, but largely – on one area of expertise, because once you establish a reputation in an area, it's much easier to get work. And hone your interviewing skills. Interview relatives, friends, your dog. Take notes even when you have a tape recorder, because tape recorders tend to break when someone's about to say something interesting. And never, *ever*, turn the TV on during a work day.

Biography?

I was orphaned at an early age and taken in by a man named Fagin who taught me to steal wallets from . . . No, wait, that was someone else entirely. I've been a newspaper reporter (a zillion years ago), a trade magazine editor and, for the past twenty-one years, a freelance writer. I've written for the *New York Times*, *TV Guide*, *American Baby*,

Entertainment Weekly and many other publications, have written an obscene number of unproduced screenplays and, so far, six published mystery novels (and one or two unpublished), and two non-fiction books on raising a child with Asperger syndrome. Someday, I hope to decide what I want to be when I grow up.

4
How to write features
Digging for news

Much of the high-adrenalin excitement from writing features comes from knowing you've hit a tight deadline, and from seeing another angle on a story people may think they know well. News features fit this category perfectly. Features allow for more detailed and in-depth analysis of big news stories. So news features, backgrounders and investigative features deserve some space of their own.

News features are always topical. You'll generally find them on the news pages in newspapers, rather than languishing in a supplement somewhere. But that's not to say that topical features don't pop up elsewhere in papers, The *Guardian*'s G2 supplement is quick off the mark for covering in depth what's in the news. Sunday papers are also fond of news features, as they have extra time to develop and analyse what's been in the news that week.

Expect a news feature either to be issue-based or to provide a fresh twist on a news story. And with the extra word count it almost always has, its examination of any story is going to be more in depth. So while the news item may give the bare bones and quote a couple of people, the news feature has the time and space to expand on the story and to pull more people into the discussion.

Bear in mind that it can be tricky to differentiate between a news story and a news feature at times – although in many ways that doesn't particularly matter. What is important is an ability to write to a tight deadline and to provide a fresh and in-depth look at the day's (or week's) big story.

Take the Budget, for example. Most papers will lead on this, and the front-page story will focus on the main points, be they a planned rise in fuel duty, 10p on a packet of cigarettes, alcohol going up ahead of inflation, or changes in child benefit. But inside the paper, news features will expand on the Chancellor's announcements and analyse what they will mean for businesses and the person in the street. Specialist writers, be they political, financial or business, will almost certainly contribute to these features – some of which are likely to be backgrounders.

BACKGROUNDERS

Backgrounders do exactly what they say – explain and analyse in detail the background to a big news story. They often examine in depth a range of issues and/or personalities associated with the story. If they are focused on a big event, such as a G8 summit, the piece will aim to set the scene and to speculate on what might happen during the conference. Historical background, or discussing what's happened at previous events, often comes into play as well.

BBC History magazine's series 'Events in context' looks at the background to world events. The December 2006 edition contained a feature by David Keys on the historical context of the war in Darfur in Africa, where, at the time, up to 400,000 civilians had been killed, another two to three million driven from their homes and up to 2,000 villages destroyed. Keys's feature looks back at the important dates affecting the Sudanese province, as well as examining the influence of neighbouring Chad and Eritrea on the conflict. It's a clear and accessible piece of writing, which points out that the region is the size of France, with just one major tarmac road. It's accompanied by pictures from the files, a graphic showing the key events in and around Sudan, thumbnail portraits (in pictures and words) of three main figures in the story of Darfur from the nineteenth century to the present day, and half a dozen suggestions for further reading on the topic.

Backgrounders are often prepared in advance – for example, if there is a major court case, expect to see some detailed features in the media as soon as the verdict is announced. With the twenty-four-hour news culture we have now, websites can react very fast to breaking news, which means they can present a range of background features that have been worked on in advance and are all ready to go once they get the nod.

Staff reporters who either have specialist knowledge of the area or have raided the cuttings library for information may write these features. Or the publication might ask an outsider with particular knowledge to write a piece. What backgrounders offer above news stories is a chance for the reporter to explain, analyse and often predict what's going on with a big story. They can often call on a wider range of sources to contribute to the debate, too.

A NOSE FOR WHAT'S IN THE NEWS

Have a browse through a variety of publications and you'll soon spot topical features galore. The challenge is coming up with an angle that your rivals won't have. When England reached the 2007 Rugby Union World Cup final, both news and sports pages carried any number of topical features, many of them based on the players and coaches of the two finalists. But I rather liked the *Independent*'s quirky angle as part of their 'Countdown to the final' series, where they did a double-page feature on the balls used during the tournament ('The curious case of the funny-shaped ball', 18 October 2007). The angle was that some of the game's most accurate kickers – including England star Jonny Wilkinson – had missed kicks they'd usually convert in their sleep. So journalist Jonathan Brown talked to Ian Savage from Gilbert, the British firm who made the balls, and the man charged with the responsibility of personally weighing and measuring (four times) each of the 288 balls used for the tournament. He also interviewed David Curtis of the Sports Engineering Research Department at Sheffield Hallam University, in whose labs the balls had been tested before the World Cup.

The floods which swamped parts of the UK during the summer of 2007 provided the media with countless dramatic news stories – Tewkesbury cut off, Cheltenham and Gloucester left without running water for almost a fortnight, people being rescued from their homes, a number of deaths, and the dramatic battle by the emergency services and the army to save an electricity sub-station from being submerged (had it been flooded, Cheltenham and Gloucester would almost certainly have needed to be evacuated). Inevitably, news features concentrated on the human interest angles and the scale of the floods. The *Guardian* went back to the source – literally – as reporter John Harris tracked down the origins of the River Severn in the Welsh mountains and followed it through Wales and into Worcestershire and Gloucestershire, talking to people who had been affected as he went ('From source to the sea: a journey down the river that created a disaster area', 28 July 2007).

The *Observer* went in search of more human interest stories as the floods began to abate ('As the floods recede, the yarns flow in', 29 July 2007). Reporter Tim Adams visited the Severn Valley and found a man in

Maisemore, near Gloucester, who'd got out just in time: he'd sold his house on the day the rains came. But over in Tewkesbury there was a family who had been due to complete on the sale of their house that week. Then there was the headteacher who had retired on that fateful Friday, and returned home to find her cottage about to be submerged: 'Her leaving present from her colleagues was a rose bush called "Carefree Days". She points it out to me, with a laugh. It now sits on her front patio entirely covered in mud and silt.'

The double-page spread also took a look at the Civil Contingencies Secretariat (CCS), a unit within the Cabinet Office set up to prepare for national emergencies – and the four potentially biggest crises (extreme weather, disease, industrial accidents and terrorism) were all examined in three or four paragraphs.

For a more off-beat angle, the *Mail on Sunday* went with a feature headlined 'Thank God for the 3rd Tewkesbury Scouts!' (29 July 2007), which had the strapline 'There was no rape, no looting, no Bob Geldof . . . when disaster struck Gloucestershire, people simply knew what they had to do. The *Mail on Sunday* pays tribute to some very British heroes.' There then followed a classic human interest, slightly teasing opening:

> Eddie Mills has been a Scout leader for the past 17 years. His freshly pressed khaki shirt is covered in a patchwork of badges, paying testimony to his prowess in tasks as varied as knot-tying and emergency first aid. But there is one badge that has, as yet, proved elusive.
>
> 'I don't have a Chef's Badge,' he admits. 'I've never been one for cooking, although I think over the past week I might have done enough to earn one.'

Eddie, his wife Edna and a team of volunteers had provided free food, drink and shelter in Tewkesbury's scout hut. They told reporter Elizabeth Day how they'd served 1,000 hot meals, poured 10,000 cups of tea and coffee, handed out 30 sleeping bags and got through 10 tons of food donated by local supermarkets. Note that the figures add more interest to an already striking story, and Day weaves in the background facts that the River Severn burst its banks, rose to a height of seven feet in thirty-five minutes and cut off the town's 76,000 residents, leaving them without electricity and drinking water. She also spoke to some of those residents who volunteered or took shelter at the scout hut to add an even stronger personal dimension to a classic *Mail on Sunday* feature – the Brits keeping a stiff upper lip in the face of adversity.

The BBC News website is an excellent source of news features and back-grounders which look at the issues of the day. Its 'Magazine' section runs a regular 'Who, What, Why?' feature which aims to answer some of the questions behind the headlines (and gives readers a chance to weigh in with their own views). So when a medical student with dyslexia claimed that multiple-choice exam questions discriminate against people with the condition, the Magazine tried to find out why people with dyslexia find such exams difficult. Its reporter interviewed the student, Naomi Gadian, Dr John Rack, head of psychology at Dyslexia Action, and Sue Flohr from the British Dyslexia Association ('Why can't people with dyslexia do multiple choice?', http://news.bbc.co.uk/1/hi/magazine/7531132.stm, 29 July 2008; accessed 30 July 2008).

Topical features can pop up in all parts of a newspaper. Britain's gold medal successes in the 2008 Beijing Olympics provided plenty of features for the sports pages, news pages and assorted supplements – even business and travel. A few of the more unusual features included:

- A mix of serious and tongue-in-cheek list-based feature – 'Mansfield needs a new bus and Nadal does his own washing – 100 things we learned in Beijing' (*Guardian*, 23 August 2008).
- A picture-based feature continuing the countdown to London in 2012 which shows an aerial view of the city with the various sites marked and the corresponding copy below updating readers on the progress – 'So will London be ready? (And within its budget?)' (*Independent*, 25 August 2008).
- A business feature on how Olympic euphoria has set the sales of sportswear soaring, but analysing whether this will last until 2012, and discussing which retailers might benefit – 'The real Olympic winners' (*Independent*, 27 August 2008).
- A travel piece where a reporter who can't swim attends an intensive course in Sicily (It's possible that this feature had been stockpiled for a while. If that's the case, a sidebar headlined 'Inspired by the Olympics? Five more sports breaks' and focusing on sailing, cycling, running, kayaking and riding was a quick and easy way of making an already enjoyable travel piece very topical, too.) – 'In at the deep end' (*Observer*, 31 August 2008).
- A photoshoot which glams up five of the female gold medallists in long golden dresses (funny how the men never get shown in smart suits!) – and, yes, it's headlined 'Golden girls' (*Sunday Mirror*, 31 August 2008).

- An online piece by a business reporter on the BBC site looking at how British success might profit businesses in Dorset, where the sailing will take place in 2012 – 'Dorset in spotlight in sailing success' (http://news.bbc.co.uk/1/hi/business/7570894.stm, 21 August 2008; accessed 21 August 2008).

Journalists need to react very fast to big events such as the Olympics and be able to generate a lot of copy as quickly as possible. And the more unusual the angle, the more your features editor will love you. It's the one occasion, too, where the so-called 'minority' sports get some time in the spotlight. After Britain won Winter Olympic gold in the women's curling in 2002, journalists flocked to Scottish ice rinks to give the sport a go.

THE MAGAZINE MARKET

Writing news features is more problematic for the magazine market because of the fact that editions tend to be prepared several months ahead. This makes reacting quickly to a story tricky. So the focus is very much on issues-based and human interest stories, such as *eve*'s account of women so desperate for babies that they will cut open other women and steal the unborn child ('Kidnapped by Caesarean', July 2005). *Marie Claire* was one of the first women's glossy magazines to go for more substantial features over and above the usual celebrity, fashion and beauty diet, and it often covers issues affecting women abroad. It and similar magazines want pieces on strong women with a powerful story to tell. The July 2005 issue of *Marie Claire* carried a six-page feature headlined 'One family taking on the IRA'. It focused on the sisters and fiancée of Robert McCartney, who was murdered by members of the IRA, and their fight to bring the killers to justice. It's a bleak, hard-hitting feature which takes us straight into the action:

> At 22 Albert Bridge Road, Belfast, the phone never stops ringing. The air is thick with cigarette smoke and cups of strong tea are constantly on the go. This is no longer just an ordinary, neat, working-class terrace in the small Catholic enclave of Short Strand. Home to mature student Paula McCartney, it has become the unofficial headquarters of the McCartney clan – Paula and her sisters, nurse Gemma, lecturer Catherine, businesswoman Donna and teaching assistant Claire – plus Bridgeen Hagans, the fiancée of their late brother, Robert. Bridgeen, 27, a former shop assistant, is mother of Robert's two boys, Brandon, two, and Conlaed, four.

It is from here that the McCartneys and Bridgeen sat together and planned their campaign to bring the Irish Republican Army (IRA) killers of Robert McCartney to justice. Their quest has brought out extraordinary qualities in six ordinary women.

Expect, too, to see issues-based features in women's magazines which reflect the fears and concerns of the target market – this might be career women taking drugs or living beyond their means, or unusual takes on stress. The feature in the August 2006 issue of *Red*, headlined 'Scared of mummy', focused on busy and stressed-out women emotionally or physically abusing their children.

As with almost any feature, the issues-based ones stand or fall by the quality of the case studies in them. The tradition in the magazine market – unlike newspapers – is that surnames are rarely used, and names are frequently changed. Whatever feature you're writing, you need to collect all the relevant personal details about people and then abide by the house style of the publication you are working for. In some cases, you may be able to get someone to talk to you only if you agree to keep their name out of print – that's something you have to discuss with the features editor.

The *Red* feature starts with a classic personalised angle:

> When her son Peter, three, was born, Beverley, 31, became depressed. A former teacher married to a doctor, she couldn't understand why she wasn't coping. Antidepressants didn't help – they just made her feel more lethargic and paranoid. One day she snapped, hitting her son so hard she left an imprint on his cheek. Her partner threatened to leave her and take their son with him, compounding Beverley's belief that she could never be a proper mother. 'I can't believe I hit him,' she says. 'It's only now that I'm starting to feel better that I can tell people how bad it was for me.'

The feature quotes the chief executive of Parentline Plus, an NSPCC adviser, a university psychologist and social work professor, two psychologists and authors, and two more stressed parents – one of whom's story is told first person in a separate box. Finally, there is a fact box – a common extra to accompany features. It's tagged 'For parenting advice and information on courses' and provides contact details for eight charities and support groups. Get into the habit when you're working on features of collecting useful tips that might fit into such a box – travel features use them a great deal to present information on flights, currency, places to stay and sites to visit.

THE LOCAL ANGLE

Regional papers are fertile ground for news features, as they concentrate on the issues that affect their readership, or provide a local spin to a national story. A dispute over a gypsy camp, a long-running row over a bypass, and differing views on a town's street art have all been turned into strong topical pieces – the latter in particular enhanced by some eye-catching pictures. Get into the habit with any feature of thinking about pix – they often play a vital role in features spreads, as we shall see in Chapter 7.

If you work on a local paper, you should expect to be asked frequently to find an angle on a national story. If there's been a big survey on homelessness, or concern about twenty-four-hour opening for pubs, find contacts in your patch who can turn this into a feature relevant to your area. With the Olympics, they'll be looking for star athletes from the locality – and maybe those who just missed out, or who will be prospects four years down the road.

With news features – and almost any other features, for that matter – don't neglect follow-ups. You can frequently revisit an issue a month, six months, a year, or even further down the line to see how the story has progressed. Always make a note in your diary to make some calls periodically to see if a follow-up piece is warranted.

WRITING A NEWS FEATURE

In many ways news features are elongated news stories. The up-to-date news angle must be featured prominently, and you'll need to ensure readers are up to speed on the issues. But the feature differs from the story in that you are likely to be juggling more angles and carrying out more research into the background. It's likely, too, that you'll be talking to more interested parties and/or experts to add breadth and depth to the feature. And while a news story will often have a human interest intro, the feature may require one or more case studies. So, if you're doing that feature on homelessness, expect to track down at least one person who is homeless, and maybe someone who was at one time but got back on their feet. Charities and pressure groups are often helpful when it comes to finding such case studies for your features.

When it comes to content, the reporter takes a back seat as a rule in news features, and you are also unlikely to have a lot of space for colour or description. Focus the piece on analysis, background history and the issues involved from a number of different angles and sources. In some cases there may be eyewitness accounts from the reporter – describing what they see in a gypsy camp, or, for a foreign correspondent, relaying to the reader at home exactly what is going on in a war zone or a famine area. Comment, though, will generally be kept to a minimum (that will come in opinion pieces, which we'll look at in the next chapter).

As a rule, the inverted pyramid structure will apply when writing up a news feature – the most up-to-date and striking information should be at or near the top. It's also a sound idea to lead with a person, if you can find a strong human interest angle. From then on the information should filter down the story, with the less essential material towards the end, where it can be cut without ruining the flow of the feature. The piece will need strong quotes from several sources. Occasionally, you may decide to go for the running theme approach, in which case it's important to make the final paragraph strong so that the story doesn't tail off.

An interesting – and effective – exception to these rules is the *Independent's* daily 'The big question' feature, where that big question always forms the headline for the piece, and then a series of supplementary questions make up the actual feature. There is also a summing-up question in a panel at the bottom, which is accompanied by three 'yes' and three 'no' points.

Journalist Michael Savage's big question prior to the 2007 Rugby World Cup Final was: 'Why are there so few black players in the South African rugby team?' (19 October 2007). The questions posed in the body of the feature were:

- Why are we asking this now?
- Why are there so few black players?
- Who's to blame?
- What's the situation in other sports?
- What can be done?
- Will strict quotas work?
- Will things change this time?
- Should we be hopeful about the future?

The summing-up panel at the bottom asked: 'Will the South African rugby team ever have more black players?'

The 'yes' column replied:

- At youth level, there are many black players beginning to come through.
- There is now real political will to transform the team, with targets being introduced next year.
- With star winger Brian Habana playing so well, he could act as a role model for non-white players in the future.

The 'no' column responded:

- If South Africa win the World Cup, it will be hard for supporters to accept a dip in performance.
- Rugby authorities have proved that they are unable to tackle the problem of a lack of black players.
- The coach should be allowed to pick a team on merit alone. Picking someone for their skin colour will just cause more problems.

The piece includes some quotes from Andy Colquhoun, editor of the *SA Rugby Annual*, but it is much more a backgrounder/analytical look at the issue.

Working through a news feature idea

One of the challenges of writing news features is coming up with an angle that won't have been done in every other publication. So an ability to think imaginatively and come up with unusual angles is a much-prized skill among feature writers.

One long-running topic that challenged writers to find a fresh angle was the gay age of consent. The critical dates were:

- **1967**: Homosexuality was legalised in England and Wales in this year (1980 in Scotland, 1982 in Northern Ireland).
- **1988**: The controversial Section 28 of the Local Government Act, which outlawed the promotion of homosexuality by local authorities, came into force under a Tory government. It was eventually repealed by Labour in 2003.
- **1994**: The age of consent was lowered to eighteen.
- **1997**: European Commission of Human Rights case (after 1994 appeal).
- **2000**: Age of consent was finally lowered to sixteen (with the help of the Parliament Act) after an amendment to the Crime and

Disorder Act (1998) had been agreed in the Commons but thrown out by the Lords. The government's response was to introduce a new Sexual Offences (Amendment) Bill in 1998, and it was this that was passed in November 2000.

A number of strong angles could be pursued in news stories:

- *Historical background* – pull together all the material, and interview some of the pioneers who fought for equality, including social reformer and Labour MP Leo Abse, who piloted the 1967 Bill through the House of Commons.
- *Gay youngster as a case study* – essential, as this provided the human interest angle. Euan Sutherland, who was sixteen in 1994, eventually took the British government to the European Court of Human Rights.
- *What the law is elsewhere* – France and Ireland provided particularly good and topical angles because of recent legislation.
- *Talk to pros and antis* – including Stonewall (the gay pressure group), hardline Tories and church groups, youth and health workers (many of whom wanted equality) and 'out' celebrities, including gay MPs.

The personal angle generally worked best – particularly thanks to the articulate teenager Euan Sutherland – rather than focusing on the issues, which were well known and had been covered in the past.

INVESTIGATIVE FEATURES*

Virtually every journalist will have dreamed of front-page leads based on uncovering corruption or dirty dealings at the highest level. Those of us of a certain age will always associate investigative journalism with the likes of John Pilger, and the *Sunday Times* 'Insight' team in the 1970s under the editorship of Harold Evans. Read Evans's *Good Times, Bad Times* (1994) for a compelling account of the cases the team exposed, including the thalidomide scandal, where mothers were given medication that later caused their children to be born with physical disabilities.

Investigative stories are based on original research which produces something new. They may unearth hidden information and may also involve

---

* Thanks to Cleland Thom for all his help with this section.

wrongdoing or negligence. Investigative reporter Cleland Thom points to the following types of story:

- people being taken advantage of (maybe illegally)
- official cover-ups
- sex scandals and sleaze
- people's health and safety in jeopardy
- people in power misusing their influence/wealth/authority
- fighting readers' battles
- crime
- consumer affairs
- security and intelligence
- local government
- financial misdemeanours.

Conducting an investigation

Researching investigative features can take time – Nick Davies of the *Guardian* spent two years investigating the British criminal justice system (http://www.guardian.co.uk/criminaljustice/0,,996518,00.html; accessed 28 August 2008). And that's something editors will always bear in mind before giving an investigation the OK – how long is it likely to take, and how many stories is it likely to generate? They will also want to weigh up the benefits, risks and resources and any ethical implications, such as going undercover.

It's almost impossible to imagine any publication devoting the amount of resources to investigative journalism that the *Sunday Times* did back in the 1960s and 1970s. After all, investigative journalism can be expensive. You have to pull a reporter (or several reporters) off general news or features desk duties, perhaps for a long time. You might have to budget for overseas travel – the *Guardian* finally cracked the Jonathan Aitken perjury case when reporters uncovered vital paperwork in a Swiss hotel. And there's the possibility of a court case if the other side takes exception to your findings.

Researching the feature can take time. Cleland Thom suggests the following sources:

- your office (cuttings, phone book, reference book, archives, colleagues across all departments)
- internet (news groups, discussions lists)
- library (year books, the electoral register, specialist books, magazines, information on local societies)

- council offices (Local Government Access to Information Act, planning applications, register of childminders, register of old people's homes, pollution data, fire precautions, safety notices at sports grounds)
- company reports and accounts
- government documents and reports (Freedom of Information Act)
- university libraries
- consumer protection organisations
- specialist groups
- quangos
- experts
- whistleblowers and axe-grinders.

Meticulous record-keeping is essential when you're working on investigative features, as your paperwork may be required in the event of a legal challenge. You'll need to keep extensive and immaculate notes (so don't write rude observations in your notebook!). Tape interviews if you can and make sure everything is filed within easy reach. If possible, get the people you interviewed to sign your notebook or a transcript of the interview they gave. Keep a separate, chronological logbook of your investigations, and note every relevant activity. If the case goes to court, your behaviour will come under the spotlight. It goes without saying that you *always* protect your sources.

Getting people to talk may be tricky, so you'll need to go in well prepared. Don't be pushy – remember that no one *has* to speak to you. You may have to coax them along, or appeal to their sense of injustice. Ask some non-threatening questions first to get them talking, and encourage them to tell their side of the story.

Going underground

Going undercover as a reporter isn't an everyday occurrence, and it's not something that should be undertaken lightly, as the risks will need to be weighed up. The operation must be planned meticulously, and it can't happen until you know there's a worthwhile story there.

Realistically, most of your investigations will take place from the comfort of your own home or the newsroom. Sadly, fewer papers seem to be devoting time and space to the big investigations, mostly because of staffing and financial constraints.

Peter Cole, in an article for the *Independent on Sunday* (5 March 2006) headlined 'Tessa, Ashley, Jonathan and the death of investigative journalism', said:

> Sentimentalists regard the 1960s and 1970s as the golden era of investigative journalism, and the *Sunday Times* under the editorship of Harold Evans, ITV's *World in Action* and *Private Eye* with Paul Foot's Footnotes as the leading exponents of the genre. What distinguished investigative journalism was that it was demanding of time and talented people, and always ran the risk of producing nothing at the end of the process. Powerful investigations like the *Guardian*'s of Jonathan Aitken posed a constant danger of back-firing.
>
> Today, publishers are obsessed with cutting costs; editorial staffs are smaller; editors are less likely to invest in investigation, and anyway audiences are thought to be more interested in bedroom than balance-sheet activities. But we are still, happily, concerned about the integrity, or lack of it, of those in power over us and we still see one of the roles of the media as holding them to account.
>
> Appropriately enough, given its investigative history, the *Sunday Times* kicked off the past Jowellgate week with a story linking Tessa Jowell to her husband's £350,000 'gift'. The story appeared under the Insight logo, which the paper has used since the supposed great days of investigation. Then there might have been eight or 10 members of the team; now it might be one or two.

Cole argues that there is now a new approach to 'investigative' journalism, where reporters do a bit of research and then ask questions rather than answer them – he gives the example of the *Sunday Times* headline which read: 'Questions Jowell must answer on payoff'. He points out that no one is obliged to answer a question just because a newspaper asks it, but that the pressure of stories being run may force some action.

Investigative journalism can carry physical risks. Don Hale, former editor of the *Matlock Mercury* in Derbyshire, is best known for his campaign which freed Stephen Dowling, who had been in prison for twenty-seven years for a murder he didn't commit. Hale's book, *Town Without Pity* (2002), tells how his life was threatened on several occasions, including high-speed car chases through the Derbyshire countryside.

Not all investigative journalism is as dangerous as that, though. Much of the time it is about meticulous, careful attention to detail, trawling through lots of paperwork, and interviewing and re-interviewing people.

And it's often overlooked that there are strong stories in need of investigating at the grassroots level. *Doncaster Free Press* journalist Deborah Wain proved this when she shared the 2007 Paul Foot Award with David Leigh and Rob Evans of the *Guardian*. Leigh and Evans investigated corruption in the British arms trade; Wain produced a series of articles on the Doncaster Education City – the most expensive education scheme in England and Wales – and uncovered how much taxpayers' money was being spent on consultancy fees, luxury flights, entertaining and a hefty pay rise for the chief executive. She said: 'Who is best placed to scrutinise the workings of local authorities? Those of us living and working in the communities they serve, of course' ('Communities need local heroes', *Guardian*, 22 October 2007). She used the Freedom of Information Act to force Doncaster council to hand over data, and was given time off from her regular duties to meet contacts, trawl through files in the college library and conduct research via the internet and the newspaper's own archives. Wain continued: 'We showed that investigative reporting doesn't have to be about weighty budgets and large staffs. Persistence and attention to detail are the key requirements.' And she felt that the FOI Act is underused: 'Reporters need more training so they can use it effectively; queries must be carefully worded and it can take time to get comfortable with the procedure.'

Former *Western Daily Press* editor Ian Beales recalls an investigation that won the paper a *Press Gazette* Award. It was an exposé of privatisation deals at West Wiltshire District Council and led to a property company, West Wiltshire Holdings Ltd, being returned to full council control and millions of pounds of council assets being recovered from a privatised computer company ('The paper that gets things done – official', *Western Daily Press*, 18 April 1991). Beales recalled (interview with the author, 9 September 2008):

> The problem was that some of the council's senior officers had proposed a deal that they should take over certain council functions, including the computer services department – which had pioneered potentially valuable local government software – and run it as a private business, with the council chief executive at its head.
>
> At the same time, the legal services department would also be privatised – with the council's legal officers handling the council's legal affairs for profit through a private practice.
>
> These proposals raised serious issues of transparency and substantial risks of conflict of interest, as the people advising the

council were also potential beneficiaries. Yet it was all done remarkably quietly and normal good practice rules of arm's length deals, such as inviting alternative bids or consulting independent advisors, appeared to have gone out of the window.

Our investigation was a classic case of the press acting as a watchdog to protect the public – but it might easily not have happened.

Another local paper had been contacted about the story but had baulked at running it, possibly for fear of legal action, and so a whistleblower came to us. We investigated, stood the story up and ran it with more revelations emerging daily, despite a flurry of legal threats.

After the *Western Daily Press* exposé, the council chief executive resigned, police were called in and – although all those involved were cleared of criminality at a Crown Court trial – the privatisation deals were largely unravelled. We were justified, and the ratepayers protected.

But investigations such as these are increasingly risky because of the chilling effect of libel laws and of lawyers offering no-win, no-fee deals (conditional fee agreements) to plaintiffs. The chilling effect is a very real danger to investigative journalism, especially in the regional press.

There are seemingly small-scale investigations, but these may have profound effects on ordinary people. And, as you will recall from earlier, human interest is the focus of almost all stories. These people, who may have been ripped off by a loan shark or a mobile phone company, could buy your publication. National newspapers run a variety of columns based on securing 'justice' for Joe and Josephine Public. The *Daily Mirror*'s Andrew Penman and Nick Sommerlad investigate scams that affect ordinary people, such as a conman fleecing sports fans with an Olympic tickets scam.

One investigative reporter who polarises opinion is the *News of the World*'s investigations editor, Mazher Mahmood, known as the 'Fake Sheikh'. Mahmood, who often disguises himself as an Arab sheikh, sets up 'stings' to entrap celebrities – the Countess of Wessex, the actor John Alford, *Blue Peter* presenter Richard Bacon and DJ Johnnie Walker all ended up in the paper. He has also produced exposés of paedophiles, brothel owners and alleged terrorists.

The *Independent on Sunday* reported:

an Old Bailey jury acquitted three men accused of involvement in an alleged terrorist plot – the 'red mercury' case – after they were caught in a sting orchestrated by the *NoW*'s investigations editor Mazher Mahmood (a.k.a. the Fake Sheikh). He had posed alongside an undercover Scotland Yard agent as a possible seller of the chemical which could be used in a terror attack. The accused walked free following defence claims that the 'sensationalised' story was published solely to bring the *NoW* 'commercial gain' and for Mahmood's 'personal kudos'.

In the same feature, Professor Steven Barnett of Westminster University said:

> They have been found out. We are seeing the lid ripped off some of the lurid and unacceptable techniques of red-top tabloid journalism . . . There is a place for high-quality tabloid investigations. There is nothing wrong with exposing incompetence, laziness and scrounging. The Royal Family does not deserve to be sacrosanct. But at one end of the tabloid industry journalists have started to go further. These are grubby money-making scams, designed to sell newspapers and nothing else. There is no public interest involved.

However, Bill Hagerty, the editor of the *British Journalism Review*, said: 'You can question the Fake Sheikh's tactics, but he has got an awful lot of people arrested' (*Independent on Sunday*, 13 April 2006).

You'll find the term 'investigation' tagged on to a variety of articles or columns which may not, at first glance, appear to involve a great deal of digging. Jessica Gorst-Williams's Saturday column in the Your Money section of the *Daily Telegraph* has a 'Jessica investigates' strapline on the top. There are similar columns elsewhere, where people who have been grappling with large financial institutions, such as banks and building societies, discover that a journalist phoning a press office on their behalf can often work wonders. Penman and Sommerlad's column in the *Daily Mirror* operates along similar lines, albeit with more digging. 'We're here to expose injustice, so if you've been ripped off, we want to know about it,' they say. They have their sights set on dodgy businesses and fake charities, with the added use of photographs to name and shame conmen.

The women's magazine market isn't particularly known for its investigative approach. Campaigns, yes, but harder-edged features are very much of the human interest sort, as we've already seen. And the exposé-style piece is very mindful of its market – *Glamour* magazine, the first handbag-sized publication on the market, sent four writers undercover for its July 2005 issue to work for businesses run by celebrities ('Undercover as an

A-list employee'). In its next edition reporter Sarah Duguid went under-cover to work at an estate agent's. The piece, 'Over-valued properties, fake offers and aggressive sales tricks', tells of the reporter's experiences during a two-week stint with what is described as an 'upmarket west London estate agents'. (We'll look at this feature in more detail in Chapter 7.) While the July feature focuses on one of *Glamour's* principal areas of interest (celebrities), the August article caters to another (life-style), as it plays very much on the fears of the twenty-something woman desperate to get on the housing ladder.

CAMPAIGNS

Editors like campaigns. They make a publication look public-spirited and ensure a steady stream of copy once the campaign takes off and readers are on board. Campaigns can vary from controversial (such as the *Independent on Sunday's* efforts to legalise cannabis, which dates back to 1997), to intensely local (such as helping a disabled youngster to get special hospital treatment), to very specific (such as a women's glossy magazine's attempts to stop date rape).

You don't start a campaign lightly. For one thing, you have to be certain that it has legs – that is, that people will care about it, and that it will have plenty of mileage. And you can't miss a day/week/month/edition – if you're running a campaign, there has to be some sort of story related to it in every issue of the publication. After a while a good campaign will more or less run itself, and members of the public will come forward with stories. But for the campaign to have maximum impact, there needs to be a range of stories and photos – short, sharp news stories to keep it ticking over alongside features and profiles of the main protagonists.

The *Citizen*, Gloucester's evening paper, ran a high-profile 'Back Badge' campaign, a classic example of an emotive issue close to the county's heart. Under army reorganisation plans, the Glosters regiment was due to be amalgamated into a giant South West regiment. The Glosters were unique in having both a back and front badge on their caps – and the *Citizen* set out to save the former.

Assistant editor Matt Holmes recalls how the campaign struck a chord with readers, including widows of soldiers from the regiment and sur-viving veterans. The paper started a petition, lobbied politicians, printed comments from readers both online and in the print edition and gen-erated a steady stream of stories, including one focusing on a Glosters veteran who had been blinded in Northern Ireland, and another on a woman who had lost three relatives serving in the regiment.

> An ex-Glosters corporal who lost his sight in an horrific terrorist attack in Northern Ireland has backed the campaign to save the regiment's Back Badge.
>
> Receiving a top Rotary award for his charitable work yesterday, Ray Peart, 59, of Abbeydale, explained the pride he felt in wearing the famous badge. 'It's never been worn on another uniform,' he said. 'Since 1801 at Alexandria we have always had that badge and we're still proud of it. You knew that was one of your battle honours and you wore that badge with pride. We are a family regiment and the recruitment around here is done through the Glosters and that badge. It denotes the Gloucestershire area.'
> (*Citizen*, 13 November 2004)

'Our approach was very simple. The only way to make the campaign successful was to humanise it,' says Holmes.

His tip is never to start a campaign where you don't have a chance of succeeding. In the case of the Back Badge, the *Citizen* was successful and the badge stayed.

CASE STUDY – CLELAND THOM, INVESTIGATIVE JOURNALIST

How did you get into investigative reporting?

I was working as a reporter on the *Islington Gazette*, north London, during the 1970s and 1980s – so it was very difficult not to get involved in investigative journalism. It was an area high in crime and social deprivation, so almost every story you handled had an investigative slant to it. But I found myself drawn towards several big cases which required a lot more digging and research. Luckily, my editor, Tony Allcock, gave me the time and freedom to follow them up – and it went from there.

What are the most memorable stories you've worked on?

Two particularly stick in my mind. The first involved the wrongful conviction of two men for the murders of two gangland figures. They were framed by the Metropolitan Police, who fabricated statements from them. This story ran for twenty-five years – that's how long it took me to get the evidence that led to the Court of Appeal overturning their convictions in 2003. I think this may hold the record as being the longest-running story! The story was featured on *Rough Justice* and a number of other TV and radio shows. Another one involved a rogue landlord, who was ripping off illegal immigrants by taking deposits on flats that did not exist. This led to him going to jail for fraud.

What's your approach to undertaking an investigation?

Every story's different. You have to draw up a strategy, a battle plan. This involves listing all the people/sources of information, and also 'long-shots' – people who might know something, or who might know someone who knows. You also have to get your timing right – it's essential that the people you're investigating don't find out until the last minute. So I tend to work from the 'edge' of the story into the 'middle' . . . researching all the background and peripheral material first, and gradually closing in on the 'target'. It's important, though, to do a 'pre-investigation' first – to find out whether the story stands up, whether I am capable of dealing with it (it might be a specialist area that would be better handled by someone else), and what the story will involve in time, resources, risks and so on. I tend to pursue tip-offs only when they are verified by at least two other people. This ensures I don't waste a lot of time chasing wild geese.

What qualities does a good investigative journalist need?

You need to be an individual – to enjoy working off the 'normal' news agenda and being prepared to listen to the non-spokespeople. You should be nosy, persistent and meticulous – and be motivated by a strong sense of justice. You shouldn't be a clock-watcher, or someone who's put off easily. And you must be prepared to be hugely unpopular: people don't like it when you start rocking the boat – even editors and colleagues don't always appreciate the investigative reporter!

What are your top tips for investigative reporting?

- Make contacts with the people who matter – that's not always the 'boss' or the 'big name'. Secretaries and caretakers are usually better sources of information.
- Be passionate about what you're doing – a byline or a cheque should not be motivators in themselves. You'll need more than that if the going gets rough.
- Be prepared for the fact that some editors aren't keen on investigative reporting these days – it costs them too much in time,

resources, legal actions. Sad, but true. So you may have to rock the boat within the media before you can get to work on a story.

- File everything – every email, every notebook, every document, every text message . . . the lot. You never know when you might need them, sometimes years later.
- Play to your character. I'm quite shy, so I do better hanging around listening to conversations, rather than being the forthcoming journalist who has plenty to say. This works well – people tend not to notice me. So you should use your own character, skills, abilities, strengths and weaknesses to shape the way you work – you'll never be someone that you're not!

Biography?

Reporter, chief reporter, news editor and chief sub at the *Islington Gazette*. Group editor of the *Enfield Independent* group. Worked for the *News of the World* and *Sunday Mirror* on investigations, and freelanced for all the national newspapers, radio and TV. Now run Potential.gb.com – a journalism and media training business. I have trained more than 1,000 journalists in the past six years, and am legal adviser to the *Manchester Evening News*, the Local Radio Company, *Essex Independent* newspaper, *TNT* magazine and *Manchester Electronic Weekly Media*.

5
Developing an ego

Being paid to rant as much as you like? Sounds like a dream job, doesn't it! That's exactly what happens if you're a newspaper or magazine columnist. On some of the UK national papers, columnists are among the highest-paid journalists. And it's not unknown for newspapers to 'poach' columnists from their competitors by waving a blank cheque at them. Over the past few years, newspapers and magazines have vied to sign up celebrity columnists, so you'll often find TV presenters and MPs treating us to their views on life, the universe and everything.

Newspapers in particular use big-name columnists in their advertising. The *Daily Mail* carried blurbs to advertise the arrival of Richard Littlejohn as a columnist. And in the 1990s, when it was unusual for national newspapers to advertise on television, the *Mail on Sunday* used their widely differing columnists of the time, John Junor and Julie Burchill, as the focus of an advertising campaign.

Over the past few years, the number of columns in UK papers has increased greatly. These have ranged from heavyweight commentators such as the *Independent's* Robert Fisk, through Peter Hitchens's right-wing agenda in the *Mail on Sunday,* to the feisty straight-talking of the *Mirror's* Jane Moore. As for the *Indepedent's* Cooper Brown, with his 'He's out there' column, readers can't quite decide whether the brash and outspoken Brown is real or a figment of some other writer's overactive imagination!

Writing a column may sound glamorous, but it's also a big commitment. We'll see later in the chapter the function of one-off opinion pieces, where you can sound off on a topic of national or personal interest. But it's clearly much more of a challenge when you're faced with a weekly or monthly column – you have to stay fresh and ensure you can turn out good, snappy copy each time. And that's why editors like columnists. If they are doing their job properly, they'll get readers talking and, even better, writing letters to the newspaper, either to agree or disagree with what's been written. You might think the columnist is talking rubbish, but their brief is only to get the readers thinking. No one wants a bland columnist who sits on the fence. Instead, editors want a writer who will build up a clear and recognisable personality and style that will have readers thumbing through impatiently to find the column each time (a reason, incidentally, for the column to appear in the same spot, whenever possible).

Columnists will build up their own recognisable 'voice'. Some go all out to be controversial. Others are off-the-wall. Others aim to be a thorn in the side of the government. Richard Littlejohn, formerly of the *Sun* and now at the *Daily Mail*, has become known for his trenchant anti-Labour, anti-*Guardian*-reader, anti-political correctness pieces, often ending with his slogan 'You couldn't make it up'. His column focusing on the end of the Beijing Olympics (25 August 2008) seemed like a typical deliberate attempt to court controversy:

> Just imagine if I had written a parody of the Olympic handover ceremony, which had included a portrait of Fred West, a simulated suicide bombing and a stabbing.
>
> I'd have been accused of tipping a tsunami on the parade and belittling Britain's achievements – not only in Beijing, but in winning the honour of staging the Games in 2012.
>
> Steady on, Rich. You've gone a bit too far this time.
>
> But even I couldn't have made up what we got on the night.
>
> In the Bird's Nest stadium on Sunday, the decapitated double-decker looked just like the bus blown up in Tavistock Square on July 7.
>
> And who thought it would be a good idea to show a promotional video featuring a picture of Myra Hindley, one of our most notorious murderers, tastefully made up of thousands of children's handprints?
>
> Back home, security jobsworths were busy turning away hundreds of people with tickets from the celebrations in the Mall, and the big screens beaming back events in China broke down.
>
> Over in East London, plans to show the closing ceremony to a crowd at the site of the 2012 Games were abandoned after a teenager was stabbed to death.

Oh, and elf 'n' safety warned anyone intending to go to Heathrow to cheer our returning athletes to stay away.

Welcome to Britain. Have A Nice Day.

TYPES OF COLUMNS

You'll find a wide range of columns in newspapers and magazines. What they have in common, though, is one person's take on current issues, or something that affects the columnist's life.

Personality

These can range from the weekly hard-hitting personality columns, much beloved of the tabloids, where the columnist is given carte blanche to comment on issues in the news, to the so-called 'id' columns, where the columnist is the star turn. Examples of the latter have ranged from the late Miles Kington, the king of idiosyncratic humour, in the *Independent* (who can forget his columns where the deities from all the religions met to sigh heavily over the ways of the world?) to the likes of William Leith in the *Observer*, bemoaning at some length in his introspective columns that his girlfriend doesn't understand him, or Liz Jones in the *Mail on Sunday*, sharing every last detail of her tangled married life with the reader. The thing to bear in mind here is that you must make your readers care about what your chosen subject, rather than rolling their eyes and muttering: 'So what?' or 'Get a life!'

A different sort of personality column became a talking point in the late 1990s when a number of terminally ill journalists, including John Diamond in *The Times*, Ruth Picardie in the *Observer* and Oscar Moore in the *Guardian*, used their columns to chart their illnesses.

Politics

These include the Black Dog column in the *Mail on Sunday*, which provides a caustic, slightly gossipy look at what goes on in Parliament (http://www.mailonsunday.co.uk/news/article-1040915/The-Queen-clears-holiday-diary.html) and the more orthodox 'sketch' columns, where the likes of Simon Hoggart in the *Guardian* report on the day's proceedings in the House of Commons in a slightly tongue-in-cheek manner

(http://www.guardian.co.uk/politics/2008/may/08/houseofcommons.
gordonbrown).

Sport

The sports pages of newspapers attract their fair share of straight-talking
columnists. There was the late Ian Wooldridge's long-running column in
the *Daily Mail* and Patrick Collins's in its Sunday sister paper. Collins
shows how understatement will often work far better than overstatement.
In his column of 1 October 2006 ('Shankly would show withering contempt for the game today'), he uses his memories of former Liverpool
manager Bill Shankly to show how soccer has changed for the worse. He
starts off in a nostalgic vein:

> The decades have drifted past, yet still I recall those Sunday after-
> noons when Nessie Shankly's kindly voice would come crackling
> down the line. 'I'm sorry, Bill's not here,' she would say. 'He's over
> the park, playing football with the kids. When will he be back, you
> say? When he wins, of course.' And you could hear the chuckle as
> she put down the telephone.
>
> Half-an-hour later the man himself would come on, a touch breath-
> less, to tell of his part in the nine-goal thriller and of how he had
> laid on the winner, with the park-keeper tapping his watch and the
> mothers calling them in for their tea. And then Bill Shankly would
> talk football.
>
> And I, the rawest of rookies, would listen, scribble and revel in the
> tutorial.

A little later, Collins concludes the column with:

> I mention these things because he died 25 years ago this weekend.
> I often wonder what he would have made of the modern game
> with its thrusting, grasping agents and towering mountains of
> money.
>
> I should love to have heard him on the subject of bungs, with his
> language ripe and his contempt withering.
>
> As well he never knew such times. As well he lived in the age he did.
> As well he died knowing just how much we loved him. There is a
> line on his captivating statue at Anfield which says, quite simply:
> 'He made the people happy.'
>
> Bill Shankly would have settled for that.

It's a masterful example of column writing, as it pays affectionate tribute to one of soccer's great names, uses the twenty-fifth anniversary of Shankly's death as a peg for the piece, and is able to ponder on how the former Liverpool boss would view today's money-obsessed game.

Frank Keating has also employed nostalgia in his columns for a number of newspapers and magazines. There is often a slightly starry-eyed feel to his reminiscences about his boyhood in Gloucestershire as he reflects on his sporting heroes from those days. Such relaxed, personal columns provide a good counterpoint to the more hard-hitting, topical ones.

Gossip

Gossip columns have undergone radical changes over the past few years. In the 1990s and before, the first name mentioned if a journalist were asked about gossip columns would almost certainly have been Nigel Dempster of the *Daily Mail*. These anachronistic columns were based largely on sightings of vaguely famous people – minor nobility, well-connected people, and B-list actors. The gossip columnists had an unrivalled network of contacts, including hotel doormen and restaurant maîtres d', who could tip them off in an instant if a celebrity arrived. Writers like Dempster gave the impression of being 'in the know' – little asides such as 'I understand' or 'so I'm told' would litter the columns. But these columns from another age have largely been elbowed out by the C-list celebrity society – so the likes of the Bizarre column in the *Sun* or the 3 a.m. column in the *Daily Mirror* focus on actors, pop stars and reality TV names. The growth of the internet has ensured cult followings for the likes of celebrity-based gossip column Popbitch (http://www.pop bitch.com), via both its website and its weekly email updates which go directly into subscribers' inboxes, and the celebrity blogger Perez Hilton (http://perezhilton.com).

Diary

Diaries are also gossipy in approach, and often end up as a dumping ground for snippets that can't find a home elsewhere in the paper – off-beat stories of famous people, misprints and lightweight anecdotes. The *Guardian* diary, fronted for several years by Matthew Norman, gained a cult 'so corny it's funny' following by highlighting how useless it was at finding stories. Norman loved collecting appropriate names (Mr De'Ath the undertaker, Mr Book the librarian . . .) and sending up badly written press releases but also fixated on certain people (members of the clergy, MPs, journalists) who took his fancy, usually much to the bemusement of the subject.

Specialist

These can cover pretty much any area – motoring, medical, TV, arts and so on. You'll find them in newspapers, often written by big names (Jeremy Clarkson in the *Sun*, for example) or by particular experts. The latter often appear in the question-and-answer format in magazines or supplements. You may also come across 'ghosted' columns which appear to be written by, say, top sports stars, but are generally compiled by a journalist interviewing the big name, then writing it up to appear as if it's the star's own work. 'As told to . . .' tends to be the giveaway here.

BEING A COLUMNIST

Writing a column is a regular commitment, not something you dabble at when you fancy it. Columns tend to appear on a set day, or in each issue of a magazine, so that a reader knows when to watch out for them. They will generally be in the same place in each issue. Editors like it if readers start to associate a columnist with their particular publication – it was always said that loyal cabals of readers bought the *Daily Mail* solely for the late Lynda Lee-Potter, and the *Sunday Express* for the late John Junor (the man with the 'pass the sickbag, Alice' catchphrase). A columnist needs a distinctive voice and an opinion on anything and everything. Sitting on the fence is boring – editors want their letters bag overflowing with missives from readers taking issue or agreeing with what a columnist has said.

Good columnists can react quickly to issues in the news and give them their own individual spin. Victoria Coren took an unusual and provocative line in the *Observer* on the story of a woman who was pushed on to a railway track after telling two men to stop smoking on the platform:

> Britain is gasping in sympathy with Linda Buchanan, the hapless Kent commuter who was pushed on to a railway track by two men she had 'ticked off' for smoking. Everyone is shaken by the idea of this ghastly, nightmarish experience. We are all standing closer to walls as we wait for trains. Poor, terrified Linda Buchanan.

Having said that ... On a bad day, I'd have shoved her off the platform myself.

Of course, this is a horrible story. But not just because there are people who push other people on to railway tracks. This was not a meeting of good and evil. It was a meeting of bad and worse.

Mrs Buchanan, who was helped off the track with a hurt wrist, has been hailed as a hero in the press. Shouting at the smokers, she did 'what any good citizen might do'. She is 'a woman unafraid to intervene when something is wrong'. She 'highlights what ordinary people risk by confronting thugs'.

Bollocks. This woman is not a Ben Kinsella (stabbed to death trying to break up a street brawl) or a Philip Lawrence (killed trying to protect the children at St George's school, where he was head-master, from a gang of bullies), although one newspaper had the tasteless nerve to compare her to both. Mrs Buchanan wasn't being a hero, she was being a busybody.

('There's no smoke without ire – that's the real outrage', 10 August 2008)

Columnists need to know their market inside out. Jon Gaunt in the *Sun* plays up his plain-talking man-of-the-people role, often referring to himself as 'Gaunty', while Richard Littlejohn in the *Daily Mail* takes frequent pot-shots at 'lefties' and political correctness. Other papers take delight in featuring opposing columnists: the *Mail on Sunday* has the right-wing Peter Hitchens on one page and the more left-leaning feminist Suzanne Moore on the next.

All good columnists will build up a consistent approach, be it satirical, serious, balanced, off-beat or ranting. Readers would be most confused if they turned to your page one week to find you delivering a hard-hitting condemnation of the government and the next week found you taking an off-the-wall look at your pet chinchilla's ingrowing toenail.

WRITING THE COLUMN

Developing a 'voice' and remaining fresh week after week are the main challenges for a columnist. No one wants a bland columnist who drones on for 800 words and never jumps down from the fence. If you write a column, you're expected to have an opinion and to express it forcefully and convincingly, or with an individual slant.

Commentator and columnist Paul Stokes, who has written for a range of publications, including the *Spectator*, the *Sunday Times* and *Scotland on*

Sunday, says: 'I once worked as a Mr Angry columnist on a tabloid but soon discovered I was more a Mr Mildly Annoyed.' So he found that a more off-beat – albeit still serious – take on the stories worked better for him. 'You can make serious points using humour,' says Stokes, who says he has tried to develop a recognisable style for himself which he hasn't had to tailor a great deal for different publications. If he is producing a weekly column of about 1,300 words, he will plan it over the course of the week, storing up useful nuggets, and then spend up to a day writing it. 'I do a lot of reading – other columnists, American writers, other opinion pieces, magazines and essays. And I do research. What I like in reading columns is being surprised.'

If you're producing a current affairs-based column, know what's in the news, react to it fast and be prepared to give it an idiosyncratic spin if necessary. The snappier and brighter you can make your writing, the better the column will be. Columnists in the tabloids tend to go for one main story and then surround this with a handful of shorter pieces, some throwaway paragraphs or even individual lines. Jane Moore's weekly column in the *Sun* features one lead story, maybe half a dozen shorter pieces, a picture caption and the 'bloke quote' and 'not the bloke quote'. In 27 August 2008's column, she leads on the row over Prince William's girlfriend Kate Middleton not getting a job while allegedly sitting around waiting for the prince to propose to her ('Waity Katie's stuck in the Middleton'). The shorter pieces, ranging from half a dozen paragraphs down to one, include an article using Olympic swimming double-gold-medallist Rebecca Adlington as the starting point for some comments on British stoicism, Madonna courting controversy by flashing up pictures of US Republican presidential candidate John McCain alongside images of Adolf Hitler and Robert Mugabe, Liberal Democrat leader Nick Clegg saying he now has to shop at Sainsbury's instead of Waitrose because of the credit crunch, and a sharp little single-paragraph piece on the new fifteen-pound suit from Tesco, which mentions that the model in the photo is hunky, it's just a shame about the cheap suit . . .

Writing ego columns is another matter altogether. Here, you have to convince the reader that they care about your spat over frozen peas in the supermarket, or about the row you had with your girlfriend. Some newspapers have gone for the cult-following approach – the *Gloucestershire Echo* used a weekly column on the news pages by its soccer writer Derek Goddard. His deadpan offerings, featuring living in a mobile home, Harley his moped, his drinking mates, his broken marriage and people from a long time back, garnered a 'so awful it's good' reputation.

THINK PIECES

Think pieces are one-offs. They can range from a serious, densely argued piece on the situation in the Middle East to an in-your-face, explicit article in a gay men's magazine on why barebacking (sex without condoms) is wrong. You'll sometimes hear them called opinion or comment pieces – and I shall use the three terms interchangeably – but the idea is the same. They are analytical first-person pieces by a (usually) bylined reporter whose brief generally includes one or more of the following prerequisites:

- provocative
- controversial
- entertaining
- thought-provoking
- topical.

They are written either by a staff reporter or by an outsider with special interest or expertise. Dr David Webster, a colleague of mine who lectures in religion, philosophy and ethics, is often called on to do think pieces on ethical issues. The *Citizen* in Gloucester asked him to give his views on 2005, a year which included Hurricane Katrina in New Orleans, an earthquake in Pakistan and the terrible aftermath of the tsunami in Asia, under the headline 'Why would God deal humanity such blows?' (2 January 2006).

You'll find that specialist writers can also provide more light-hearted opinion pieces that still carry a topical message. Janine Gibson, the editor-in-chief of *MediaGuardian*, used the BBC drama *Bonekickers*, which had been savaged by the critics but nevertheless had developed a cult following, to talk about the importance of TV drama. Her column appeared under an 'Opinion' heading in the Monday supplement (18 August 2008), and the intro is a nice example of building up the tension and then providing an amusing little sting in the tail:

> Right now, or at least over the next few days and weeks, the BBC will take a momentous decision. One that has reached seminal status in the eyes of many of its stakeholders. Viewers, critics, writers and, crucially of course, columnists await the announcement that for many will define the course of the corporation for the next 18 months. Will they, or will they not, recommission *Bonekickers*?

Newspapers such as the *Guardian* and the *Independent* devote several pages each day to their comment sections, and often ask a mix of people to contribute. The former's Comment and Debate section covers three pages and features a balanced range of opinion pieces. In the issue of 1 September 2008, you would have found the following:

- *Guardian* writer Gary Younge looking at what George Bush was allowed to get away with by America's political class during his time as president.
- David McKie lamenting the number of professions that have disappeared in the past century. He tried to track down a candlestick-maker after Radio 4's *Farming Today* programme interviewed a butcher and a baker about the credit crunch, but claimed they couldn't find the third type of artisan. McKie had no more luck.
- Former *Daily Telegraph* editor Max Hastings talking about the issues around the hiring and firing of people from minorities in senior posts because there are so few of them, in the light of Metropolitan Police Assistant Commissioner Tarique Ghaffur's claims that he was the victim of racial, religious and age discrimination.
- Former *Guardian* editor Peter Preston highlighting the financial bubble that Premier League soccer has been in, and how it may be about to burst.
- Political journalist Jackie Ashley focusing on how there is no chance of economic recovery unless Gordon Brown and his ministers can present an optimistic vision of what comes next.
- Luke Harding writing on how he witnessed the worst ethnic cleansing since the war in the Balkans in South Ossetia.

Preston's first two paragraphs are particularly effective and sharp:

> This was, by precise design, a dream come true. A six-year-old lad puts on his beloved team's kit, clutches the captain's hand and walks on to a Premiership pitch as the crowd roars its welcome. He's ball boy for the afternoon, famous for two minutes in a small, touching ritual you've seen a hundred times – the familiar moment when our greatest game seeks to show a soft heart.
>
> And – oh yes! – it cost his dad £200 cash, up front. Doesn't the relentless, tatty avarice get you down?

Opinion columns in newspapers are generally found on or near the opposite editorial (op ed) page. If it's part of a series, such as soccer magazine *Four Four Two*'s Rant, it will show up in the same place in each issue.

Opinion pieces must respond to issues in the news. And whereas a feisty columnist may be able to get away with a degree of ranting and 'because I say so' comments, the writer of a think piece will generally need to argue their corner coherently and logically. Of course, they may be addressing highly controversial issues that could provoke anger and debate on the letters page. For instance, the *Independent's* Johann Hari wrote a 1,200-word think piece headlined 'We need to stop being such cowards about Islam' (14 August 2008). The article starts with: 'This is a column condemning cowardice – including my own.' The first and second paragraphs then discuss a novel called *The Jewel of Medina*, which tells of a nine-year-old girl being married off to a fifty-year-old man who subsequently became known as the Prophet Mohammed. Random House, who had bought the rights as part of a two-book deal with author Sherry Jones, cancelled its publication after stinging criticism of the subject matter from an American academic and warnings that it could be another *Satanic Verses*. Hari wrote:

> In Europe, we are finally abolishing the lingering blasphemy laws that hinder criticism of Christianity. But they are being succeeded by a new blasphemy law preventing criticism of Islam – enforced not by the state, but by jihadis. I seriously considered not writing this column, but the right to criticise religion is as precious – and hard-won – as the right to criticise government. We have to use it or lose it.

The angle and the style of a think piece will depend very much on the publication and on the writer's expertise. The *Daily Mail* is more likely to run a comment piece from a family values campaigner on why gay civil partnerships are wrong than from a gay rights activist saying how welcome they are. Someone with an interest in the issue can often give a personalised dimension to the news.

Some publications go for the 'for and against' approach, where they present both sides of the argument from different writers. The *Daily Mirror* (17 August 2005) took this approach following England's thrilling Ashes win over Australia. Beneath the news story headlined '7.7 million not out . . . record TV audience tunes in for final Ashes day drama' was the question 'Is cricket better than football?' Bill Borrows took the 'yes' side, opening up with: 'The back pages are full of it and you can't get on a radio phone-in to rant about Omar Bakri Mohammed for middle-aged women going on about Andrew "Freddie" Flintoff. Cricket, it seems, has arrived. Or rather, returned.' On the 'no' side was Darren Lewis, who argued: 'Here we go. Five days of fun with the red cherry and cricket is suddenly the number one sport in this country. What a load of rubbish. Yes, this has been one of the most thrilling Test series of all time. Yes, it would be great if England win the Ashes. But fans from Hackney to Humberside get just as much excitement – and more – every week watching football.'

The explosion in blogging means everyone thinks they can be a journalist and have an opinion. Some newspapers – including the *Guardian*, with its Comment is Free section – devote significant website space to blogs and comment pieces.

Online magazine *spiked* (http://www.spiked-online.com) focuses on provocative, opinionated writing, advertised by a weekly email to interested readers. It describes itself as:

> an independent online phenomenon dedicated to raising the horizons of humanity by waging a culture war of words against misanthropy, priggishness, prejudice, luddism, illiberalism and irrationalism in all their ancient and modern forms. *spiked* is endorsed by free-thinkers such as John Stuart Mill and Karl Marx, and hated by the narrow-minded such as Torquemada and Stalin. Or it would be, if they were lucky enough to be around to read it.

A typical (if such a thing exists) issue of *spiked* ranges from Russia and China, through Salman Rushdie's libel case against a publisher, to a provocation picnic in Hyde Park in London protesting against bans on public drinking, and to Patrick West's piece ('Who does Jerry Springer think he is?') on TV celebrity Jerry Springer as the subject of BBC1's *Who Do You Think You Are?*, where he says:

> I'm not anti-Jewish. In fact, I am exactly the opposite. I'm very pro-Israeli, because I think the Jews are a nation of geniuses. You can always spot a loser in life if he is anti-Semitic. This is the politics of envy. Hitler hated the Jews because he thought they were clever; the philosopher Friedrich Nietzsche loved the Jews because he thought they were clever. Hitler, the *über*-anti-Semite, was an über-loser. Never trust anyone who hates Jews.

> But Holocaust stories have become very tiresome, especially when people alive today claim victimhood status on behalf of their ancestors, which is not only boring but despicable. Jerry Springer shed many a tear on behalf of his grandparents who were rounded up by the Germans in Czechoslovakia. But what about the people who actually survived Auschwitz, Bergen-Belsen and the like, or the

children of the survivors and the dead who do actually remember the trauma they endured? This programme felt like an insult to genuine Holocaust survivors.

These were the cheap words of a cheap TV presenter who has made his career from deriving cheap thrills from the misfortunes of others. He has made a living from parading and creating 'victims' by humiliating them on American and international TV, and now parades himself as an ersatz victim on the BBC.

(http://www.spiked-online.com/index.php?/site/earticle/5656/, 28 August 2008; accessed 29 August 2008)

WRITING A THINK PIECE

People starting out often think writing a comment piece is easy – but it's not unusual to run out of steam halfway through and wonder how you will reach the 800-word limit. Most of us have strong opinions on a wide variety of issues (I can rant for England on the UK railway system or on the obscene amounts of money paid to Premiership footballers). But just because you feel strongly about a subject that doesn't necessarily mean you can knock out a comment piece on it. You may simply not be able to argue your corner coherently, or find enough to say on the issue, or discover a sufficiently punchy spin on it. If I had a pound for every comment piece I've read on why cannabis should be legalised, or why fox hunting should be banned, I'd now be reclining regally on a beach in the Bahamas! But if you asked me to point to a particularly convincing piece on one of those subjects, I'd be hard-pressed to do so – simply because both topics have more or less been done to death. That's not to say there shouldn't be debate about them, but the topics might be better served by another kind of feature – the elderly woman with multiple sclerosis who has to go to a drug dealer to obtain cannabis for pain relief, or a day out with a drag hunt, perhaps.

A comment piece must be argued logically and coherently – and it goes without saying that the writer should have strong opinions on the matter. It's hard to write passionately about something you're really not fussed about, although there are likely to be times in your journalistic career when you will have to do just that. And you must react fast with a comment piece – it's not usually much good publishing it a week after the main story has broken, unless, of course, you have a strong new angle on a running story.

A good writer can use the big story of the day as a jumping-off point for other issues. There are two excellent examples from the *Independent*, a paper with a strong tradition of opinionated writing: Johann Hari uses two *Big Brother* contestants to illustrate a piece on the appalling state of the UK education system ('*Big Brother* and the failed generation', 2 August 2007); and David McKitterick weaves in the momentous occasion of England playing Ireland at rugby at Croke Park (the home of Gaelic games) with a look at the Irish elections and Anglo-Irish relations ('Triumph of this new Anglo-Irish alliance', 27 February 2007).

Resist the temptation to be pompous and to overstate your case – the best and most accessible writing is sharp and focused. The style, naturally, should depend on who you are writing for: you wouldn't expect to see a think piece on the war in Iraq written in exactly the same way in the *Sun* and the *Guardian*.

As with writing a column, it's fine to push yourself to the front – but within reason. It's obvious to the reader that it's a personal piece, as it will have your byline on it, and in some publications there may also be a photo. But overusing the word 'I' will leave the reader feeling that you think you are more important than the issue itself.

LEADER WRITING

The leader – also known as the editorial – is an opinion piece with a difference. It's where the paper nails its colours to the mast and presents its stance on the big stories of the day. Clearly this can be significant, particularly when it comes to general elections and a newspaper makes it clear which political party it is supporting.

The leader appears in the same place in each issue of the paper – although you might occasionally see it transplanted to the front page when there's a particularly large story in the news. It is the focus of that part of the paper known as op ed (opposite editorial), which also includes comment pieces and sometimes the diary column.

Each big national newspaper has a team of leader writers, whose job it is to select and write the editorials. On smaller papers, the editor is more likely to write them, sometimes with the help of a reporter who may have been working on the related news story and may therefore have deeper knowledge of the issues. Leaders are not bylined – this is the paper's view and the paper's stance. There's a party line and as an individual journalist you don't break ranks, irrespective of whether you agree with the view being expressed.

The point of the editorial column is to provide the paper's take on that day's key stories and, to some extent, to influence the readers' views. Again, this is significant during a general election, or when a campaign is up and running.

Leader columns are fixed in length – if you're running the column vertically in that same space every day there's obviously nowhere else you can go. Most papers will feature several topics in the editorial, the final one of which may well be an off-beat or lighter piece.

Magazine editorials tend to fulfil a different requirement – usually they are a cheerful, chatty welcome from the editor introducing the reader to some of that month's contributors and picking out some of the keynote features in the issue.

WRITING LEADERS

Opinion pieces ('I') are your view. Leaders ('we') are the paper's view – and the paper must always have an opinion. You can't sit on the fence when you write leaders. They must be tightly, persuasively and authoritatively written as you are aiming to influence people's opinions and to make them back your paper's stance. And the leaders have to be topical and to focus on what's in that day's paper – hence, they can't be written ahead of time.

A good leader is hard hitting, accessible, well argued and makes the reader think. The style and language will clearly depend on the publication. Look at the differences between a leader in the *Sun* and one in the *Independent* on A-level results:

'A' WAY TO GO

Congrats from the *Sun* to all students celebrating their A Levels.

The pass rate and A grades both hit a new high – a huge credit to teenagers and teachers.

There are the usual claims that A Levels have been dumbed down.

But this is no time for carping. Today's exams may be different but they remain tough.

The question for Labour is why they cannot raise standards at the other end of the classroom.

Every year A Level results get better while the worst-performing children show no improvement.

This month's SATS show a third of 14-year-olds can't read properly.

The *Sun* believes EVERY child deserves a decent education.
(*Sun*, 15 August 2008)

The *Sun*'s angle is careful to praise teachers and pupils, but uses the leader as a chance to take a pot-shot at the government for uneven standards in schools. As befits a red-top tabloid, the style is brisk, direct and unequivocal.

The *Independent*, by contrast, takes a different angle on the same story:

Two trends emerged from this year's record crop of A-level results in England and Wales – one hopeful, the other ambiguous. The hopeful one is that there has been a swing back to traditional subjects, such as maths, sciences and foreign languages. This suggests that the message is getting through to schools that reputedly difficult subjects are worth taking and improve pupils' chances of admission to a good university and employment thereafter.

The increased take-up of maths is particularly encouraging, with more candidates than at any time in the past. Chemistry, physics and biology have also increased in popularity. A decade of decline has been reversed.

On the arts side, there has been a welcome rise, albeit small, in the take-up of foreign languages. Although German continues its decline, the numbers taking French and Spanish have risen. Minority languages, such as Chinese, Arabic, Russian and Polish, are also on the rise. How far this reflects greater encouragement given to migrant children to capitalise on their language skills, and how far it reflects a more enterprising approach to language teaching in schools may be worth a closer look, but in either event, it is a promising development.

The ambiguous trend is the revelation of a stark North–South divide, with a much greater improvement in overall performance in the South of England than in the North, and a particular gap between the South-east and the North-east. It is the first year the figures have been broken down regionally, so it is not clear whether the disparity is new or ingrained. But a separate breakdown shows that, as last year, the biggest improvements were at selective schools and in the independent sector.

It would be consoling to believe that the greater improvement in the South-east represents a return on vastly increased state investment. If, however, it reflects the greater proportion of independent

and selective schools in the region, then the distinction relates less
to geography than to the type of school. In that case, questions
need to be asked about how effectively the money has been spent.
As so often, the provision of one new set of statistics shows a need
for even more data in order to interpret them.
(*Independent*, 15 August 2008)

The tone of the *Independent*'s editorial is far more analytical, looking
beneath the actual results and noting trends in languages, science and
maths – and pointing to a possible North–South divide.

It's worth noting which other news items are deemed worthy of editorial
space in that day's papers (headlines in brackets). The *Sun* also focused
on:

- An NHS report showing that more youngsters need help for drug-
  related mental disorders (Drug menace – the lead editorial).
- Rookie Emma Ford, aged seventeen, graduating from army college
  less than a year after her brother Ben was killed serving in
  Afghanistan (Salute her – third editorial).
- Relations between Russia and Georgia after the ceasefire (Russian
  bullies – fourth editorial).

The *Independent* also went for:

- The Zimbabwean opposition needing to be on their guard during
  the political negotiations over who rules the country (Beware a
  despot bearing gifts of shared power – the lead editorial).
- BBC presenter Jeremy Paxman dubbing Scottish poet Robert Burns
  'a king of sentimental doggerel' (Sentimental journey – third
  editorial).

For some political contrast, the staunchly anti-Labour *Daily Mail* (which
leads on the A-level results under the headline 'Who wins when you
can't FAIL exams?') uses all three of its leaders that day to criticise the
government. The other two deal with:

- The elderly missing out on basic care for osteoarthritis, osteoporosis
  and other crippling conditions (Ageism in the NHS).
- Former local government minister Hilary Armstrong taking up a
  job advising SITA, one of Europe's largest waste companies (Muck
  and brass).

Looking for the local angle

You will almost always find that local papers stick to their own patch when it comes to writing leaders. They may put that patch's slant on a national story, but it's more likely that the leader column will remain rooted in grassroots issues where they can criticise council decisions, praise heroes from the area, or query why such-and-such an event was allowed to happen.

The people featured in local paper leaders may not be big names, but they may well be familiar to readers. The *Gloucestershire Echo* focused on a young man from Cheltenham who needed a bone-marrow transplant, and supported the attempt to find a perfect match for him. One lead editorial – 'News we all wanted to hear' (5 September 2008) – announced that a match had been found and that the next step was a transplant. The second editorial that day mentioned ingenious money-raising methods and gave full marks to a sponsored midnight walk for women through Cheltenham. Both editorial items were firmly community-based and aimed to pull readers into that community.

FORMULAIC COLUMNS

Those of us of a certain age (i.e., over forty) will probably remember the questionnaires that used to appear in soccer magazines in the 1970s. Weekly magazines such as *Shoot!* posed a set of questions to the stars of the day. Inevitably, their favourite meal was always steak and chips, their favourite band was Genesis, and the person they longed to meet was the Queen.

These formulaic features are still around today in myriad forms. They range from the *Observer*'s My Space (a descendant of its A Room of My Own feature) to the *Radio Times*' back-page One Final Question, to the *Independent*'s pithy I Am . . ., which focuses on just three questions. The *Sunday Times* magazine has carried several such features at the same time, including the long-running Relative Values, where family members discuss their relationship; Best of Times, Worst of Times, where the subject discusses key points in their life; and A Life in the Day, where the person outlines what their typical day is like.

Regular features like these are a great way to fill pages. They also ensure a steady stream of celebrities – and often not so well-known people who provide snappy responses to the questions. Local papers are more likely to choose interviewees from their patch – the *Weekend* supplement from the *Gloucestershire Echo* and sister paper the *Citizen* asks familiar faces from around the county to share their idea of a dream weekend. Readers, as well, will often build up a relationship with these sorts of features and be quite miffed when they are discontinued. The important thing for the editor is to make sure they have lined up an equally good one to slot in its place.

Don't think, though, that these are easy space-fillers. The best formulaic features have staying power or quirky questions – or both. A good editor or features editor will know when to kill the column off before it gets stale. The *Guardian*'s Passnotes column, a tongue-in-cheek spin on issues in the news, disappeared when the paper changed size from broadsheet to the current narrower and shorter Berliner format. A similar column then appeared in *The Times*. This chatty, off-beat take on a topical item had gathered a cult following among readers.

I've always been rather fond of the long-running Mad Hatter's Box column in Irish music and current affairs magazine *Hot Press*. Subjects – pictured wearing fetching headgear – are asked thirty questions, ranging from those that will elicit short answers, such as favourite book, favourite film and favourite author, to more off-beat enquiries that will get people talking:

- Most embarrassing moment of your life?
- Your concept of heaven?
- Your concept of hell?
- What would be your dying words?
- Period of history you'd most like to have lived in and why?
- If you weren't a human being which animal would you have chosen to be?
- If you were told that the world was ending tomorrow morning, how would you react/what would you do?
- Humanity's most useful invention?
- Humanity's most useless invention?

Off-beat questions can generate fantastic answers. Dan Snow's great response to 'Have you ever had a same-sex experience?' in the *Guardian* magazine's Q&A column (22 October 2005) was: 'Does wanting to kiss Wayne Rooney during Euro 2004 count?' And it goes without saying that, as a general rule, closed questions aren't a lot of help. You're looking for a sparky, open question that will help encapsulate the subject in a single phrase or a sentence or two.

Formulaic features are often carried in specialist publications or sections. The *Guardian* carries a My Media column every Monday in its Media supplement with the barest of bare-bones headings – Newspapers, Magazines, Books, TV, Radio, Ads and New Media – which places a lot of trust in the interviewee to answer the question fully. And the *Independent on Sunday*'s ABC section carries the This Cultural Life feature, where performers are invited to answer questions such as:

- What was your cultural passion at fourteen?
- What do you cling on to from childhood?
- What are you reading in bed?
- What's the least disposable pop song?
- What's the most disposable piece of classical music?
- Which painting most corresponds to your vision of yourself?
- What's the most fashionable thing you own?
- Who should play you in the Hollywood version of your life?

Sometimes you don't even need the same questions or, indeed, questions at all. Relative Values and A Day in the Life, both long-running fixtures in the *Sunday Times*, and Last Word in the *Daily Express*'s Saturday magazine are interview-based and therefore depend on finding some good talkers as subjects. A more recent approach, favoured in the *Mail on Sunday*'s This Much I Know, is to interview the subject and then present the feature in crisp sentences, with the first half a dozen or so words in bold text.

Formulaic features offer the chance for the off-beat as well. The *Word* magazine runs a two-page 20 Best/20 Worst feature every month. The September 2006 issue tells us that among the twenty worst duets are Mick Jagger and David Bowie's rendition of 'Dancing in the Streets', and Russell Watson and Shaun Ryder massacring 'Barcelona', with Paul McCartney and Stevie Wonder taking the top spot for 'music's most deathsome duo' for 'Ebony and Ivory'. Over the page, the best duets include Blur and Phil Daniels bawling along on 'Parklife', Kirsty MacColl and Shane MacGowan on the sublime 'Fairytale of New York', with the accolade of best duet going to the Pet Shop Boys and Dusty Springfield's 'What Have I Done to Deserve This?'

This particular formulaic feature benefits from short, snappy verdicts – the Watson/Ryder collaboration is described thus: 'Because what every bit of MFI opera needs is Baron Baggy hoarsely bellowing the chorus like Grandpa Simpson in the middle of a truss malfunction. Piss-yourself hilarious.' Meanwhile, the verdict on 'Parklife' is: 'Daniels can't sing but it doesn't matter for here is all the raucous daftness of Britpop encapsulated – and subtly commented upon – in a few lairy minutes.'

If you have a regular feature series in mind, don't even think about running it until you have stockpiled at least half a dozen – and preferably more. A sports desk I worked on had the excellent idea of running a 'where are they now?' on a 1960s League Cup-winning football team. The reporters, enthused by the project, did a couple of interviews and the series started running. Sadly it ran out of steam after about six people – it turned out that a couple of the team were dead, one or two had emigrated, and the rest couldn't be traced. The sports desk received more queries about when the rest of the series would be published than on virtually any other topic. Suffice it to say that some research in advance would have helped enormously.

Some formulaic features do require a fair amount of detective work from reporters. Several magazines, including the *Observer*'s monthly colour sports supplement, run a 'frozen in time' style feature. This focuses on a significant sports photo from the past where the reporters have done a short, sharp 'then and now' report on each of those in the picture. Occasionally, though, they have to admit defeat and say that they haven't managed to track down a person. This kind of feature stands or falls by the strength of the picture and the quality of the research.

You will also come across 'ghosted' pieces that belong under the formulaic heading. These tend to be much favoured on sports pages, where, traditionally, a reporter can smarten up copy from monosyllabic sportspeople (more often than not footballers) and make it look as if they have written the column. I worked on a sports desk where we had to interview footballers for a 'talk of the town' column which appeared weekly under the relevant player's name. You can probably guess why some players were featured more often than others – we got very good at focusing on the good talkers!

The same problems that beset question-and-answer-style interviews may also hijack formulaic features. If you've got a waffler, be prepared to edit what they say tightly. And it goes without saying that we can live without the 'erms' and 'errs'. Go for open questions (those that won't elicit a 'yes' or 'no' answer) to give yourself the best chance of people responding to them fully.

CASE STUDY – LAWRENCE BOOTH AND THE SPIN

How did you get into column writing?

I was offered the chance to write the Spin, my weekly cricket column for the *Guardian*'s website, in the summer of 2002. I had spent plenty of time working at the *Guardian*, first as the custodian of the old Wisden.com website, which was run from the *Guardian* offices, then as a freelancer working casual shifts. Since most of the other guys – and it was mainly guys – on the sports desk were interested primarily in football, I was the only obvious candidate to write the cricket column they wanted to get off the ground. Six years later it's still going strong(ish), with more than 10,000 weekly subscribers.

Which columns are you most proud of?

The grinding nature of writing a weekly column means you barely have time to rest on your laurels, let alone compile a list of your five favourite pieces. I do remember writing an item about the shoddy treatment of a young woman – the girlfriend of the brother of a friend – who had tried and failed to gain access to a bar in the Lord's pavilion. I slated the Marylebone Cricket Club (MCC) for their outdated views on equality and was gratified when the bar in question later threw open its doors to women as well as men. Vanity insisted I double-check that the catalyst for the decision had been my column. It was a rare example of sports journalism actually making the blindest bit of difference.

What particular stories stick in your mind?

'Stories' is not quite the right terminology for the kind of thing that appears in the Spin, which is more a mixture of opinion, anecdote and puerility. But I remember engaging in a running battle with several readers who felt it was the height of folly to pick Kevin Pietersen for the 2005 Ashes. I was quite adamant he should be picked and only narrowly resisted the temptation to gloat uncontrollably when he made 158 to secure the urn at the Oval. But columns always produce plenty of material to bring you back down to earth. I was a big advocate of Andrew Flintoff assuming the captaincy for the next Ashes series, in 2006–07. England lost 5–0 and I felt obliged to refer to my faulty tip every time I mentioned the series after that.

What's your approach to column writing, from thinking up an idea to delivering the finished product?

I try to ensure I have a point to make and I try to make it as clearly as possible. My worst columns are the ones I start writing without a clear thought process, as if the argument will simply formulate itself as the words appear (which, sometimes, if you are very lucky, it does). The best ones write themselves and allow me to indulge in a few jokes and digs along the way. I will write one draft, then go over it again, possibly the next morning – it's funny how many times a good night's sleep helps you to see things differently.

How do you adapt to writing for different markets?

In terms of regular column writing, the Spin has been my only one, and I hope I know the *Guardian* audience quite well now. They like strong, plausible views topped up with a smattering of humour and a lack of self-importance. I think! I once wrote a daily diary from India for the Cricinfo website, where my brief was to give the English perspective on the brand-new Indian Premier League. I tried to combine wide-eyedness with insight – to both English and Indian readers. And, Cricinfo being a specialist cricket website, I naturally threw in some obscure stats to keep the anoraks happy.

What are the top tips you'd give a young columnist?

Don't overwrite. First-time columnists will understandably feel the need to impress, but the best impression is made by an argument that is cogent and easy to follow. Think of the reader: you don't want him or her to keep having to go over each sentence trying to decipher your elegant prose. Don't be afraid to be controversial, but don't be controversial for the sake of it: you'll be found out quickly if you can't marshal your facts properly. Humour is good if you can do it, but it's not easy and is best avoided if it's not working. And read as widely as you can to discover what style works best for you. A writing style can take years to develop, so be patient.

Biography?

I graduated from Cambridge with a degree in modern languages in 1998 and immediately took up a work-experience position at *Wisden Cricket Monthly* magazine. A year later they offered me a job and I was employed by *Wisden* until 2002, when I went freelance. Since then I have written on cricket – county and international – for the *Daily Telegraph*, the *Sunday Times* and the *Guardian*, as well as the *Wisden Cricketer, Wisden Cricketers' Almanack* and several other publications at home and abroad. I have written three books, the most recent of which – *Cricket, Lovely Cricket? An Addict's Guide to the World's Most Exasperating Game* – was published recently by Yellow Jersey.

6
Writing reviews

Reviewing is one of the most enjoyable aspects of being a journalist – after all, doesn't it sound like a dream job to be paid to go to gigs or to the theatre, and to receive free books and CDs? It's a much sought-after perk on newspapers and magazines, and also provides a good freelance opportunity, although most freelancers will tell you that they cannot make a living from just reviewing.

A review is a critical view of an arts event or product. It is highly opinionated, but also aims to be informative, thought-provoking and, in most cases, entertaining (the latter won't be your main focus if you are writing reviews for, say, academic journals, where good scholarship and discussion of the text are more important). Areas that are reviewed include:

- theatre
- television
- radio
- cinema
- music
- fine art
- books (including audio books)
- computer games and software
- restaurants.

THE ROLE OF A REVIEWER

A good reviewer will provide an honest and constructive analysis of what they have seen or read. Doing a hatchet job on something is all too easy – but generally not terribly helpful or fair. There are very few occasions where you cannot find at least one positive thing to say in a review. I've been reviewing books and music for twenty years, often turning out three or more reviews a week, and in that time I have reviewed only half a dozen books and just one CD where I couldn't find anything good to say about them. The fact that I remember the precise number suggests what a rare occurrence hatchet jobs are – or, at least, should be.

A reviewer has to analyse. The biggest mistake many inexperienced – and sometimes not so inexperienced – journalists make is simply to retell what they have seen or read. That's not a review; it's a précis. I can ask my five-year-old niece to tell me what's happened in the book I've just read to her and be pretty confident she will be able to relate in some detail what the story was about. She won't be so hot, though, on analysing the book.

A reviewer needn't necessarily have an intimate knowledge of the area they are reviewing, but it helps a lot if they do. I have no qualms about reviewing books, theatre and popular music, but I'd be a little more nervous about reporting on fine art or classical music, which are areas I know little about. Reviewing the non-verbal offers different challenges – and pity the poor reviewer confronted with avant-garde composer John Cage's '4′ 33‴' of silence!

As well as that analytical role, a reviewer needs to act as a bridge between the practitioner and the audience, particularly when it comes to interpreting new and challenging work. A well-informed reviewer will be able to set what they see in the context of previous work, as well as comparing it with what contemporaries are doing. It's up to a reviewer to argue persuasively and authoritatively that their view is right, although there is sometimes space to be able to step back and say, 'This is good, but it isn't my cup of tea . . .'

At the bottom line, though, a review should allow the reader to make an informed choice as to whether the product being reviewed is worth their time and money.

WHAT ARE YOU LOOKING FOR?

We've established that you're not simply parroting the plot of a book, a play or a film, nor are you simply listing the tracks on an album or a set list from a gig. So what should you mention in your review?

- *Stunning performances*. This includes good as well as bad! Mention, if relevant, any strong supporting roles. Discuss why the actors were right or wrong for their roles.
- *Sets/scenery/location*. If it's a modern-dress Shakespeare, did it work? Reviewers writing about BBC1's adaptations of Shakespeare plays commented that transferring *Much Ado about Nothing* to a local TV newsroom worked. Peter Brook's famous 1970 production of *A Midsummer Night's Dream* took place in a white box resembling a squash court with the actors on trapezes, and it's often still mentioned nearly forty years on as a point of reference in reviews.
- *Memorable lyrics/words*. It's OK to quote short extracts from books or lyrics without breaching copyright. If you are a regular book reviewer, you will encounter ARCs (advance reading copies). These are bound, unchecked proofs, sent out by publishers to reviewers ahead of the release date in an effort to ensure that a review appears near to that date. But it's not safe to quote from them, as the author may yet make changes. Request a copy of the finished product if you want to quote from it. CD lyrics are often printed on the accompanying booklet and are fair game to be quoted. But remember this is a review, not an English literature essay; it's rarely necessary or desirable to quote more than a few lines in reviews.
- *Striking image*. Is there a particularly striking moment that sticks in your mind from the product? It might be a cinematic device, or an incident during a play, or a scene in a book that makes you catch your breath.
- *Production/direction*. This comes into play when you are reviewing films or plays. Reviewers unfamiliar with these areas might not feel they can comment on these absolutely vital but behind-the-scenes roles. But people reading theatre reviews would expect to be given some idea of what the director's overall concept was, and whether it was successful.
- *Technology*. This applies to films and computer games in particular. Reviewers covering big-budget movies brimming with special effects will want to comment on how these were achieved.
- *Plots/structure*. Keep an eye open in books, films and plays for well-structured or creaky plots. But be careful what you give away. I spotted a significant plot flaw in a book recently, when a teenage girl jumped off a moving train. I was almost certain that slam-door trains no longer existed on that line – a fact that was easily checked

by phoning up the train company's press office (which, of course, the writer could and should have done, too). However, it was tricky to mention this in the review without giving away too much of the plot (I shall discuss spoilers in more detail below), so I just had to hint at the glitch.

TYPES OF REVIEW

There are several different types of review, depending on your market. You may be asked to knock out a couple of sharp, witty paragraphs for a tabloid paper or for the review section of a women's glossy magazine. Never let anyone tell you that it's impossible to do justice to a product in a short review. It might not allow you to go very deep, but you can certainly give readers a fair idea of what to expect. I was always a fan of Jeremy Jehu's book reviews on Channel 4's Teletext – he was first rate at providing a flavour of the plot, a point of reference for the reader, and then giving his verdict, all in three paragraphs. *fRoots* magazine manages even crisper reviews – as well as their more detailed review sections, they carry 'And the rest', which is subtitled 'successes, disasters and retreads: enthusiasm, tedium and dismay noted in passing'. These one-paragraph reviews are accompanied by a thumbs up, thumbs sideways, or thumbs down, depending on the reviewer's verdict. Here's a taste of a thumbs-down review from the November 2007 issue, which manages to squeeze in some kind of comparison to give a would-be buyer an idea of what they'll be getting:

Dr Strangely Strange Halcyon Days

Ten tracks from 1969/70, some produced by Joe Boyd for the Irish hippy trio, plus three new ones. So most of this has been unreleased for 37 years, and, brutally, one can see why. There's fey, and then there's this lot, like a straighter, less quirky Incredible String Band . . . doesn't stand the test of time.

Tabloid papers often blur the lines between a columnist and a reviewer – expect to see a photo byline of TV reviewers at the top of a full-page column in papers such as the *Sun* and the *Mirror*. Ian Hyland in the *News of the World* is bylined as 'the toxic TV critic'. Columns such as this will have a lead item of several hundred words, then about a dozen shorter pieces, ranging from four or five paragraphs to one cutting aside. We're not talking deep and meaningful analysis here; the emphasis is on sarcasm and humour. In his 13 August 2006 column, Hyland focuses on *Big*

Brother, under the headline 'Nik all our money say housemates'. Here are the opening paragraphs, describing previously evicted housemate Nikki's return to the house:

> Re-entry night at BB7 and Big Moutha had this question: 'Can it possibly get any more exciting?'
>
> Let's hope not, Davina. Because if it does there's a very real danger you'll give birth live on telly.
>
> And the last thing this year's show needs is a screaming infant who needs picking up by the legs and having their a*** smacked.
>
> Because we've already got Nikki.
>
> Yes, in the most altruistic vote in history (let the poor Tourette's kid have his way, it might make us look good) the housemates have invited Nikki to come and steal their prize money. Whatever happened to it being a game show, you morons?

The shorts tend to be along the same bitchy lines. For instance: 'Sources on the new Bond movie claim 007 will grapple with a burly six-footer and finish him off in a public toilet. Sounds like George Michael's dream night out.'

Broadsheets or specialist publications may well allow reviewers the luxury of longer reviews, but by the same token will expect more than just witty, throwaway comments. Indeed, the review may be written by someone with expert knowledge of the area covered in the book, rather than by a journalist. And scholarly reviews, such as those to be found in the *Times Literary Supplement*, the *London Review of Books* or academic journals, are targeted at a much narrower market, one which almost certainly knows a great deal about the subject area, is going to expect specialist knowledge and authoritative writing from the reviewer and will be very unforgiving of errors or lack of research in the review.

Many local papers are strict in what they review. The general rule is often that there has to be a link to the paper's circulation area, be it the book's setting or that the writer lives in the patch, or the fact that a top band is playing at a venue in town later in their tour. Local papers will generally aim to review plays and concerts in their area – and this will almost certainly lead you into the thorny area of what you do about the amateurs.

Reviewing the amateurs

Most reporters have had the dubious pleasure of sitting through excruciatingly bad amateur dramatics – and then wondering how the heck they review it fairly. After all, is it reasonable to treat Little Snodrington Amateur Dramatics in the same way as you would the Royal Shakespeare Company? Some local papers take the line of least resistance and provide a bland summary of what they have witnessed, lumping as many names of the cast and crew as possible in the review in the hope of boosting sales.

Others – and I'm in this group – take the view that once people are charged admission, or sold a book, then the product is fair game for constructive criticism. This is becoming a big issue in book reviewing with the increase in self-publishing, and where authors who have paid to see their work in print may get very defensive when anyone criticises it.

The keyword, though, is 'constructive'. It may be easy to do a hatchet job on something – and occasionally this approach may be called for if the book, play or album is beyond redemption – but as a general rule you should aim to be fair in your reviewing and give both praise and criticism where they are warranted.

PUTTING THE REVIEW TOGETHER

When you are setting out to write a review, bear the following in mind.

Don't forget the usual questions

News writing traditionally adheres to the who/why/what/when/where/ how approach – and review writing is no different. Readers will want to know who was in the play, why the film is successful, what is the best moment, when the run finishes, where it's taking place and how much tickets cost. Try to put yourself in the reader's place and ask yourself what you want from a review. Ultimately, though, they want to know whether the product is any good and if it's worth their time and money.

Include vital details

You should always mention (as appropriate):

- title
- author
- publisher
- record company
- price
- dates
- venue.

Your publication's style will dictate whether these details are interwoven in the review or summarised at the top or the bottom of the review. Some publications may request even more information, such as the ISBN number for books or catalogue numbers for CDs, or the author's or band's website from which to purchase the item. If in doubt, check the publication or ask the features editor.

Spoiler alert!

One of the cardinal sins of reviewing is providing spoilers – giving away key parts of the plot. This will have your readership twitching and cursing when you ruin the ending or reveal a crucial plot twist. So be sparing in how much plot summary you include – a couple of paragraphs is generally more than enough. If in doubt, leave information out, rather than running the risk of ruining someone's enjoyment of the book or play by including it.

Beware of libel

You can libel someone in a review just as easily as you can elsewhere in a publication. Make sure honest criticism doesn't become malicious points-scoring. In the 1980s actress Charlotte Cornwell took the *Sunday People* to court – and won – after reviewer Nina Myskow (whose byline included the description 'the bitch on the box') made a personal remark about the size of her backside and her acting ability.

Classy writing

Reviews are almost always bylined, so it's not usually necessary to keep repeating 'I . . .', which will ruin the flow of your review. And in any case, the reader will have gathered that it's your opinion! Resist the temptation to overdo the adjectives or to throw in vague 'it was quite good' phrases. Reviewing, like all writing, calls for precision and fluency. Remember that a review should be entertaining and informative, but it also needs to be appropriate for the market at which the publication is targeted. The first paragraph of Rick Martin's review in *NME* (23 August 2008) of Brett Anderson's new album *Wilderness* knows exactly what the readership will stand in terms of rather earthy language:

> Masturbation and cocaine addiction may, generally speaking, be considered the highest forms of self-indulgence, but they have got nothing on a Brett Anderson solo album. Once Britpop's snake-hipped pretend-bisexual clown prince, Anderson is a far more introspective character these days – the sort who'd rather don a rollneck sweater and retire solemnly to the piano in his shed than hit the suburban streets and get psycho for sex and glue.

By contrast, here are the opening paragraphs of Alastair Sooke's review in the *Daily Telegraph* (22 July 2008) of the Hadrian exhibition at the British Museum, which is both accessible and strong on descriptive powers:

> It's easy to assume that ancient history is, well, ancient history, the dusty province of antiquarians poring over old texts and artefacts. What more is there to learn about classical Greece and Rome?
>
> Think again. The British Museum's magisterial new exhibition about the life and times of Publius Aelius Hadrianus, ruler of one of the mightiest empires the world has ever seen, reveals the extent to which our understanding of the ancient world is fashioned from fragments of historical evidence.
>
> It also reveals how it is constantly evolving, as hitherto unknown objects are discovered. Ancient history may be the stuff of marble statuary, but, it turns out, it is anything but set in stone.
>
> Take one of the show's highlights, a colossal marble head of Hadrian spotlighted as you enter the Reading Room, where the exhibition is held. It was dug up last August in south-west Turkey, like a whopping great gemstone plucked from the earth's crust.
>
> Once the apex of a statue 5m tall, Hadrian's head now looms above visitors like the presiding spirit of the entire show. It is a gleaming wonder, intricately chiselled, and as valuable-looking as an over-sized Fabergé egg. Looking at it is as close to coming face-to-face with a Roman emperor as it's possible to get.

Naming the names

When you're reviewing theatre and film, the reader will want to know who's in the cast and who was particularly impressive, or spectacularly miscast. Aim to weave the names in fluently as you move through the review, rather than dumping them all at the end with a rather weak 'and there were good performances from . . .' Listing every name in the cast is a local paper tradition that should have gone out with the ark!

Developing a voice

The best reviewers develop their own distinctive voice when they review, and there are times when you can go for the off-beat. This should be used sparingly, however, or you will be in danger of becoming a one-trick pony. Marina Lewycka had fun and games reviewing Martin Sixsmith's book *I Heard Lenin Laugh* in the *Guardian* (31 July 2006). All you need to know is that Lewycka is the author of a novel called *A Short History of Tractors in Ukrainian*:

> This Martin Sixsmithevich was formerly a pretty important big wheeler and spinning doctor in Novaya Rabotnaya Partiya (OK, I explain: Novaya in Russian is mean New and Rabota is mean Labour, and you can guessing rest) and after departing in strange and clouding circumstance he is writing famous satire novel *Spin* and also contributing in TV politdrama *The Thick of It*. Now he is turning attentions on to former Soviet reality, and maybe also reliving his times as BBC Moscow correspondent in ending of cold war era.
>
> This new novel is concerning life of unfortunate Zhenya Gorevich from Vitebsk who is all time seeking opportunity for escaping from Soviet reality by making podvig to capitalist false paradise of England to be reunite with his father who is English aristocrat. You think this is sounding improbable? Wait until you reading about Mr VI Smirnov, manager of collective farm, who is big arching enemy of Zhenya after he denouncing him for making joke disrespectful to glorious Soviet Union, and his son Vova Smirnov, who is becoming world famous footballer, and Great Lenin himself. All is pretty bit improbable and crazy and is therefore good depicting of unreal Soviet reality.
>
> Anyway, this Zhenya Gorevich is arriving in London Khitro airport in time for World Cup 1966 and all around is happening swinging 60s with devushkas in meanie-skirtings and everybody is smoking special cigarette and going on big manifestation of popular sentiment outside fascist US embassy.

The story is telling in naive voice of Zhenya in this type of Sovietese, which is amusing, but sometimes you getting fed up because it not always easy for reading, like in this review.

GENRE TIPS FOR REVIEWERS

Many reviewers tend to stick to one field. But if you are freelancing or starting out, you need to be versatile and prepared to review anything that will get you noticed. You may find the following briefings useful when you set out to review different areas.

Books

Book reviewing is a very satisfying part of journalism. Yes, there are lots of free books, but don't expect to make a living out of it – many journalists do it as a sideline. However, you may find that once you have built up a specialism, as discussed earlier in the book, publications will call on you to review books in that particular area.

Many newspapers, particularly local ones, don't use a lot of book reviews, and those that they do publish have a clear relevance to their patch. When I worked for a West Country morning paper, the sort of book you would see reviewed might include a history of the SAS in Hereford, a photographic account of the Somerset Levels, the history of Gloucestershire cricket, or a crime novel by a Bath-based author.

Magazines, too, will often restrict the books they review. Weekly current affairs magazines such as the *New Statesman* and the *Spectator* will review a wide range of books, although more often than not they will have a political or current affairs theme. But with the specialist magazines, the requirements are much more specific – you would not see *Harry Potter* reviewed in the football magazine *Four Four Two*, nor a book on corruption in soccer reviewed in a glossy women's magazine.

A recent development is that there is now a large number of websites dedicated to book reviewing. Whatever genre you're looking for, there's bound to be something out there. I edit a crime fiction review site, which puts up twenty new reviews each week – clearly many more than your average newspaper or magazine has space for. Our rules state that we will review crime fiction, true crime and related fantasy and science fiction (that is, with a mystery angle to it). But we frequently have to explain politely to publishers that, no thanks, we don't want a history book on the Alamo or a fluffy chicklit novel.

When you receive a book from a publisher, it will almost always be accompanied by a press release. Scan through them, but don't rely on them – they're not always accurate. And unless you are doing a separate interview with the author, you are unlikely to want to include much biographical matter in the review, as that's not what's wanted. A good book review will consider the plot, themes, setting, characters, style and language. It will not simply parrot the plot. Of course, it's useful to give the reader some idea of what the book is about, but a couple of paragraphs should suffice. And, naturally, you must not give away what happens in the end.

Do some research about the writer and, if appropriate, the subject area. With non-fiction (and, to some extent, in fiction as well), it's important to watch out for factual errors. If you're reviewing the book for a specialist audience, this is particularly vital. They won't want to spend their hard-earned cash on an expensive hardback history book, for example, only to discover that it's full of mistakes.

As with any writing, it's best to get into the habit of typing your review straight on to screen. But it's also worth briefly noting your reactions and page numbers as you go along. That way, if you need to quote something in the review, or want to refer to a particularly good or bad section, you can find it quickly. (I also use those multicoloured sticky tabs.) Incidentally, it depends very much on your market and the sort of book you're reviewing as to how much (if any) you quote. If you're writing for an academic publication, or turning out a more lengthy review for a serious readership, quoting briefly from the book may be necessary. Or, if you're reviewing fiction, you may need to give examples of particularly sparkling or leaden prose or dialogue.

Reviewing audiobooks is a fairly recent addition to many books pages. Nowadays, the audiobook is often published simultaneously with the print version. The key things to note are whether it's an abridged (cut) version of the book and who the narrator is. As people buy audiobooks because they are fans of particular actors, it's important to tell them who is doing the reading.

Television

Being paid to watch television sounds like a breeze, but in fact it is more of a challenge than you might think. Imagine turning out a daily column based on the evening's TV and having to make it fresh each time. The

Guardian has got round this by having a roster of TV critics. And while large newspapers may receive preview tapes or DVDs, or be invited to advance screenings of significant new programmes, the TV critic on a smaller newspaper will find the job plays havoc with their social life. So, depending on where you work, you'll have the luxury of writing the piece in advance or will have to get used to knocking it out very quickly late at night.

If you're reviewing for a newspaper, the chances are they won't want your column devoted to just one programme, unless it's a particularly epic one. The usual approach, no matter whether you're working for a heavy or a red top, is to focus on several shows from the previous evening (or week, if it's a Sunday paper). While major new programmes always feature strongly, critics will often return to old favourites, such as soap operas or reality TV shows. If you're writing the column for the tabloids, you may end up filling a full page, as you would with any other column – selecting one show as the main focus and using bite-sized pieces for the other reviews. Elsewhere, though, the challenge is to knit the column together smoothly – sometimes with a linking line to take you from one review to the next.

Theatre

Theatre critics often need to be able to be quick off the mark. London theatres traditionally hold a press night with a slightly earlier start time than usual. This allows reviewers to catch the final edition of the next day's paper. If you live out in the sticks and get an earlier edition, expect to see the review a day later, accompanied by the words 'this review appeared in yesterday's later editions'.

If you cover theatre, you have to be versatile: one night you may be covering something jaw-droppingly shocking like Sarah Kane's *Blasted*; the next you might be attending an Alan Ayckbourn comedy. And you should have a wide knowledge of the drama world. Certainly, pretty much anyone can review the local am-dram group's pantomime, but if you want to make a name for yourself as a theatre reviewer, readers will expect you to set the work in context, to draw comparisons with what the playwright's contemporaries did or are doing, and to know what the director and the leading actors have done in the past.

And it's not just a matter of commenting on how well the actors per-formed. You also need to consider the set, costumes, incidental music, direction and even the lighting. For instance, reviews of the stage version of Philip Pullman's *His Dark Materials* trilogy commented on how puppets wielded by black-clad operators were used to represent the daemons. The opening paragraphs of Michael Billington's review in the *Guardian* (5 January 2004) show the critic utilising his knowledge of English and international literary classics to explain the problems of transferring a complex text to the stage:

> Nothing is more tempting than the apparently impossible. But, although director Nicholas Hytner and his creative team display heroic courage in turning Philip Pullman's epic trilogy into two three-hour plays, they are ultimately overcome by the vastness of the enterprise. There is much to admire in the staging; yet the result, inevitably, is like a clipped hedge compared to Pullman's forest.
>
> Partly, it's a problem of scale: Pullman's 1,300 pages have to be condensed to manageable proportions. Shrewdly, the adapter, Nicholas Wright, begins at the end with Pullman's protagonists, Lyra and Will, meeting on an Oxford park-bench while existing in parallel worlds. What follows is a retrospective guide to their amazing adventures. Wright has also axed several key characters including Mary Malone, the scientist who stimulates Lyra's sexual awareness, and the militant angel, Metatron. Although Wright avoids a linear plod through Pullman's inverted *Paradise Lost*, he cannot hope to match the amplitude of the original.
>
> But there is a more specific problem in adapting Pullman for the stage. Part of his intention is to rewrite Genesis, as well as Milton, and to rescue humanity from a Christian culture based on sin and guilt. But, in so doing, he creates a quintessentially literary work where much of the pleasure lies in the cascading references. Apart from Milton, Pullman's books draw heavily on Homer, the Icelandic Sagas, Dante, Blake, Wordsworth, the Shelleys, Wagner, Barrie and Tolkien. I even detect a nod to Kingsley Amis's *The Alteration*, which assumes the Reformation has not taken place. You can obviously pick up many of these allusions from the stage, but I can't think of any recent fiction that depends more on an intertextual complicity with the reader.

In the course of the review, Billington mentions the actors, the director, the adaptor, the designer, the composer and the puppet designer. His review is accessible and intelligent, although I have noticed that he does tend to consign his comments on the actors to one big clump at the end. Weaving them into the body of the review does avoid an 'Oh, and before I forget . . .' conclusion.

Fine art

Whereas you may well be asked to review a book or a play in the course of your job, covering fine art is less common, unless you are an expert. Even if you have strong views on what you reckon constitutes art, it's not a genre you can busk. You need to have done your homework on the artist/sculptor and his/her work. You need to know something about the ethos and aims of the particular gallery. And you need strong descriptive powers, as what you are doing is essentially interpreting the non-verbal – and that's not easy.

Music

The music market is colossal, so before you even start, know your target audience. A classical music fan won't have the same expectations as a reggae fan (aside from wanting to know whether the gig or the CD was any good). Again, this is an area where background knowledge is almost essential – you'll get found out pretty quickly if you haven't done your homework. My area of expertise is roots and world music, so I'd be very wary of reviewing a classical concert. Even within my specialism I know that I have to keep as up to date as possible. Acquiring a wide knowledge of your area of music will make it much easier to set what you're hearing in the context of a band's previous work, or what their contemporaries are doing, or even what has influenced them from the past.

The music magazines devote a lot of space to album reviews. *Q*, for example, grades each album out of five stars, and includes a 'download' line at the end to highlight a particular track that offers the best introduction to the rest of the album.

Film

People assume that reviewing a film is easy – that it's simply a matter of sitting back with popcorn and a Coke and describing what you see on the screen. As with books and theatre, though, just parroting the plot is inadequate. You need to consider the acting, the setting, the music, the direction and even the use of technology, including special effects. And readers will expect the film to be put in context, based on the director's and actors' previous work. There may also be the need to comment on the quality of the script, in terms of both dialogue and plot.

The film magazines are particularly heavy on reviews and require them to be written to a formula, which, like the music magazines, includes grading methods. There will also be a lot of space dedicated to background information about the film, including details of the production team.

Computer games/software

Reviewing computer games and software is pretty much the domain of specialist computer magazines and websites. The main consideration for the reviewer is, therefore, whether the audience is expert or non-expert. This will dictate how technical you need to be. Whichever, you'd be expected to compare the game or software with previous versions of it, to point out any bugs or glitches, and to make clear which platforms it plays on and what the system requirements are.

Restaurant reviews

These used to be the domain of Sunday papers, with reviewers spending their time trying out snooty London restaurants. It often seems that not a lot has changed – but local papers will often include a column for restaurants in their patch. On the nationals, the likes of A.A. Gill and Michael Winner have made their reviews more about themselves than the restaurant and the food. Take a look at Gill's review of the London restaurant Tendido Cuatro in his Table Talk column in *The Times* (17 August 2008):

> Wouldn't you just know that the world centre of excellence for dog cloning is South Korea. Of course it is. Where else would it be, in a world that patently works as a manga version of Grimm's fairy tales? Naturally, the Koreans clone dogs. They have two laboratories competing to corner the market in copycat dogs. One is led by Hwang Woo-suk (the h is silent), a disgraced scientist who's been tried for fraud, the other by his protégé, Lee Byeong-chun, who has, surprise, surprise, also been accused of fraud. It's plainly obvious that clones breed clones and that fraud breeds fraud and, anyway, what else would cloners be guilty of except duplicity. Apparently, the Roslin Institute in Scotland is pissed off at the Koreans for cloning their patented cloning technology. 'No. You do sheep. We do dog. Scot person eat disgusting haggis from sheep arse. Korean eat yummy dog. You sod off back to fat-battered Gorbals and take your sporran with you.'

After insulting both Koreans and Scots in his first paragraph, Gill then starts a meandering monologue about dogs. Seven (long) paragraphs later, he briefly mentions the food (and insults Sloane Rangers – who apparently frequent the tapas restaurants of London – and the Spanish for good measure): 'The food is far better than they deserve, or notice. It's good value, the room smells of deep-fried Basque, and there's weird piped music. But then, Spanish music all sounds like someone stamping on seagulls. The service was Spanish in the *Fawlty Towers* sense . . .' Thirteen words out of a 1,300-word feature are devoted to what he ate.

Writing decent restaurant reviews that *do* focus on the food and the restaurant is harder than it seems. You don't want a chronological ramble through the evening, beginning with you turning up and ending with you paying the bill. As with any colour piece (and that's partly what a restaurant review is), you may need to start in the middle of the evening and recap, or choose a particular incident as your focus. And there's nothing more boring than ploughing through a list of what you and your companion ate.

As well as the food, it's important to mention the decor and the service. A good reviewer will also give an idea of what else is on the menu – but, sadly, few of them bother to enlighten us vegetarians as to what we could eat at these places.

CASE STUDY – LEV RAPHAEL, REVIEWER

How did you get into reviewing?

In the early 1990s I was starting to get known in Michigan, and the *Detroit Free Press* – which had done an interview feature after my first novel came out – invited me to review for them. I had a very good feeling for the book editor, who was literate and good-natured, so I said yes. I reviewed everything but sports and religion for her (since specific editors handled those topics), and after a few years we agreed to add a monthly mystery column to my portfolio.

Who do you review for?

I have reviewed for the *Washington Post, Jerusalem Report, Forward* (a New York weekly), the *Fort Worth Star-Telegram, Boston Review* and

Lambda Book Report. I also did a five-year stint on an NPR (National Public Radio) show as guest reviewer, and have had my own book show on a public radio station in mid-Michigan. Right now my primary responsibility is for a public radio station in East Lansing, Michigan, where I cover books that are 'under the radar', broadly defined.

When you were doing the monthly column, how many books do you reckon you read per month/per year?

When I did the column, I read a minimum of three books for that, sometimes four to five, and was also reviewing other books for the *Free Press* as well as for other outlets, so in a busy month I might have been reading ten to twelve books for review a month. There were long stretches of time where my life revolved around deadlines and there was always something due. And then of course I'd have to read books now and then for pure pleasure, so I read quite a lot. It was heaven to take a whole week off and reread an old favourite like *Middlemarch* and fall in love with George Eliot's vision and humanity all over again.

What's your approach to reviewing?

Be open. Be informed. Read about the author. Read something else by the same author if there's time. Ignore the publisher's hype. And polish, polish, polish.

What do you believe are a reviewer's responsibilities?

Henry James wrote that one should grant each author his option; in other words, write about the book that is there, not the book you wish had been written. That's key. You also have to remember you're providing a service for readers/buyers. Should they spend money and time on this book? Don't make excuses, don't sugar coat, be honest.

How do you approach reviewing a book you absolutely loathe?

With fingers pinching my nose. Seriously, the first thing to do is to get over the loathing, that initial rush of disgust, so that the review isn't intemperate. If you can accomplish that, then you can be balanced. Bashing doesn't help readers at all. If you find the book dreadful, explain it, without being needlessly cruel. However, if I think a book is beyond the pale, I will decline to review it. Conversely, once or twice I've done 'Summer Book Warnings', telling readers or listeners about books that were getting great press but that I thought were terribly overrated.

What are your biggest reviewing bugbears?

Reviewers who tell too much of a story or give away significant plot points, especially with any book that has a mystery or thriller component to it even if it's literary fiction. Reviewers who are snarky to no purpose. Reviewers who ignore bad writing. I see too many thrillers praised – even by the *New York Times* – when the writing is appalling or just bland.

How do you set about writing and structuring a review?

I make some notes along the way but usually let the review shape itself when I'm done. Having written so much over so many years in so many different genres, and hundreds of reviews, I don't rely on formulae but trust my unconscious to give me the right 'entrance' to the review. A door always opens, eventually.

Of which reviews are you proudest?

I did a very long review for the *Boston Review* of an Alan Furst novel which referenced Rebecca West's *Black Lamb* and *Grey Falcon*. It was the only review I read that traced his vision of the Balkans to that seminal work. I'm also proud of reviews I did of books by Roth and Ozick, Mark Leyner, Anita Brookner and Andrei Makine. And I like being able to champion a book that's been ignored or misunderstood, like Andrew Bergman's very dark, hilarious *Sleepless Nights* or Terrill Lankford's amazing thriller *Shooters*.

What tips would you give to someone who wanted to start writing reviews?

Find a small local outlet, study what they review, pitch a review. Read widely, read reviewers not just for books but film, theatre, art. When you find someone you like, study that person's reviews. I read the *New Yorker* mainly for Anthony Lane's movie reviews, for instance, and Salon.com sometimes has great movie reviews by Andrew O'Hehir and Stephanie Zacharek.

Biography?

Lev Raphael is the author of nineteen books in a wide array of genres and hundreds of reviews, essays and articles. His work has been translated into nearly a dozen languages and is taught in colleges and universities across the US, which means he's become homework.

7
Packing a punch
Features spreads

Think of all the big stories of recent years and the chances are you'll be able to envisage newspaper front pages, ranging from the jaw-dropping images of 9/11 and the London Tube and bus bombings to the far more ludicrous 'Freddie Starr ate my hamster' (*Sun*, 13 March 1986). But move inside the newspaper or magazine, and you'll soon see the value of features spreads, where the big issues are dissected minutely for the reader.

You'll see the various features discussed in this book used to different effect. But it's not just a matter of words on the page – the most striking and effective features spreads marry words and pictures to pack a real punch. A good features editor will weigh up the value of copy against images and ensure there's a strong balance to tempt the reader.

The make-up of features desks varies hugely between publications. Whereas national newspapers will have a features editor, various deputies, writers and a team of subs, smaller newspapers will rely on a features editor who both writes and sub-edits and may have only one or two colleagues to help them out. Bigger newspapers may also have a graphic designer who will work on the more elaborate layouts and can provide graphics. It's common on national papers for the design of a page to come first and the content second – but on smaller papers usually the latter dictates the former. The magazine market relies a great deal on freelances, with features directors or features editors generally doing the commissioning. Staffers usually do the production work, with the articles coming from both staff and freelance writers. Many print publications now expect their production staff to be able to handle online copy as adeptly as the traditional print medium.

Whatever the make-up of the team, copy and pix will come in from a variety of sources. Staff will generate ideas; freelances will push for their proposals to be used; there will be an avalanche of press releases to be sifted through on a daily basis and decisions to be made on what's worth following up and what's destined for the wastepaper basket. Features desks are often the dumping ground for bizarre gimmicks dreamed up by press officers: some may make an off-beat feature; most are binned hastily. Pictures will come from staff photographers, agencies and freelances, or from picture libraries if it's an unusual or hard-to-find shot.

When it's a big features spread, the features editor will liaise with news colleagues, and you'd expect to see a front-page lead cross-referencing the feature inside the newspaper. Coverlines on the front of a magazine advertise what's contained within, and then the contents page will steer readers to the relevant pages. As important stories are signalled by their presence as a page lead, so features spreads are signposted by their place-ment in a publication, by the size of headlines and pictures, and by the way copy is selected and displayed.

SELECTING THE COMPONENT PARTS

A features spread isn't just a matter of slinging a long article and a couple of pix on to the page and hoping for the best. For the maximum effect, a features editor and their team must slot together their pages like a sophis-ticated jigsaw puzzle.

Features pages often use different layout techniques from the rest of the paper. You'll generally find a much wider use of colour in magazines than you will in newspapers. And it's not unusual, for instance, to find more copy on features pages set across bastard (that is, non-standard single-column) measure. Drop capitals and pull quotes may also be used to dress up the pages. Pix will most likely be bigger; they may also be cut out partially or fully, or used as a collage effect. Headlines may well be less straight down the middle and more of a teasing variety – and they may be placed anywhere but at the top of a story. Expect to see graphics used where appropriate to add understanding to a story, and fact boxes supplying extra useful information to the reader. Captions may not be under the pic in the usual newspaper style but, for example, superimposed on the image.

Other creative layout designs can be used to reflect the focus of the piece. A feature in the health section of the *Sun*, 'We were saved by second opinions' (24 August 2006), was presented in the form of medical notes with tabbed profiles of each of the four case studies. Meanwhile, *SFX* magazine's Anatomy of a Classic regular feature took a close look at the film *Back to the Future* in its June 2008 issue. The double-page spread was laid out to look like scrapbook pages, complete with a large cut-out pic of Michael J. Fox, an assortment of other photos – with sticky tape to hold them in place – and cuttings (some designed to look like they'd been raggedly torn from a notebook).

SHOWCASING BIG STORIES

For some idea on how to cover the story of a lifetime, think back to how newspapers covered the 7 July 2005 bombings in London. Everyone recalls the picture of the bus at Tavistock Square, with its top deck blown away, which was used big on most of the next day's front pages. There were also emotive pictures of people such as former firefighter Paul Dadge helping an injured woman in a burns mask at Edgware Road Tube station. If you analyse the coverage of the bombings both the following day and subsequently (remember that this truly is a story that has run and run), you'll be struck by the sheer range of copy that was used and from how many sources. News reporters were turning out huge amounts of copy, but the features desks were kept equally busy for months and even years afterwards ('one year on', 'two years on' and 'three years on' features and supplements have been published). News features examined what happened from every angle and asked terrorism experts to comment. There were features on the bombers, survivors and eyewitnesses, on the emergency services, and on how the Muslim community reacted.

It's a challenge for any editor or features editor to find fresh angles on big stories. After all, there's a chance that a proportion of the copy will have originated from agencies such as Reuters and the Press Association, and one thing editors hate is seeing stories from other papers appearing word-for-word in theirs. Which is why staff journalists get so used to rewriting agency copy and putting a more appropriate angle on it for their publication.

If you're a magazine editor, you've got different pressures and different deadlines to handle. Take, for example, magazine coverage of big sporting events, such as the 2006 Football World Cup, held in Germany, and the 2007 Rugby Union World Cup, which took place in France. Newspapers kept their coverage of these events ticking over with match reports, features and profiles of key people – both players and behind the scenes – and diaries from the finals. But where does that leave a monthly magazine? Every media outlet in the universe – newspapers, TV, radio, online – with deadlines well ahead of yours will have done the match reports and news stories to death, so upcoming magazine editions must find a different focus. In effect, readers often want the magazines to be souvenir issues, so they will expect the next available issue to carry match reports of every game, extensive facts and figures, detailed analysis of key events, and features on behind-the-scenes people who might not have been deemed worthy of coverage in the other media. *Four Four Two* (September 2006), for example, carried a question-and-answer interview with Horatio Elizondo, the Argentinian referee who sent off both England's Wayne Rooney in the quarter-finals and French captain Zinedine Zidane in the final. Note, too, that publications often rush-release separate souvenir magazines which stand alone from the normal daily, weekly or monthly publication.

FEATURING A RUNNING STORY

Never mind the Edinburgh Festival . . . the best show in Scotland in the summer of 2006 was a court case that had the lot: sex, drugs, alcohol, lies, tears, politics, excessive body hair, Scrabble and a glamorous wife. The defamation case featuring Tommy Sheridan, a member of the Scottish Parliament, made the headlines both north and south of the border – and abroad. The then Scottish Socialist Party MSP won a civil action he brought against the *News of the World* over articles which made all manner of allegations about his private life, including the claim he'd been unfaithful to his wife and that he had frequented swingers' clubs where he'd snorted cocaine and drunk champagne. The court case was a gift for the front pages. Sheridan, a flamboyant hard-left politician, has rarely been out of the news in Scotland over the past two decades. He's known for his passionate oratory, sharp suits and year-round sunbed tan, was thrown out of the Labour party in 1989, formed his own political party after the dramatic court case, lost his seat at the 2007 Holyrood election and has spent time in prison for protests against the poll tax and nuclear weapons. Sheridan, who sacked his legal team halfway through the case and ended up representing himself in court, successfully convinced the jury that he was a happily married teetotaller and that all the other claims made against him were untrue. 'You will hear of my addiction to Scrabble and sunbeds, not champagne, cocaine and swingers' clubs,' he said. At the time of writing, the story looked set to keep running, as the *News of the World* was appealing against the verdict, and Sheridan had been charged with perjury.

The quotes that emerged from the case were the sort to make a journalist's eyes light up and their shorthand go into overdrive – and they provided pegs on which to hang any number of articles. One of the first features to appear on the BBC Scotland online site once the verdict had been announced was a collection of the choicest quotes from the case. Most memorable were those from the MSP himself and from his formidable air-hostess wife Gail, whom Sheridan himself cross-examined in the witness box. He asked if she believed the claims and she replied that neither of them would have been standing in court if she had: 'You would be in the Clyde with a piece of concrete tied round you and I would be in court for your murder.' Then she added: 'You're like a monkey, so anybody that was rolling an ice cube round your body would have had a hair ball in their throat.' Turning to the jury, she clarified: 'He looks like a gorilla. He's covered in hair from head to toe. There's more hair on his body than there is on his head – but there is no mention of that [in the paper]' (*Guardian*, 1 August 2006). Sheridan, in his closing speech, referred to this and offered to strip for the jury: 'If I am a hairy ape, if challenged, I am sure my lord will allow me to disrobe. I would be prepared to do that.'

The jury were sent out to consider their verdict on the morning of Friday, 4 August. Within two and a half hours they had voted seven to four in Sheridan's favour. The websites reacted fast. By early evening, the front page of the BBC Scotland site contained a lead story: '**Sheridan victory in court battle**' (http://news.bbc.co.uk/1/hi/scotland/5246378.stm). This was rapidly followed by a number of features, each adding a different dimension to what was already a huge story north of the border, and gaining significance further afield. Links to reports from previous days were there, but now the case was over it was time to reflect on the enormity of the verdict (the highest damages ever awarded in a Scottish court) and the political ramifications of so many of Sheridan's own party colleagues testifying against him. Some of the features to appear included:

- '**Key figures in the Sheridan case**' (http://news.bbc.co.uk/1/hi/scotland/5231208.stm)
- '**Split on the cards for Socialists**' (written by the BBC Scotland political correspondent; http://news.bbc.co.uk/1/hi/scotland/5246956.stm)
- '**In quotes: Sheridan case**' (memorable quotes from the four-week hearing; http://news.bbc.co.uk/1/hi/scotland/5239222.stm

He shouted, he cried,

... but Tommy Sheridan's sensational victory in court is not the end of the story, writes *Eddie Barnes*

HIS wife was wearing her customary ear-to-ear smile, but Tommy Sheridan looked grim. As he arrived at the Court of Session in Edinburgh on Friday morning, the most charismatic Scottish politician of his generation appeared to have lost some of his usual sparkle. "I am hoping for the best but preparing for the worst," he had told friends the previous night. Sheridan was expecting to lose.

Around seven hours later, as the couple emerged from the court building to the cheers of supporters and dozens of waiting journalists, photographers and TV crews, Gail and Tommy Sheridan raised their clenched fists in triumph. From a window above, Lord Turnbull – the case's judge – took in the spectacle of the melee. The jurors who had just delivered their verdict lingered among the crowd, eager for one last look at the man who had persuaded them to find in his favour. Dabbing her eyes, one of Sheridan's sisters, Lynn, who had sat behind her brother for much of the previous month in court, insisted the verdict was all that she and her family had been expecting.

And then Sheridan did what he does best. With the world's media hanging on his every word, the bombast began, as he denounced in thunderous Glaswegian tones those who had so nearly ruined his reputation and his marriage with accusations of champagne and cocaine-fuelled orgies. Across the road on the Royal Mile, hard-up actors in Edinburgh for the festival were attempting to persuade passing tourists to come and see their shows. They might as well have packed up and gone home: there was only one act in town that mattered.

For some, Sheridan is, in the words of the News of the World's QC Mike Jones, "a monstrous ego". It is an ego that has driven him through a 17-year political career which has captivated the Scottish public. From his emergence on the public stage in 1992 when, jailed for contempt of court following his refusal to pay the poll tax, he was elected as a Glasgow councillor while still in Saughton prison, to the remarkable rise of the hard-left Scottish Socialist party which he founded in 1998, Sheridan has known nothing but victory.

But he had never faced a tougher fight. This time he was forced to take on not just the courts and the might of Rupert Murdoch's media empire, but also his oldest and once dearest friends, including his best man, and his closest political colleagues. His win leaves many of them open to perjury charges and the party he founded in ruins. The long road which took him to triumph on Friday is strewn with broken friendships, shattered reputations and bitter feuds. And he has not reached its end.

It all began on October 31, 2004, when the Scottish edition of the News of the World dropped a bombshell. Anvar Khan, a columnist with the newspaper, revealed she had had sex with an un-named married MSP. With typical tabloid flourish, the paper declared how the MSP liked to be "spanked", enjoyed "romping at swingers' parties" and had "even asked her to arrange a threesome". At Holyrood, fevered speculation began about the identity of the man in question.

There was an even greater frenzy inside the SSP. Party policy chief Alan McCombes claimed in court that two years earlier he had spoken to Sheridan about similar rumours involving the Socialist convener. After Khan's claims were published, an emergency meeting of the SSP's executive committee was called, and before the night was over, Sheridan had stepped down.

'Just after 11am on Wednesday last week, this master of the political arts delivered his masterpiece'

Some of those present – including McCombes, current convener Colin Fox and MSP Carolyn Leckie – told the court that Sheridan admitted at that meeting to having twice attended a swingers' club in Manchester. Others, including MSP Rosemary Byrne, insisted he did not. Fox and McCombes said they urged Sheridan to either ignore the story or to pre-empt it by admitting to his infidelity.

But Sheridan was insistent: if he was named, he would sue.

"All at the meeting were concerned because I epitomised the party," Sheridan told the court last week. "As convener, legal action could mean the financial involvement of the SSP. If I insisted on legal action, it was agreed I would have to stand down... I agreed."

When, that weekend, the News of the World backed their story up by reporting he had been having a sexual relationship with party worker Fiona McGuire, Sheridan followed through with his pledge.

His plan, according to allies in the party, was to keep the News of the World's second story about his alleged affair with McGuire separate from the first story, involving Khan. Even party colleagues who took the stand against him agree he has always vehemently rejected the claims about McGuire.

"Tommy has always denied the Fiona McGuire story," said one party chief who did not back him in court.

"He always hoped to keep the two stories separate so that the evidence would solely be on that case."

With that plan in place, Sheridan believed right to the end that the News of the World would eventually agree to settle. Convener Colin Fox said: "He always thought that they would drop the case, even in the week beforehand."

But they did not. Instead, a third woman – Danish-born 31-year-old Katrine Trolle – was brought forward by the News of the World, with her own substantial allegations of a sexual relationship. Thus Sheridan was catapulted into a dog-fight for both his political and family life.

It was a fight for which he was prepared to sever the most long-lasting of his political ties.

Glasgow councillor Keith Baldarassa had been one of Sheridan's three best men at his unorthodox wedding in 2000. Now Sheridan accused him and others of using the controversy to mount a vicious political campaign to topple him as leader. Ultimately, this was to prove the centre-piece of his successful defence.

Yet for Sheridan, the first eight days of the trial were an unmitigated disaster. Lurid evidence from both McGuire and Khan, combined with damning evidence from McCombes, who declared both that Sheridan had admitted to being a swinger and that he would deny it was true, appeared to have left him facing defeat. It was then that he made what may well have been the move that saved his skin. Sacking his entire legal team, Sheridan decided to defend himself. Every night, he, his two sisters and party ally John Aberdein – "the best amateur legal team in Scotland," Sheridan claimed after his victory on Friday – would convene to plan their line of attack.

By doing away with his legal middlemen, the way was left clear for Sheridan to focus his considerable oratorical talents on the jury directly. It was, lawyers admitted afterwards, a brilliant tactical move.

For one thing, the make-up of that jury – six men and five women – had not gone unnoticed. "The jurors were all under 40," said Fox. "One of them came to court one day wearing a Che Guevara T-shirt and another had a stud through her lip."

In other words, Sheridan's allies realised they might just have a sympathetic ear. Sheridan began to weave his magic. And just after 11am on Wednesday last week, this master of the political arts delivered his masterpiece.

He had been up all night writing it. Sheridan believed his trial had parallels to another court case 88 years ago. In 1918, a Glasgow schoolteacher called John MacLean had also appeared in court, on trial for sedition, after he called on workers to follow the Russian revolution. MacLean, who led the so-called Red Clydeside uprising, was a mythical figure for the hard left and had been a hero of Sheridan's ever since, aged 17, he was given MacLean's biography by his ever-influential mother. MacLean is best remembered for the words he gave at that trial: "I am not here, then, as the accused: I am here as the accuser of capitalism, dripping with blood from head to foot," he told the courts. Sheridan decided to write the same words into his own speech.

With typical understatement, Turnbull later described it as a "powerful" offering. In fact, it blew the jury off their feet. First Sheridan cleverly drew a contrast between himself, the amateur, and the might of the News of the World's finest legal brains. Then, he told the jury of his 14-month-old daughter, Gabrielle, and how the most difficult part of the trial had been not seeing her every day. He spoke of how the first News of the World story had broken when Gail was three months pregnant.

"They endangered my wife and my child and, do you know what, they endangered Fiona Maguire as well. They can't care less because the bottom line is to sell newspapers."

He shouted; he whispered; he broke down; he begged the jury for mercy. By the end he was referring to them as "brothers and sisters". As one SSP official quipped on Friday: "The cry will now go through the courts: call for Sheridan!"

'The smart money is on Sheridan deciding to mount a leadership bid to take back control of the party he founded'

There can be little doubt now that the speech won him the case. And yet few were expecting the verdict when it came. Haggard reporters who had been following the case for four weeks shook their heads outside court in disbelief. In Glasgow, McCombes could barely talk. "It's totally incredible," he said, moments after hearing the verdict. In Canada on holiday, Rosemary Byrne got the news via a text message. "Wonderful news," she said.

Those contrasting moods within the SSP offer evidence of the turmoil that now threatens its continued existence.

Members of the party are continuing to dispute Sheridan's evidence. On Monday, Gail Sheridan told the court that at the party conference in 2005, Trolle told her the News of the World had offered her money to reveal an affair with Sheridan. Party secretary Allan Green has now stepped forward to dispute this.

"She [Trolle] was not listed among the delegates or as a visitor by any of the branch submissions in advance of the conference," Green told Scotland on Sunday. "I have gone through every visitor, delegate and there is no sheet with Katrine's name on it. So according to the records, Katrine wasn't at the conference."

The 11 SSP members who claimed Sheridan did have an affair are now considering whether to make an official com-

Floaty skirts and

STANDING outside Court Six in a sharp black suit and high heels she towered over a couple of drably-dressed middle-aged women, tossing her immaculate hair and gesticulating as they discussed proceedings in the room beyond.

Against the austere and hushed backdrop of Edinburgh's Parliament House it could be a conversation between a high-flying lawyer and her client. In fact this is Gail Sheridan talking to members of her own extended family.

Before her husband's £200,000 victory against The News of the World newspaper on Friday, much was being made of his air hostess wife's wardrobe, hair, handbags and sunglasses, symbols of her self-assured style and polished glamour which thrilled the public almost as much as the lurid allegations inside the courtroom.

But off-camera and behind the carefully constructed facade, 42-year-old Gail Sheridan is far more than just a clothes horse and trolley dolly. Highly competent and hugely confident, she is a controlling presence in her husband's life, and in the last few weeks helped mastermind a PR campaign which ultimately had a major impact on the outcome of the case.

One of the main reasons Tommy Sheridan took on the might of a tabloid newspaper was to prove himself not just to the public but to his formidable wife, with whom he has an extraordinary relationship in which the distribution of power is far more complex than simply that of a woman standing by her man.

Born Gail Healy, the daughter of two care workers from Cardonald, she met her future husband at Glasgow's Lourdes Academy, where he thought she was a teacher's pet and she thought he was rough. The pair started dating in the 1990s after she sent him postcards in prison from the exotic locations she had travelled to in her job with British Airways.

They married six years ago when he was the only Socialist MSP at Holyrood, and she is said by those close to the couple to be the smarter and more sophisticated of the two, and a significant force behind his success.

One source who spoke to Scotland on Sunday about the couple said: "Gail is a hugely competent woman. As an experienced member of cabin crew there are very few issues that she has not come across. They have to portray a degree of authority and are trained to deal with many different situations."

Gail Sheridan's way of dealing with her husband's political career and the factions within his party was to avoid too much

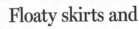

Original layout as published in *Scotland on Sunday*. Reproduced by kind permission of The Scotsman Publications Limited.

he begged for mercy

SEX, LIES AND SOCIALISM: THE TRIAL IN KEY WITNESSES' OWN WORDS

DAY 1
Allison Kane, 38, SSP treasurer, right
Asked if Sheridan had admitted going to Cupid's swingers' club. "Yes. He said he had gone on two occasions with friends."

DAY 2
Douglas Wight, 33, former News of the World news editor reading a transcript by Fiona McGuire
"He liked to dominate me. He liked rough stuff. He likes uniforms and stuff."

DAY 4
Alan McCombes, 51, policy chief of the SSP
"He acknowledged that this had been reckless behaviour and had been, in hindsight, a mistake. He said he was confident there had been no proof in existence about his visit to the club."

DAY 5
Anvar Khan, 39, columnist with the News of the World "He and I got undressed and started to have sex... I saw Tommy have sex with Katrine (Trolle) and Andy (McFarlane, Sheridan's brother-in-law) was part of the threesome."

DAY 6
Helen Allison, 52, who claimed to have seen Sheridan having group sex at the Glasgow Moat House hotel
"He smiled at me. I was devastated... I realised I had been asked to some kind of orgy."

DAY 7
Fiona McGuire, 32, party worker
"He was very much the instigator. He was jollying us all in having a good time. He was just up for anything."

DAY 8
Anne Colvin, 54, on the alleged Moat House incident
"Mr Sheridan looked at that moment as though he was completely spaced out. He just stared into space."

DAY 9
Tommy Sheridan, sacking his legal team
"I have been less than satisfied... in relation to my defence. I was incandescent with rage yesterday."

DAY 10
Katrine Trolle, 31, right, SSP member who alleged an affair with the MSP
"Tommy kept saying how liberal he thought Scandinavian people were, much more open about their sexuality than the British."

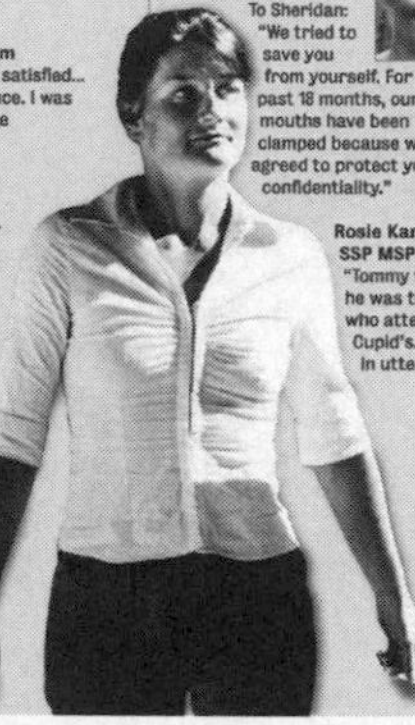

DAY 11
Colin Fox, 47, convenor of the SSP, asked if he made up what happened at the SSP's 2004 meeting when Sheridan was confronted over sex rumours
"I am not mistaken. I am absolutely categorically clear on what took place at the meeting."

Allan Green, 48, SSP national secretary, on the same meeting
"He accepted his behaviour was reckless and he apologised... Everyone was absolutely shocked."

DAY 12
Carolyn Leckie, 41, SSP MSP
To Sheridan: "We tried to save you from yourself. For the past 18 months, our mouths have been clamped because we agreed to protect your confidentiality."

Rosie Kane, 45, SSP MSP
"Tommy told us he was the MSP who attended Cupid's. I was in utter shock – personally and politically. It's not something I could forget or make a mistake about."

DAY 13
Tommy Sheridan
"What you have heard over the last three weeks has been a complete and utter fabrication... I feel I am the mild mannered Clark Kent of Scottish politics and Superman by night."

DAY 14
Tommy Sheridan
"You will hear of my addiction to Scrabble and sunbeds, not champagne, cocaine and swingers' clubs. The evidence I will lead will establish the truth about me as an individual and a Socialist."

DAY 15
Patricia Smith, 60, party worker, on the 2004 meeting
"It was rancorous, heated, emotional. They were anxious about how to deal with the sniggers, sneers and salacious comments."

DAY 16
Steve Arnott, 44, SSP member, describing the claims Sheridan had admitted to sexual liasions
"Bullshit."

Mike Gonzalez, 63, SSP member, asked whether he was telling the truth
"I would hardly risk my hard earned professional reputation by telling a lie in court."

Jock Penman, 56, party worker
"I got the impression this was like a family fall-out because the people who were the most vociferous were the ones who had known you the longest... I thought there are quite a few people who have taken gossip too far."

DAY 17
Bob Bird, Scottish editor of News of the World
"We would not have printed the story if we had not believed it was true."

DAY 18
Gail Sheridan, 42, asked if she would give evidence if she believed Sheridan had lied
"There is no way I would be here. Neither would you. You would be in the Clyde with a piece of concrete tied round you and I would be in court for your murder. You are like a monkey. Anyone rubbing ice cubes round your body would have ended up with a hairball in their throat."

DAY 20
Tommy Sheridan
"If I am a hairy ape I am sure, if challenged, my lord will allow me to disrobe. I would be prepared to do that."

DAY 21
Tommy Sheridan on his victory
"What we have done in the last five weeks is the equivalent of Gretna taking on Real Madrid in the Bernabeu and beating them on penalties."

EDDIE BARNES

plaint to the police against him, hoping to spark an investigation for perjury. It seems likely that he has not seen the last of the courts.

Sheridan has spent the weekend holed up with the Daily Record, who have paid £30,000 to get his and Gail's story (Gail, it is rumoured, has even been awarded a fashion column at the tabloid paper). As for his £200,000 damages, legal experts believe he may have to wait 18 months before he finally gets his cheque, with the News of the World embarking on a lengthy appeal.

His next move is being watched keenly. Some of those close to him believe he may quit Scottish politics altogether. Others predict a potential link-up with Respect, the party founded by George Galloway, with whom he now shares the scars of courtroom battles.

But the smart money is on Sheridan deciding to mount a leadership bid to take back control of the party he founded and which he still views as his personal property. If he does, the Scottish Socialist party will almost certainly split. The United Left faction – led by MSPs such as Leckie and Rosie Kane – will not countenance having to work under Sheridan once again.

A bloody civil war will unfold at the party's conference this October. Few would now bet against Tommy Sheridan emerging victorious.

Battle-hardened: Tommy Sheridan, with his wife Gail opposite, was victorious last week, but could face further investigation as 11 SSP members who claimed Sheridan did have an affair consider whether to pursue a police complaint against him

How a team of top lawyers isn't always enough to win

IF TOMMY Sheridan's David versus Goliath victory over the News of the World surprised many, it was predictable to those familiar with the law.

While the News of the World could muster 18 witnesses and a top legal team, Sheridan's case was initially dogged by problems. He sacked his lawyers and conducted his own case against Mike Jones, a top QC.

And observers might have thought that the News of the World was home and dry when they heard the judge's directions to the jury.

Lord Turnbull told them that if they believed any one of the newspaper's 18 witnesses, that would be enough to make them give a verdict to the News of the World.

In the event, the jury decided by a seven to four majority in Sheridan's favour, a verdict which has left the former SSP leader £200,000 better off.

The News of the World, which is appealing, must now argue before a panel of judges that "no reasonable jury" could come to the judgment reached last Friday.

Senior legal insiders have described the newspaper's task as "well-nigh impossible". Should the paper win its appeal, that would not overrule last week's verdict but only allow a re-run of the case.

Robert Black, professor of Scots law at the University of Edinburgh, said: "Numbers of witnesses are not enough unless the evidence is of good quality, and it obviously wasn't if it failed to impress the jury.

"Tommy Sheridan made a very good fist of it. He succeeded in calling into question the credibility of the other side's witnesses, enough to undermine the paper's case."

Alistair Bonnington, secretary of the Scottish Media Lawyers Society and the co-author of *Scots Law for Journalists*, said: "If you study major defamation trials, of which there have been a number in England, though not so many in Scotland, there's a clear message in them that juries don't particularly like tabloid journalists. In fact, they find them quite repulsive. And this parade of witnesses, with prostitutes and ex-prostitutes and people who wanted money for their stories and all that was very unimpressive."

'This parade of witnesses, with prostitutes, ex-prostitutes and people who wanted money for their stories – all that was very unimpressive'

Solicitor Campbell Deane, who provided Sheridan with legal advice, said: "It's not quite accurate to say it was all him because there were months of preparation work and interviews done by lawyers which gave him the ammunition. But fair play to him, Tommy did brilliantly.

"He was helped, too, by the fact that he knew all the people he was questioning and cross-examining inside out.

"Also, not having the lawyers crystallised it in the eyes of the jury – it was no longer one lawyer against another lawyer, but they could see it was Tommy Sheridan against the News of the World. There is another lesson in this: a newspaper which is going to print things about people must be very sure of their facts or they're going to get stuffed."

A senior QC said: "Why on earth did anyone think that the News of the World were going to win? A collection of prostitutes and ex-prostitutes and people who seemed to have an axe to grind? Not an impressive collection.

"Also, Sheridan played a blinder. His final address to the jury was 90 minutes, while Mike Jones's was over six hours. You need a balance between putting your case and not boring and annoying the jury.

"You could argue, correctly in my mind, that His Lordship's direction to the jury was pro-newspaper. But juries don't like being told what to do."

Another leading QC added: "The only News of the World witness I thought seemed credible was SSP activist Katrine Trolle. I thought that if anyone could have brought him down it was her. The others didn't impress at all and might even have done more harm than good."

Veteran criminal trial QC, Gordon Jackson – the MSP for Glasgow Govan – said: "This was a case of juries do what juries do and they are hard to predict. What people who might have been observing this case will forget is that the onus of proof is on the paper. It's not as high a standard of proof as in a criminal trial, where it's beyond all reasonable doubt. But it is still up to the paper to prove their case.

"What goes on in jurors' minds, no one can know, but some will believe one side, some the other. But quite a few will not believe either side particularly, and in those cases they would go against the side with the case to prove.

"In a murder trial, that means the Crown, in a case like this it means the paper.

"It's probably just as well I am leaving law to focus completely on being an MSP. No one will want a lawyer after this. The way to winning a case seems to be getting rid of them."

MURDO MacLEOD

wrap dresses – but Gail is happiest wearing the trousers

contact with outsiders and instead surround herself with a trusted clique of family and friends. Gail's Catholic family are very close-knit, with her parents, sister and assorted aunts, uncles and cousins all living within a few streets of the Sheridans' home.

Surprisingly, although she is a socialist herself, she has always had little to do with the other powerful women in her husband's life – including SSP MSPs Carolyn Leckie and Rosie Kane – or many of the party faithful. As one source put it: "She is nothing like them and they are nothing like her."

Instead of marching in the streets with banners, she prefers to sip wine, smoke cigarettes, keep an immaculate house and work hard on her looks. The Sheridans both use tanning booths regularly and she watches her figure carefully with Scottish Slimmers and Weight Watchers. But she is also a cunning PR woman.

"In many ways, she is a lot more worldly-wise and rounded than he is," another source said. "She is the brains behind a lot of the things which have been done to boost the human side of his image and keep him in the public eye."

For example in 1999, Gail called in to a phone-in radio show after her husband had made a series of wise cracks about her cooking. Putting on a fake posh accent, she called to lambast men who were useless at DIY, a dig at her then fiancee aimed at showing his human side. A party source said: "The point of things like that was to build up the image of Tommy as a human kind of guy combining family and a love life with his principles. It moved him away from any image of a stern, shouting, humourless Socialist."

On another occasion, a colleague saw them together at an event just before he was due to speak. "Gail straightened his tie, brushed him down and made sure his jacket was straight. She was clearly very conscious of his image and he just stood there and let her do it," the source said.

Described by those who have forged friendships with her as upfront, honest and deeply in love with her husband, Gail Sheridan is also said to have been utterly convinced of his innocence. One friend said of the trial: "Tommy is doing this because of his love for her. She believes him, otherwise she wouldn't be there. She will have been supporting him at the end of each day after they have got home."

In some ways, she appears to have accepted a rather diminished role in Tommy Sheridan's life, bowing graciously to politics as her husband's No.1 priority, not a concession many wives would make.

In an interview with Scotland on Sunday shortly before their wedding in 2000 he referred to politics as "the constant in my life". He added: "Gail is realistic enough to know politics is always going to be first in the pecking order." She acknowledged: "I fight two mistresses. Politics and football."

'She is the brains behind a lot of the things which have been done to boost the human side of his image and keep him in the public eye'

Despite this, the signs of her wilful nature are unmistakable. The wedding, which took place after the couple had been together for seven years, was at her insistence, not his. And despite his atheism, the ceremony took place at her local chapel, Our Lady of Lourdes Church in Cardonald, with 200 guests, three bridesmaids and two flower girls. Film director Peter Mullan and novelist William McIlvanney attended.

Sheridan had suggested a wedding in Cuba but the bride refused to be upstaged by Fidel Castro on her big day. She also got her own way over the name of their 14-month-old daughter, Gabrielle. She chose the name against his choice of Poppy and underwent an elective caesarean, saying she was not "too posh to push", rather "too smart to suffer".

However, it is her performance over the last few weeks of his court case that has really focused attention on Gail's powerful role in her marriage.

In a trial which has seen women portrayed as liars and prostitutes, Gail Sheridan has played another female stereotype, the loyal and glamorous wife, to perfection. On camera she waged a propaganda campaign that started with the fashion show, paused for dramatic effect in the courtroom and ended with the smiles of triumph outside the Court of Session. Trumping her far less glamorous rivals, Anvar Khan, Katrine Trolle and Fiona McGuire, her entire image dared anyone to believe her man would have bedded these woman when she was keeping the home fires burning.

There was the floaty white polka-dot skirt with strappy sandals and tailored black shirt, the Diane von Furstenberg-style wrap dress, the fitted pale trouser suit and the pinstripe trousers with open-necked white shirt. The lipstick was always fresh, the hair was salon-styled and she was constantly at her husband's side.

In court she declared her faith in "hairy" Tommy as he quizzed her in front of a packed courtroom. If the allegations were true, she declared: "There's no way I would be here and neither would you. You'd be in the Clyde with a piece of concrete tied round you and I would be standing in court for your murder."

Off camera, those present described her as "gallus". One said: "She would chat to the photographers as she sat at the outdoor cafe next to the court. She would take off her heels, put them in her briefcase, put on some comfy flip-flops and joke to the photographers not to take unflattering snaps. She would come into court with shopping bags and show her friends and family her latest buys. She chatted to everyone. She bonded with the photographers, as if she thought she was a real celebrity. I think she'll have withdrawal symptoms now the court case is over."

Party insiders also noticed a remarkable body language between the two in recent weeks as Sheridan battled the system to save his reputation.

One SSP source said: "It's been very interesting and something many of us have noticed. Gail has been taking his hand in the way a mother would take a child's hand and lead the wee one off. It's very protective, quite unlike like the way a man and wife would normally hold hands."

Gail Sheridan is now said to be taking a break from the cameras, to spend some time with her husband and the daughter she has barely seen over the past few weeks. But it is unlikely we have seen the last of the most glamorous woman in Scottish politics.

With the SSP in disarray, Tommy Sheridan's own future is as uncertain as that of his party. What is clear, however, is that he is a more formidable force with Gail Sheridan at his side.

KATE FOSTER

He shouted,

. . . but Tommy Sheridan's sensational victory in
court is not the end of the story, writes *Eddie Barnes*

Battle-hardened: Tommy
Sheridan, with his wife Gail
opposite, was victorious
last week, but could face
further investigation as
11 SSP members who
claimed Sheridan
did have an affair
consider whether
to pursue a police
complaint
against him

he cried,

His wife was wearing her customary ear-to-ear smile, but Tommy Sheridan looked grim. As he arrived at the Court of Session in Edinburgh on Friday morning, the most charismatic Scottish politician of his generation appeared to have lost some of his usual sparkle. "I am hoping for the best but preparing for the worst," he had told friends the previous night. Sheridan was expecting to lose.

Around seven hours later, as the couple emerged from the court building to the cheers of supporters and dozens of waiting journalists, photographers and TV crews, Gail and Tommy Sheridan raised their clenched fists in triumph. From a window above, Lord Turnbull – the case's judge – took in the spectacle of the melee. The jurors who had just delivered their verdict lingered among the crowd, eager for one last look at the man who had persuaded them to find in his favour. Dabbing her eyes, one of Sheridan's sisters, Lynn, who had sat behind her brother for much of the previous month in court, insisted the verdict was all that she and her family had been expecting.

And then Sheridan did what he does best. With the world's media hanging on his every word, the bombast began, as he denounced in thunderous Glaswegian tones those who had so nearly ruined his reputation and his marriage with accusations of champagne and cocaine-fuelled orgies. Across the road on the Royal Mile, hard-up actors in Edinburgh for the festival were attempting to persuade passing tourists to come and see their shows. They might as well have packed up and gone home: there was only one act in town that mattered.

For some, Sheridan is, in the words of the News of the World's QC Mike Jones, "a monstrous ego". It is an ego that has driven him through a 17-year political career which has captivated the Scottish public. From his emergence on the public stage in 1992 when, jailed for contempt of court following his refusal to pay the poll tax, he was elected as a Glasgow councillor while still in Saughton prison, to the remarkable rise of the hard-left Scottish Socialist party which he founded in 1998, Sheridan has known nothing but victory.

But he had never faced a tougher fight. This time he was forced to take on not just the courts and the might of Rupert Murdoch's media empire, but also his oldest and once dearest friends, including his best man, and his closest political colleagues. His win leaves many of them open to perjury charges and the party he founded in ruins. The long road which took him to triumph on Friday is strewn with broken friendships, shattered reputations and bitter feuds. And he has not reached its end.

It all began on October 31, 2004, when the Scottish edition of the News of the World dropped a bombshell. Anvar Khan, a columnist with the newspaper, revealed she had had sex with an un-named married MSP. With typical tabloid flourish, the paper declared how the MSP liked to be "spanked", enjoyed "romping at swingers' parties" and had "even asked her to arrange a threesome". At Holyrood, fevered speculation began about the identity of the man in question.

There was an even greater frenzy inside the SSP. Party policy chief Alan McCombes claimed in court that two years earlier he had spoken to Sheridan about similar rumours involving the Socialist convener. After Khan's claims were published, an emergency meeting of the SSP's executive committee was called, and before the night was over, Sheridan had stepped down.

he begged

SEX, LIES AND SOCIALISM: THE TRIAL IN

DAY 1
Allison Kane, 38, SSP treasurer, right
Asked if Sheridan had admitted going to Cupid's swingers' club. "Yes. He said he had gone on two occasions with friends."

DAY 2
Douglas Wight, 33, former News of the World news editor reading a transcript by Fiona McGuire
"He liked to dominate me. He liked rough stuff. He likes uniforms and stuff."

DAY 4
Alan McCombes, 51, policy chief of the SSP
"He acknowledged that this had been reckless behaviour and had been, in hindsight, a mistake. He said he was confident there had been no proof in existence about his visit to the club."

DAY 5
Anvar Khan, 39, columnist with the News of the World
"He and I got undressed and started to have sex . . . I saw Tommy have sex with Katrine (Trolle) and Andy (McFarlane, Sheridan's

brother-in-law) was part of the threesome."

DAY 6
Helen Allison, 52, who claimed to have seen Sheridan having group sex at the Glasgow Moat House hotel
"He smiled at me. I was devastated . . . I realised I had been asked to some kind of orgy."

DAY 7
Fiona McGuire, 32, party worker
"He was very much the instigator. He was jollying us all in having a good time. He was just up for anything."

DAY 8
Anne Colvin, 54, on the alleged Moat House incident
"Mr Sheridan looked at that moment as though he was completely spaced out. He just stared into space."

DAY 9
Tommy Sheridan, sacking his legal team
"I have

been less than satisfied . . . in relation to my defence. I was incandescent with rage yesterday."

DAY 10
Katrine Trolle, 31, below, SSP member who alleged an affair with the MSP
"Tommy kept saying how liberal he thought Scandinavian people were, much more open about their sexuality than the British."

DAY 11
Colin Fox, 47, convenor of the SSP, asked if he made up what happened at the SSP's 2004 meeting when Sheridan was confronted over sex rumours
"I am not mistaken. I am absolutely categorically clear on what took place at the meeting."

Allan Green, 48, SSP national secretary, on the same meeting
"He accepted his behaviour was reckless and he apologised . . . Everyone was absolutely shocked."

for mercy

KEY WITNESSES' OWN WORDS

DAY 12
Carolyn Leckie, 41,
SSP MSP
To Sheridan: "We
tried to save you
from yourself. For the past 18
months, our mouths have
been clamped because we
agreed to protect your
confidentiality."

Rosie Kane, 45, SSP MSP
"Tommy told us he was the
MSP who attended Cupid's. I
was in utter shock –
personally and politically. It's
not something I could forget
or make a mistake about."

DAY 13
Tommy Sheridan
"What you have heard over
the last three weeks has
been a complete and utter
fabrication . . . I feel I am the
mild mannered Clark Kent of
Scottish politics and
Superman by night."

DAY 14
Tommy Sheridan
"You will hear of my addiction
to Scrabble and sunbeds, not
champagne, cocaine and
swingers' clubs. The evidence
I will lead will establish the
truth about me as an
individual and a Socialist."

DAY 15
Patricia Smith, 60,
party worker, on the
2004 meeting
"It was rancorous,
heated, emotional. They were
anxious about how to deal
with the sniggers, sneers and
salacious comments."

DAY 16
Steve Arnott,
44, SSP
member,
describing the
claims Sheridan
had admitted to sexual
liasions
"Bullshit."

Mike Gonzalez, 63,
SSP member, asked
whether he was
telling the truth
"I would hardly risk
my hard earned professional
reputation by telling a lie in
court."

Jock Penman, 56, party
worker
"I got the impression this was
like a family fall-out because
the people who were the
most vociferous were the
ones who had known you the
longest . . . I thought there
are quite a few people who
have taken gossip too far."

DAY 17
Bob Bird, Scottish
editor of News of the
World
"We would not have
printed the story if we had not
believed it was true."

DAY 18
Gall Sheridan, 42, asked if
she would give evidence if
she believed Sheridan had
lied
"There is no way I would be
here. Neither would you. You
would be in the Clyde with a
piece of concrete tied round
you and I would be in court
for your murder. You are like
a monkey. Anyone rubbing ice
cubes round your body would
have ended up with a hairball
in their throat."

DAY 20
Tommy Sheridan
"If I am a hairy ape I am sure,
if challenged, my lord will
allow me to disrobe. I would
be prepared to do that."

DAY 21
Tommy Sheridan on his
victory
"What we have done in the
last five weeks is the
equivalent of Gretna taking
on Real Madrid in the
Bernabeu and beating them
on penalties."

EDDIE BARNES

'Just after 11am on Wednesday last week, this master of the political arts delivered his masterpiece'

Some of those present – including McCombes, current convener Colin Fox and MSP Carolyn Leckie – told the court that Sheridan admitted at that meeting to having twice attended a swingers' club in Manchester. Others, including MSP Rosemary Byrne, insisted he did not. Fox and McCombes said they urged Sheridan to either ignore the story or to pre-empt it by admitting to his infidelity.

But Sheridan was insistent: if he was named, he would sue.

"All at the meeting were concerned because I epitomised the party," Sheridan told the court last week. "As convener, legal action could mean the financial involvement of the SSP. If I insisted on legal action, it was agreed I would have to stand down . . . I agreed."

When, that weekend, the News of the World backed their story up by reporting he had been having a sexual relationship with party worker Fiona McGuire, Sheridan followed through with his pledge.

His plan, according to allies in the party, was to keep the News of the World's second story about his alleged affair with McGuire separate from the first story, involving Khan. Even party colleagues who took the stand against him agree he has always vehemently rejected the claims about McGuire.

"Tommy has always denied the Fiona McGuire story," said one party chief who did not back him in court.

"He always hoped to keep the two stories separate so that the evidence would solely be on that case."

With that plan in place, Sheridan believed right to the end that the News of the World would eventually agree to settle. Convener Colin Fox said: "He always thought that they would drop the case, even in the week beforehand."

But they did not. Instead, a third woman – Danish-born 31-year-old Katrine Trolle – was brought forward by the News of the World, with her own substantial allegations

Floaty skirts and wrap dresses – but

STANDING outside Court Six in a sharp black suit and high heels she towered over a couple of drably-dressed middle-aged women, tossing her immaculate hair and gesticulating as they discussed proceedings in the room beyond.

Against the austere and hushed backdrop of Edinburgh's Parliament House it could be a conversation between a high-flying lawyer and her client. In fact this is Gail Sheridan talking to members of her own extended family.

Before her husband's £200,000 victory against The News of the World newspaper on Friday, much was being made of his air hostess wife's wardrobe, hair, handbags and sunglasses, symbols of her self-assured style and polished glamour which thrilled the public almost as much as the lurid allegations inside the courtroom.

But off-camera and behind the carefully constructed facade, 42-year-old Gail Sheridan is far more than just a clothes horse and trolley dolly. Highly competent and hugely confident, she is a controlling presence in her husband's life, and in the last few weeks helped mastermind a PR campaign which ultimately had a major impact on the outcome of the case.

One of the main reasons Tommy Sheridan took on the might of a tabloid newspaper was to prove himself not just to the public but to his formidable wife, with whom he has an extraordinary relationship in which the distribution of power is far more complex than simply that of a woman standing by her man.

Born Gail Healy, the daughter of two care workers from Cardonald, she met her future husband at Glasgow's Lourdes Academy, where he thought she was a teacher's pet and she thought he was rough. The pair started dating in the 1990s after she sent him postcards in prison from the exotic locations she had travelled to in her job with British Airways.

They married six years ago when he was the only Socialist MSP at Holyrood, and she is said by those close to the couple to be the smarter and more sophisticated of the two, and a significant force behind his success.

One source who spoke to Scotland on Sunday about the couple said: "Gail is a hugely competent woman. As an experienced member of cabin crew there are very few issues that she has not come across. They have to portray a of a sexual relationship. Thus Sheridan was catapulted into a dog-fight for both his political and family life.

It was a fight for which he was prepared to sever the most long-lasting of his political ties.

Glasgow councillor Keith Baldarassa had been one of Sheridan's three best men at his unorthodox wedding in 2000. Now Sheridan accused him and others of using the controversy to mount a vicious political campaign to topple him as leader. Ultimately, this was to prove the centrepiece of his successful defence.

Yet for Sheridan, the first eight days of the trial were an unmitigated disaster. Lurid evidence from both McGuire and Khan, combined with damning evidence from McCombes, who declared both that Sheridan had admitted to being a swinger and that he would deny it was true, appeared to have left him facing defeat. It was then that he made what may well have been the move that saved his skin. Sacking his entire legal team, Sheridan decided to defend himself. Every night, he, his two sisters and party ally John Aberdein – "the best amateur legal

team in Scotland," Sheridan claimed after his victory on Friday – would convene to plan their line of attack.

By doing away with his legal middlemen, the way was left clear for Sheridan to focus his considerable oratorical talents on the jury directly. It was, lawyers admitted afterwards, a brilliant tactical move.

For one thing, the make-up of that jury – six men and five women – had not gone unnoticed. "The jurors were all under 40," said Fox. "One of them came to court one day wearing a Che Guevara T-shirt and another had a stud through her lip."

In other words, Sheridan's allies realised they might just have a sympathetic ear. Sheridan began to weave his magic. And just after 11am on Wednesday last week, this master of the political arts delivered his masterpiece.

He had been up all night writing it. Sheridan believed his trial had parallels to another court case 88 years ago. In 1918, a Glasgow schoolteacher called John MacLean had also appeared in court, on trial for sedition, after he called on workers to follow the Russian revolution.

Gail is happiest wearing the trousers

degree of authority and are trained to deal with many different situations."

Gail Sheridan's way of dealing with her husband's political career and the factions within his party was to avoid too much contact with outsiders and instead surround herself with a trusted clique of family and friends. Gail's Catholic family are very close-knit, with her parents, sister and assorted aunts, uncles and cousins all living within a few streets of the Sheridan's home.

Surprisingly, although she is a socialist herself, she has always had little to do with the other powerful women in her husband's life – including SSP MSPs Carolyn Leckie and Rosie Kane – or many of the party faithful. As one source put it: "She is nothing like them and they are nothing like her."

Instead of marching in the streets with banners, she prefers to sip wine, smoke cigarettes, keep an immaculate house and work hard on her looks. The Sheridans both use tanning booths regularly and she watches her figure carefully with Scottish Slimmers and Weight Watchers. But she is also a cunning PR woman.

"In many ways, she is a lot more worldly-

wise and rounded than he is," another source said. "She is the brains behind a lot of the things which have been done to boost the human side of his image and keep him in the public eye."

For example in 1999, Gail called in to a phone-in radio show after her husband had made a series of wise cracks about her cooking. Putting on a fake posh accent, she called to lambast men who were useless at DIY, a dig at her then fiancee aimed at showing his human side. A party source said: "The point of things like that was to build up the image of Tommy as a human kind of guy combining family and a love life with his principles. It moved him away from any image of a stern, shouting, humourless Socialist."

On another occasion, a colleague saw them together at an event just before he was due to speak. "Gail straightened his tie, brushed him down and made sure his jacket was straight. She was clearly very conscious of his image and he just stood there and let her do it," the source said.

Described by those who have forged friendships with her as upfront, honest and deeply in love with her husband, Gail Sheridan is also

MacLean, who led the so-called Red Clydeside uprising, was a mythical figure for the hard left and had been a hero of Sheridan's ever since, aged 17, he was given MacLean's biography by his ever-influential mother. MacLean is best remembered for the words he gave at that trial: "I am not here, then, as the accused: I am here as the accuser of capitalism, dripping with blood from head to foot," he told the courts. Sheridan decided to write the same words into his own speech.

With typical understatement, Turnbull later described it as a "powerful" offering. In fact, it blew the jury off their feet. First Sheridan cleverly drew a contrast between himself, the amateur, and the might of the News of the World's finest legal brains. Then, he told the jury of his 14-month-old daughter, Gabrielle, and how the most difficult part of the trial had been not seeing her every day. He spoke of how the first News of the World story had broken when Gail was three months pregnant.

"They endangered my wife and my child and, do you know what, they endangered Fiona Maguire as well. They can't care less because the bottom line is to sell newspapers."

He shouted; he whispered; he broke down; he begged the jury for mercy. By the end he was referring to them as "brothers and sisters". As one SSP official quipped on Friday: "The cry will now go through the courts: call for Sheridan!"

There can be little doubt now that the speech won him the case. And yet few were expecting the verdict when it came. Haggard reporters who had been following the case for four weeks shook their heads outside court in disbelief. In Glasgow, McCombes could barely talk. "It's totally incredible," he said, moments after hearing the verdict. In Canada on holiday, Rosemary Byrne got the news via a text message. "Wonderful news," she said.

Those contrasting moods within the SSP offer evidence of the turmoil that now threatens its continued existence.

Members of the party are continuing to dispute Sheridan's evidence. On Monday, Gail Sheridan told the court that at the party conference in 2005, Trolle told her the News

---

said to have been utterly convinced of his innocence. One friend said of the trial: "Tommy is doing this because of his love for her. She believes him, otherwise she wouldn't be there. She will have been supporting him at the end of each day after they have got home."

In some ways, she appears to have accepted a rather diminished role in Tommy Sheridan's life, bowing graciously to politics as her husband's No. 1 priority, not a concession many wives would make.

In an interview with Scotland on Sunday shortly before their wedding in 2000 he referred to politics as "the constant in my life". He added: "Gail is realistic enough to know politics is always going to be first in the pecking order." She acknowledged: "I fight two mistresses. Politics and football."

Despite this, the signs of her wilful nature are unmistakable. The wedding, which took place

'She is the brains behind a lot of the things which have been done to boost the human side of his image and keep him in the public eye'

after the couple had been together for seven years, was at her insistence, not his. And despite his atheism, the ceremony took place at her local chapel, Our Lady of Lourdes Church in Cardonald, with 200 guests, three bridesmaids and two flower girls. Film director Peter Mullan and novelist William McIlvanney attended.

Sheridan had suggested a wedding in Cuba but the bride refused to be upstaged by Fidel Castro on her big day. She also got her own way over the name of their 14-month-old daughter, Gabrielle. She chose the name against his choice of Poppy and underwent an elective caesarean, saying she was not "too posh to push", rather "too smart to suffer".

However, it is her performance over the last few weeks of his court case that has really focused attention on Gail's powerful role in her marriage.

In a trial which has seen women portrayed as liars and prostitutes, Gail Sheridan has played another female stereotype, the loyal and glamorous wife, to perfection. On camera she waged a propaganda campaign that started with the fashion show, paused for dramatic effect in the courtroom and ended with the smiles of triumph outside the Court of Session. Trumping

> **'The smart money is on Sheridan deciding to mount a leadership bid to take back control of the party he founded'**

of the World had offered her money to reveal an affair with Sheridan. Party secretary Allan Green has now stepped forward to dispute this.

"She [Trolle] was not listed among the delegates or as a visitor by any of the branch submissions in advance of the conference," Green told Scotland on Sunday. "I have gone through every visitor, delegate and there is no sheet with Katrine's name on it. So according to the records, Katrine wasn't at the conference."

The 11 SSP members who claimed Sheridan did have an affair are now considering whether to make an official complaint to the police against him, hoping to spark an investigation for perjury. It seems likely that he has not seen the last of the courts.

Sheridan has spent the weekend holed up with the Daily Record, who have paid £20,000 to get his and Gail's story (Gail, it is rumoured, has even been awarded a fashion column at the tabloid paper). As for his £200,000 damages, legal experts believe he may have to wait 18 months before he finally gets his cheque, with the News of the World embarking on a lengthy appeal.

His next move is being watched keenly. Some of those close to him believe he may quit Scottish politics altogether. Others predict a potential link-up with Respect, the party founded by George Galloway, with whom he now shares the scars of courtroom battles.

But the smart money is on Sheridan deciding to mount a leadership bid to take back control of the party he founded and which he still views as his personal property. If he does, the Scottish Socialist party will almost certainly split. The United Left faction – led by MSPs such as Leckie and Rosie Kane – will not countenance having to work under Sheridan once again.

A bloody civil war will unfold at the party's conference this October. Few would now bet against Tommy Sheridan emerging victorious.

---

her far less glamorous rivals, Anvar Khan, Katrine Trolle and Fiona McGuire, her entire image dared anyone to believe her man would have bedded these woman when she was keeping the home fires burning.

There was the floaty white polka-dot skirt with strappy sandals and tailored black shirt, the Diane von Furstenberg-style wrap dress, the fitted pale trouser suit and the pinstripe trousers with open-necked white shirt. The lipstick was always fresh, the hair was salon-styled and she was constantly at her husband's side.

In court she declared her faith in "hairy" Tommy as he quizzed her in front of a packed courtroom. If the allegations were true, she declared: "There's no way I would be here and neither would you. You'd be in the Clyde with a piece of concrete tied round you and I would be standing in court for your murder."

Off camera, those present described her as "gallus". One said: "She would chat to the photographers as she sat at the outdoor cafe next to the court. She would take off her heels, put them in her briefcase, put on some comfy flip-flops and joke to the photographers not to take unflattering snaps. She would come into court with shopping bags and show her friends and family her latest buys. She chatted to everyone. She bonded with the photographers, as if she thought she was a real celebrity. I think she'll have withdrawal symptoms now the court case is over."

Party insiders also noticed a remarkable body language between the two in recent weeks as Sheridan battled the system to save his reputation.

One SSP source said: "It's been very interesting and something many of us have noticed. Gail has been taking his hand in the way a mother would take a child's hand and lead the wee one off. It's very protective, quite unlike like the way a man and wife would normally hold hands."

Gail Sheridan is now said to be taking a break from the cameras, to spend some time with her husband and the daughter she has barely seen over the past few weeks. But it is unlikely we have seen the last of the most glamorous woman in Scottish politics.

With the SSP in disarray, Tommy Sheridan's own future is as uncertain as that of his party. What is clear, however, is that he is a more formidable force with Gail Sheridan at his side.

KATE FOSTER

How a team of top lawyers

IF TOMMY SHERIDAN'S **DAVID** versus Goliath victory over the News of the World surprised many, it was predictable to those familiar with the law.

While the News of the World could muster 18 witnesses and a top legal team, Sheridan's case was initially dogged by problems. He sacked his lawyers and conducted his own case against Mike Jones, a top QC.

And observers might have thought that the News of the World was home and dry when they heard the judge's directions to the jury.

Lord Turnbull told them that if they believed any one of the newspaper's 18 witnesses, that would be enough to make them give a verdict to the News of the World.

In the event, the jury decided by a seven to four majority in Sheridan's favour, a verdict which has left the former SSP leader £200,000 better off.

The News of the World, which is appealing, must now argue before a panel of judges that "no reasonable jury" could come to the judgment reached last Friday.

Senior legal insiders have described the newspaper's task as "well-nigh impossible." Should the paper win its appeal, that would not overrule last week's verdict but only allow a re-run of the case.

Robert Black, professor of Scots law at the University of Edinburgh, said: "Numbers of witnesses are not enough unless the evidence is of good quality, and it obviously wasn't if it failed to impress the jury.

"Tommy Sheridan made a very good fist of it. He succeeded in calling into question the credibility of the other side's witnesses, enough to undermine the paper's case."

Alistair Bonnington, secretary of the Scottish Media Lawyers Society and the co-author of *Scots Law for Journalists*, said: "If you study major defamation trials, of which there have been a number in England, though not so many in Scotland, there's a clear message in them that juries don't particularly like tabloid journalists. In fact, they find them quite repulsive. And this parade of witnesses, with prostitutes and ex-prostitutes and people who wanted money for their stories and all that was very unimpressive."

'This parade of witnesses, with prostitutes, ex-prostitutes and people who wanted money for their stories – all that was very unimpressive'

Solicitor Campbell Deane, who provided Sheridan with legal advice, said: "It's not quite accurate to say it

isn't always enough to win

was all him because there were months of preparation work and interviews done by lawyers which gave him the ammunition. But fair play to him, Tommy did brilliantly.

"He was helped, too, by the fact that he knew all the people he was questioning and cross-examining inside out.

"Also, not having the lawyers crystallised it in the eyes of the jury – it was no longer one lawyer against another lawyer, but they could see it was Tommy Sheridan against the News of the World. There is another lesson in this: a newspaper which is going to print things about people must be very sure of their facts or they're going to get stuffed."

A senior QC said: "Why on earth did anyone think that the News of the World were going to win? A collection of prostitutes and ex-prostitutes and people who seemed to have an axe to grind? Not an impressive collection.

"Also, Sheridan played a blinder. His final address to the jury was 90 minutes, while Mike Joncs's was over six hours. You need a balance between putting your case and not boring and annoying the jury.

"You could argue, correctly in my mind, that His Lordship's direction to the jury was pro-newspaper. But juries don't like being told what to do."

Another leading QC added: "The only News of the World witness I thought seemed credible was SSP activist Katrine Trolle. I thought that if anyone could have brought him down it was her. The others didn't impress at all and might even have done more harm than good."

Veteran criminal trial QC, Gordon Jackson – the MSP for Glasgow Govan – said: "This was a case of juries do what juries do and they are hard to predict. What people who might have been observing this case will forget is that the onus of proof is on the paper. It's not as high a standard of proof as in a criminal trial, where it's beyond all reasonable doubt. But it is still up to the paper to prove their case.

"What goes on in jurors' minds, no one can know, but some will believe one side, some the other. But quite a few will not believe either side particularly, and in those cases they would go against the side with the case to prove.

"In a murder trial, that means the Crown, in a case like this it means the paper.

"It's probably just as well I am leaving law to focus completely on being an MSP. No one will want a lawyer after this. The way to winning a case seems to be getting rid of them."

MURDO MacLEOD

- 'Sheridan's victory speech outside the court' (http://news.bbc.co.uk/1/hi/scotland/glasgow_and_west/5246764.stm)
- 'A lawyer's perspective' (http://news.bbc.co.uk/1/hi/scotland/5246716.stm).

Backgrounders which appeared within hours on the site included:

- 'Biggest challenge – Socialist MSP's sternest test in taking on newspaper' (http://news.bbc.co.uk/1/hi/scotland/glasgow_and_west/5231 626.stm)
- 'In pictures: Political career' (http://news.bbc.co.uk/1/hi/in_pictures/5238336.stm).

By the next morning, there was a vox pop pop-up section after a reporter had gone out on the streets of Pollok (Sheridan's constituency) to ask local people's views, plus a news feature: 'Fight on for future of Socialists' (http://news.bbc.co.uk/1/hi/scotland/5247842.stm). There were also links to what the Scottish newspapers were saying about the case.

Particularly important in online journalism is this use of links to other sites. The BBC site stresses, 'The BBC is not responsible for the content of external internet sites', but it includes the links as a useful aid for readers wanting to explore a topic further. With this story, some of the links went to the Scottish Courts and the Scottish Socialist Party. Also added rapidly were links to audio and video footage that had appeared on radio and TV. Of course, these aren't as user-friendly as having the newspaper or magazine pages open in front of you because a certain amount of shuttling between pages is required, and not all the video links were stored on the same page.

With stories of this scale, which run over weeks or months (bear in mind that Sheridan had resigned as leader of the Scottish Socialists as far back as 2004), writers will spend time putting together features which may not be used immediately. Furthermore, with court cases, much background cannot be released until the trial has ended. And no doubt the BBC had alternative versions of the stories stockpiled, to be used depending on who won the case.

Note that the BBC site, with its 'straight down the middle' approach, does not present heavily opinionated pieces from columnists. It relies instead on recognisable 'experts', such as lawyers and its own political correspondent. It contrast, columnists in the print media have a clear field to comment.

Such stories also provide opportunities for bloggers to react fast – the *Guardian*'s media expert Roy Greenslade had the news up on his blog within a couple of hours of the verdict being announced (http://blogs. guardian.co.uk/greenslade/). The *Guardian* is a good example of a media organisation that has embraced blogging as a serious addition to the journalist's toolbox. But my guess is that readers would be far more likely to go to an authoritative site such as the BBC's, where the story is examined in breadth and depth, rather than relying on an unknown blogger's sometimes idiosyncratic point of view. One of the disadvantages of blogs is the difficulty in deciding who is offering an informed opinion and who is simply Joe or Josephine Public having their say.

Over the weekend, much of the action took place in the print media, as Sheridan had sold his story to the *Daily Record*, a Scottish tabloid. Almost all the British heavies, including the *Financial Times*, put the story on their front pages on Saturday morning. The final day of the case and the shock verdict were discussed in depth, but there were also plenty of backgrounders and profiles of the main players. The *Telegraph* devoted a whole page to the case, with a lead story from the paper's Scottish correspondent, separate profiles of both Tommy and Gail Sheridan, and a transcript of his speech to the press, headlined with one of his own quotes: 'What we have done is the equivalent of Gretna taking on Real Madrid'. Meanwhile, the *Daily Mail*, known for its female focus, not surprisingly focused its attention on Gail Sheridan.

The Sundays had a little more time to mull over the judgement, with the *Observer* looking at the legal impact ('Sheridan win leaves Fleet Street reeling'). Not surprisingly, all the Scottish papers devoted acres of space to the story. The *Daily Record*, having bought the Sheridans' story for a reported £20,000, were the only paper to get an exclusive interview with the couple. The paper's features spread included them celebrating their win by playing Scrabble and Tommy Sheridan posing for the camera in a Gretna football shirt.

It's worth noting in the coverage of the case the differences between what was reported in the Scottish papers and what appeared in newspapers elsewhere. The former didn't need so much back story, as they would expect more of their readers to know who Sheridan is. Readers south of the border, on the other hand, needed to be brought up to speed on him. So there were recurring descriptions of him in stories and features as a socialist firebrand with a glamorous wife and a permatan who had been arrested and jailed a number of times for his beliefs.

Headline writers had a ball throughout, thanks to an avalanche of juicy quotes, and the possibilities for alliteration and plays on words. 'Tommy the Trot' and the 'Muppet Marxists' were both used, but my personal favourite was the front-page splash in the *Daily Record* on 15 July 2006, the day after Sheridan sacked his legal team – 'Tommy drops his briefs'. I hope whoever thought that up got a pay rise!

KNOWING YOUR MARKET – FEATURES SPREADS FOR NEWSPAPERS

The broadsheet *Scotland on Sunday* really went to town on the Sheridan story, providing a striking and varied features spread in its 6 August issue. Unsurprisingly, they led on the story, the news angle being 'Sheridan bid to grab SSP leadership', with the sub-deck 'Victorious politician plots coup' and 'Police probe MSP perjury claims'. The story turned on to page two, running alongside a photo of Tommy and Gail Sheridan and their daughter Gabrielle, and a separate news story headlined 'PR guru's warning as Sheridans' star rises'. The said PR guru was Max Clifford, who, along with PR experts from Scotland, was interviewed about how the couple could cash in on their fame.

The main spread, though, came on pages twelve, thirteen and fourteen. The first two were dominated by a cut-around pic of the couple – her smiling, him looking grim – which took up a good two-thirds of page twelve. The main story, running to a mammoth thirty-five paragraphs, was headlined, 'He shouted, he cried, he begged for mercy', and provided the background to the case – as well as throwing it forward in the sub-deck, which read, '. . . but Tommy Sheridan's sensational victory in court is not the end of the story'.

Running opposite and taking up half of page thirteen was a day-by-day breakdown of what went on in court, headlined, 'Sex, lies and socialism: the trial in key witnesses' own words'. This picked out a juicy quote from almost every day of the twenty-one-day trial. Also included were thumb-nail pix of key witnesses – Allison Kane, Alan McCoombes, Helen Allison, Carolyn Leckie, Patricia Smith, Mike Gonzalez, Jock Penman and Bob Bird, with a larger cut-out pic of Katrine Trolle. Beneath that was a piece headlined, 'How a team of top lawyers isn't always enough to win', which focused on the legal implications of the verdict. Interviewed in the article were: Robert Black, professor of Scots law at the University of Edinburgh; Alistair Bonnington, secretary of the Scottish Media

Lawyers Society and the co-author of *Scots Law for Journalists*; solicitor Campbell Deane, who provided Sheridan with legal advice; two unnamed QCs, described as 'senior' and 'leading', respectively; and Gordon Jackson, MSP for Glasgow Govan, and described as a 'veteran criminal trial QC'.

The anchor story at the bottom of the page, headlined, 'Floaty skirts and wrap dresses – but Gail is happiest wearing the trousers', focused, as you might guess, on Gail Sheridan. It was an intriguing twenty-eight paragraph profile of the woman, compiled from cuttings files and anonymous sources. The well-chosen quotes and incidents threw light on both Mr and Mrs Sheridan, such as this one from the middle of the feature:

> Surprisingly, although she is a socialist herself, she has always had little to do with the other powerful women in her husband's life – including SSP MSPs Carolyn Leckie and Rosie Kane – or many of the party faithful. As one source put it: 'She is nothing like them and they are nothing like her.'
>
> Instead of marching in the streets with banners, she prefers to sip wine, smoke cigarettes, keep an immaculate house and work hard on her looks. The Sheridans both use tanning booths regularly and she watches her figure carefully with Scottish Slimmers and Weight Watchers. But she is also a cunning PR woman.
>
> 'In many ways, she is a lot more worldly-wise and rounded than he is,' another source said. 'She is the brains behind a lot of the things which have been done to boost the human side of his image and keep him in the public eye.'
>
> For example in 1999, Gail called in to a phone-in radio show after her husband had made a series of wisecracks about her cooking. Putting on a fake posh accent, she called to lambast men who were useless at DIY, a dig at her then fiancé aimed at showing his human side. A party source said: 'The point of things like that was to build up the image of Tommy as a human kind of guy combining family and a love life with his principles. It moved him away from any image of a stern, shouting, humourless Socialist.'
>
> On another occasion, a colleague saw them together at an event just before he was due to speak. 'Gail straightened his tie, brushed him down and made sure his jacket was straight. She was clearly very conscious of his image and he just stood there and let her do it,' the source said.

Almost half of page fourteen, the comment and leader page, was taken up with the case. The top leader, 'This is a time for positive thinking', asked the wider question of what next for Sheridan, the SSP and the Scottish Parliament? It opened with:

> After five weeks of lurid headlines and sometimes grotesque evidence, Tommy Sheridan clearly savoured his victory last week at the Court of Session, celebrating with a glass of orange juice which pointedly eschewed the champagne he was alleged during the trial to have swilled. The erstwhile leader of the Scottish Socialist Party emerged with £200,000 and a typically mesmerising, if politically naive, victory speech – job done, proclaimed Tommy, now to the relatively minor tasks of saving Lebanon and delivering an independent socialist Scotland.
>
> Of course, the reality is somewhat different. For a start, Sheridan's trial is not yet over. The *News of the World*, stunned that the jury effectively called 18 witnesses liars, is to appeal, in the hope that a second hearing, in front of a panel of judges and with no jury to dazzle, will produce a different outcome. As we report today, several of those involved may also face perjury charges. So, while today Sheridan is a vindicated man, he faces an uncertain future.

It closed with:

> Holyrood [the site of the Scottish Parliament] has survived some difficult early years, including Henry McLeish's resignation and the £430m bill for the building itself; even two years ago, allegations of sexual misconduct would have exposed the parliament to further damaging ridicule. But, encouragingly, while the Sheridan trial has raised the profile of Scottish politics it does not appear to have tainted the institution as a whole. This may be the best evidence yet that, seven years in, Holyrood's reputation, while still fragile, is growing. We should all do what we can to ensure that continues.

Running to the right of the leader was a large cartoon. Top left was labelled, 'What teflon Tommy did next', and showed Sheridan, clad in tropical shirt and shorts, arriving with his suitcase at Cuban passport control and saying: 'I hear there's a vacancy?' Beneath this was a nine-paragraph (very long paragraphs, incidentally) comment piece from Magnus Linklater, headlined, 'The real losers in the Sheridan trial', with a sub-deck reading, 'Neither the public nor Scottish politics gain anything from a tawdry case'. The intro was a touch on the ponderous side, but then there were some telling observations about the court case and the state in which the SSP now found itself:

Robert Louis Stevenson thought there was nothing uglier than a court of law. 'Hither come envy, malice, and all uncharitableness to wrestle it out in public tourney,' he wrote. He pictured the end of a trial at the Court of Session, with the losing side counting the cost. 'To how many has not St Giles's bell told [*sic*] the first hour after ruin? I think I see them pause to count the strokes, and wander again into the moving High Street, stunned and sick at heart.'

None felt sicker last week, after the end of the Tommy Sheridan case, than those who had been branded liars, perjurers and conspirators against the course of justice. His was a famous victory, a triumph of soap-box oratory over the dull pedantry of the law. But it came at a cost, not just to the *News of the World*, which is left contemplating the largest defamation award ever made in a Scottish court, but to the party which Sheridan formed and led, the colleagues he traduced in court, the loyal workers who gave evidence against him, and who, this weekend, find their reputation in tatters.

I am thinking not so much of the high-profile witnesses, but people such as Barbara Scott, the minutes secretary of the Scottish Socialist Party, a meticulous note-taker, proud of her job, outraged at being accused of fabricating her record of a party meeting; of Catriona Grant, a founder member of the party – so passionate in her admiration of Sheridan that she was able to remember the exact time he stood up to make a speech and the time he stood down – now accused by him of perjuring herself: 'Tommy,' she protested tearfully, 'you know that I know that I'm telling the truth.' Then there were others who had never sought the limelight, each of them accused of conspiring to lie. All in all, in the course of Sheridan's pugnacious self-defence, some 18 witnesses have been branded by him as perverters of justice.

Along with their shredded testimony, a left-wing movement has been exposed to ridicule and contempt.

The last word on the case in the paper that week came on the back page of the main section in Paul Stokes's PS column. This was a lighter look at what the future held for Tommy Sheridan, headlined, 'Socialism should be Tommy's last resort' and accompanied by a not very sophisticated montage pic of Sheridan being interviewed by Jonathan Ross. The second half of a deadpan column read:

While I am, of course, very happy for Tommy, and Mrs Tommy for that matter, I cannot help but feel sad that he has missed out on the many great new opportunities that a resounding thrashing at the hands of the *News of the World* would have opened up to him.

Controversially, I always felt defeat was the best option. Now that he has won, he is stuck in the cul-de-sac that is extreme left-wing politics. He'll have to get involved in some intense battle for the future of socialism in this country. Tommy, don't do it. Nobody cares.

It is a real waste of the man's obvious talents as a performer, displayed to such good effect in court these past few weeks.

Imagine how great things could have been had he lost. Apart from the perjury case and the bankruptcy, of course. Tommy is now probably the best-known Scottish politician in Britain, if not the world. Even Paris Hilton probably knows who he is. After the mandatory celeb confessional appearance on Jonathan Ross, he could have coined it in on the highly lucrative repentance circuit.

There would have been Tommy the musical, with Tommy as himself, and years of gigs in panto. He would have been a definite pick for the next series of *Celebrity Love Rat Island*. He probably could have got his own daytime chat show. At the very minimum he could have landed a job as a presenter on Channel X.

But all that is gone now that his reputation is saved. Tommy has won his court case and handed himself a life sentence in Scottish politics.

If you ask me, it's a tragedy.

Virtually every part of the paper got in on the story, except perhaps the sports pages – but even they got their turn in subsequent weeks when various match reports and sports columns mentioned Sheridan's comment about Gretna taking on Real Madrid.

KNOWING YOUR MARKET – FEATURES SPREADS FOR WOMEN'S MAGAZINES

A fairly recent development in the magazine market has been the appearance of 'handbag-sized' publications. *Glamour* started the trend, and several others followed suit, including *Marie Claire*, which give readers a choice of size when they purchase the magazine.

Glamour is aimed at twenty- to thirty-something young professionals, and its mix of lifestyle, current affairs, fashion, celebrities and health and beauty is typical of that market. The editorial team know precisely what their readership cares about – which is why they sent reporter Sarah Duguid undercover to work in an estate agents (August 2005) to investigate dirty dealings.

The four-page feature is tagged 'G investigation' and, unusually for a magazine, features three pix that don't appear to be staged, showing the writer working in the estate agents and visiting houses. That first page is also dominated by a very long and unorthodox headline, which is almost more of a standfirst, albeit in a larger point size: 'Over-valued properties, fake offers and aggressive sales tricks. Just three of the ploys our writer discovered working undercover at an estate agents. Now read her story . . . from the inside.'

Content pointers

The feature is aimed squarely at *Glamour*'s age group, who are probably thinking about buying their own home. The writer appears to be in that age range herself, and she mentions how useful her two weeks will be if she ever buys a property.

The article starts with a classic personalised angle, although in the circumstances the writer obviously cannot name the would-be buyer. So she makes herself a key part of the feature.

> Lesson number one: do not fall in love with a property you cannot afford. East to say, much harder to do. But, in the second week of my assignment, one first-time buyer proves the point perfectly. She has viewed a flat that the estate agent believes is worth £195,000, but is advertising for £214,950. She is on a very tight budget and makes an offer of £195,000.
>
> It's rejected, as is her second offer of £200,000. Determined to get the property, she borrows a further £5,000 from her stepfather and offers £205,000.
>
> For the agent, the sale might mean a target met and a nice commission, but the buyer has been forced further into debt for a property that isn't necessarily worth the price she has paid. She may risk putting herself into negative equity – paying interest each month on a mortgage that is higher than the value of the flat – or losing money on it if she has to sell.
>
> I witnessed this scene at the upmarket west London estate agents where I worked as a negotiator for two weeks. I landed the job by faking sales experience – my references were never checked – and taking a personality test that identified me as a persuasive and aggressive salesperson. My aim was to report on how deals are done from the inside, so that other women like this unfortunate first-time buyer might avoid the same pitfalls.

Over-valued properties, **fake offers** and **aggressive** sales **tricks.** Just three of the ploys **our writer** discovered working undercover at an **estate agents.**

Now read her story . . . **from the inside**

By **Sarah Duguid** Photographs by **Ian Brodie**

Secret agent: journalist Sarah infiltrates the property world

into debt for a property that isn't necessarily worth the price she has paid. She may risk putting herself into negative equity – paying interest each month on a mortgage that is higher than the value of the flat – or losing money on it if she has to sell.

I witnessed this scene at the upmarket west London estate agents where I worked as a negotiator for two weeks. I landed the job by faking sales experience – my references were never checked – and taking a personality test that identified me as a persuasive and aggressive salesperson. My aim was to report on how deals are done from the inside, so that other women like this unfortunate first-time buyer might avoid the same pitfalls.

Sell, sell, sell

On my first day with the company, I was given a booklet outlining estate-agency law and asked to look over it "sometime". The real emphasis was on the hard sell. I was told the importance of appearing sincere, and how to employ 'psychology' in order to get buyers and sellers to increase an offer or lower their asking price.

I was also told that a potential purchaser spends more time deciding whether to buy a pair of shoes than a house. Women are often easier to persuade, apparently, whereas men can be sceptical. So, if it looks like a sale is faltering, I'm advised to call the wife or girlfriend and have a go at talking her round. If a woman doesn't like a property, they say, a couple will never buy it and it's pointless to waste any more time on it. But if the man hates it and the woman loves it, you could still have a sale as her verdict is often the final one.

The following day, even though I had no knowledge of law or of the ▶

L esson number one: do not fall in love with a property you cannot afford. Easy to say, much harder to do. But, in the second week of my assignment, one first-time buyer proves the point perfectly. She has viewed a flat that the estate agent believes is worth £195,000, but is advertising for £214,950. She is on a very tight budget and makes an offer of £195,000.

It's rejected, as is her second offer of £200,000. Determined to get the property, she borrows a further £5,000 from her stepfather and offers £205,000.

For the agent, the sale might mean a target met and a nice commission, but the buyer has been forced further

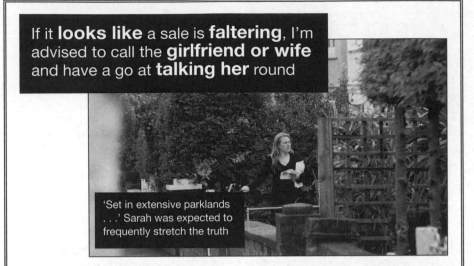

If it **looks like** a sale is **faltering**, I'm advised to call the **girlfriend or wife** and have a go at **talking her** round

'Set in extensive parklands . . .' Sarah was expected to frequently stretch the truth

◀ local property market, I was set my weekly target: 25 viewings, two sales, two home valuations and two mortgage appointments.

In May this year, the reputation of estate agents was called into question when a report in *Which?* magazine described their property valuations as more like "stabs in the dark" than professional opinion. Even though this agency signs up to a voluntary code of practice designed to protect the public from dubious sales techniques, I witnessed a number of conversations that led me to wonder if the rules are always adhered to. The phrase "everybody does it" seemed to be used a lot.

On day two of my new job, a potential buyer phoned in an offer on a flat for sale at £725,000. But at £680,000 the offer was too low and rejected. Nothing remarkable about that – until you discover that the offer was £30,000 more than the agency think the flat is worth. It had been over-valued to win the seller's business. So the seller could be about to reject what might have been a very good offer. But this won't stop Anna*,

the branch manager, trying to save the deal and hit her sales targets. "They'll pay more. We could pretend the vendor has rejected the offer to see if they'll go up," she says. But she agrees when Mark*, one of the sales negotiators, reminds her they can't do this. So she changes tack and calls the seller instead, telling him that several buyers who've seen the flat have been put off by the busy road it's situated on. One, she says, has seen a similar property selling for £690,000. Having built up his hopes of achieving the asking price, she now needs to bring them down again. The ploy doesn't work and he's not budging – he had, after all, been told that his property could fetch £45,000 more.

Later that day, I join Mark to see how a viewing is done. His client is a first-time buyer with £350,000 to spend and who is going to be shown a £310,000 flat nearby. Once in his car, Mark transforms into a silver-tongued estate agent, true to the stereotype. But inside the property we hit our first problem. The client asks where the strong smell of food in the garden is coming from. ▶

◄ "The neighbour must be doing a spot of cooking," he says. Later, though, he tells me there's a restaurant nearby and the smell was probably coming from its vent. "But obviously you'd keep quiet about something like that," he explains.

Fact or fiction

I learn quickly from my colleagues and, by day four, I am managing to hit my targets of four to five viewings a day – but not without being pretty imaginative with the facts. I describe a one-bed flat in a high-rise block as "a spacious development project", while a one-bedroom flat that everyone in the office agrees would only suit someone "willing to pay well over the odds" becomes "an exciting opportunity to get on the property ladder".

As the on-the-job training gathers speed, there's lots to remember. I'm advised by Anna to exaggerate other interest in flats in order to persuade people into buying quickly, and to gloss over facts that might prevent a sale – such as the short lease on one flat that would cost £15,000 to extend, or the estimated £15,000 worth of work needed on the windows of another. The buyer of that flat would probably only find out about the extra cost after the survey.

Worse still, in my book, I am routinely taking property hunters into flats already under offer, after buyers have begun the costly purchase process. If a flat is being advertised through a number of agents and a

Des res: our writer was asked to exaggerate interest to hasten the sale

rival office has an offer, our agency would work even harder to secure a higher one – and, ultimately, the sale.

With my lack of training and the pressure to hit targets, I was finding myself in some tricky situations. If a buyer asked about the state of the property market, I had to be bullish – even though three houses were repossessed during my two weeks at the company and bailiffs in the area were said to be booked up two months in advance. When buyers queried prices, I trotted out the standard response: "That's how it is around here. It's a very desirable area."

Against the spirit, if not the letter, of the code of practice, sellers were given inflated valuations of their property to get their business. I quickly learn that these valuations would be boosted in line with the seller's expectations rather than what the agent thought they would get for a property. Returning from a valuation one day, Anna shrugs as she explains: "I had to value the house a bit high. But you have to do that in order to get the business." The next day, she makes a similar admission. ►

I am **taking** property hunters **to see** flats already **under offer,** where buyers have begun the costly **purchase** process

◀ "Dave* [the area manager] thought I was naughty valuing that flat at £725,000. He thought it was only worth £650,000. But another agent had it on at £800,000, so the buyer has an expectation."

One homeowner had his four-bedroom house valued by different agents for figures that varied by over £100,000. He eventually chose an asking price of £685,000 that was roughly in the middle. My colleagues knew the seller was being ambitious, but agreed to take it on at that price and then privately discussed a plan whereby a developer would go round and make a considerably lower offer to bring down his expectations.

A question of trust

Ten days into the job, exhausted by the pressure and still with no verifiable knowledge of the rules of estate agency, I was sent on a sales course to learn how to close a deal.

During those two and half hours, I was told that when an agent meets a buyer, their first priority is to build a relationship of trust. Only then can you sell them a property.

In order to get viewers over the threshold, you have to exaggerate a property's qualities. "Tell them it's fabulous. Paint a picture of a lifestyle," says Dave. "Then, when you're taking them to see it, lower their expectations slightly. Tell them it's a little tired, or may need work. That way when they walk in, they'll go: 'Oh, it's not that bad'. Most of a sale is done before you actually get through the door."

After the course, I return to the office and discuss price negotiation with my colleagues. A favourite tactic, they tell me, is the 'ghost offer', when the estate agent pretends someone else is also bidding on a flat. Rebecca*, the lettings manager, reassures me: "Everyone does it. You have to. Even in lettings."

Mark, who usually earns in excess of £3,000 a month in commission, and has been known to make £6,000, confirms this: "If you're getting bollocked for not selling enough, you're going to think, fuck it, I'll do what I have to do. It's your money at the end of the day."

Eventually, almost two weeks into my employment, I was asked to take an online exam, which I finished in ten minutes, on the rules of estate agency. Had I stayed, I would have taken a more detailed exam in a month's time. But, as I'd already been doing the job, it seemed more about ticking regulatory boxes than a genuine concern that I knew the law.

During my fortnight at the agency, I was expected to work ten-hour days – longer if I'd booked evening viewings – without a lunch break. When I wasn't rushing to a viewing, I was expected to be on the phone, selling. Adding to the already unpleasant working environment was the ruthless competition. On my first day, Anna took me aside and said she wanted to stir up rivalry ▶

Sales drive: Sarah worked punishing ten-hour days to meet sales targets

◀ between Mark and me to get sales going.

On my final day, I had truly had enough. I told Anna that, despite my best efforts, I wasn't sure estate agency was for me and I needed more time to consider my future in the job. Three hours later, I was taken into a back office, told they didn't need uncommitted employees like me . . . and sacked. As I gathered up my belongings and walked, a little awkwardly, out of the office and into a bright, spring afternoon, all I felt was utter relief. I would never have to go back to the money-grabbing world of selling houses again – although, if I ever plan to buy a property, my two weeks as an insider will certainly serve me very well indeed. **G**

Don't get stung

Thinking of buying or selling? Make sure you read our inside tips before you do anything.

BUYERS BEWARE

- **Don't appear to fall in love with a property.** Feign indifference and bargain hard. Estate agents are experts in spotting someone who 'adores' a property.

- **"Beware, of the 'cool places to' live,"** says Tony Levene, author of *The Women's Guide to Finance* (Kogan Page £7.99). "These are often invented by estate agents, as are property stories in newspapers. If you want to know what the area is really like, go there with a friend at night – then you'll discover the noisy pub that's just down the street."

- **"Take a tape measure.** Descriptions of properties are often exaggerated – it's not what they put in, but what they leave out," says Levene.

- **Stick to your guns.** If your offer is rejected, be very firm that you can't go any higher. Then wait 24 hours and if the offer is still rejected only then consider going up.

- **"Beware of ghost offers.** If the agent tells you there's another offer, don't be persuaded to up your price," advises Levene. "If they are telling the truth, you don't want to get into a bidding war – if not, they'll call you."

- **"And don't get involved in an auction,"** adds Levene. "There are plenty of properties for sale. Any first-time buyer has the advantage of being able to move in quickly. And speed can often be worth more than thousands of pounds to sellers."

SELLING SAVVY

- **Research the local housing market.** That way you will be more in control if they start with the mind games. Pretend to be a buyer so you can visit estate agents and see how they price properties in the area.

- **"Don't base your plans on just one agent's valuation of your property.** Get six or seven valuations," suggests Levene.

- **Haggle to get a lower selling fee** – this can be between 1 – 2% of your sale price. Agents will be flexible to get your business.

- **Think about signing up to several agencies.** If you can negotiate a low selling fee then you're generally better off getting four or five agents to work for you than handing one the sole title. There's nothing like competition to get them motivated. Check the small print to see how long it will take you to terminate the contract if you're not happy.

- **"Be prepared to give a little,"** says Levene. "It could be a bit on the price, or the inclusion of the curtains. Furnishings can be an attractive offer for a buyer."

- **You don't have to use estate agents.** Why not try *Loot* which will give you a For Sale sign and a sales kit? You'll be surprised how much you learn when you buy and sell your property. Alternatively, try websites such as www.propertybroker.com.

*Names have been changed.

From here on, the piece is firmly focused on the reporter, outlining chronologically the fortnight Duguid spends at the agency. Other people are quoted – although we are told names have been changed – including area manager Dave, branch manager Anna, lettings manager Rebecca and sales negotiator Mark. Interestingly, there are no 'official' comments from the company, even at the end of the feature when Duguid leaves. You'd expect them to be given a chance to respond – even if all they could come up with was a revealing 'no comment'.

> On my final day, I had truly had enough. I told Anna that, despite my best efforts, I wasn't sure estate agency was for me and I needed more time to consider my future in the job. Three hours later, I was taken into a back office, told they didn't need uncommitted employees like me . . . and sacked. As I gathered up my belongings and walked, a little awkwardly, out of the office and into a bright, spring afternoon, all I felt was utter relief. I would never have to go back to the money-grabbing world of selling houses again – although, if I ever plan to buy a property, my two weeks as an insider will certainly serve me very well indeed.

There's a fact box on the final page of the feature, headed, 'Don't get stung', which contains buyers' and sellers' tips. These boxes are common in magazines, appearing alongside features as a way of summarising key information that may be useful to the reader. They may provide, as this one does, a checklist for further action. Or they can act simply as 'more information' boxes, giving names of organisations, telephone numbers and email addresses.

Design points

- *'Undercover' pix.* The quality isn't great, but that doesn't matter. The 'snatch' feel to them reinforces the secret nature of the assignment. The pix are also that rare beast in women's magazines – genuine photos of the reporter, not the usual mocked-up fare.
- *Big headline.* This takes up two-thirds of the first page of the feature.
- *Sans serif headline, body text and captions.* Not unusual for a women's magazine aimed at a younger and more relaxed market.
- *Drop cap.* A common technique used to launch a story.
- *Sub-heads.* Three are used to break up the feature.
- *Pull quotes.* Two (reversed in a box) are used to break up the feature ('If it looks like a sale is faltering, I'm advised to call the girlfriend or wife and have a go at talking her round' and 'I am taking property

hunters to see flats already under offer, where buyers have begun the costly purchase process').

- *Captions.* Reversed in a box and super-imposed on the pix.
- *Fact box.* Tagged 'Don't get stung' with bullet points in two columns ('Buyers beware' and 'Selling savvy').
- *Double thin rule.* Each of the pages is boxed in by a double thin rule all the way round, although the pix, which bleed off the pages, run over the top of it.

Even when the subject matter of the feature is serious, as it is here, magazine design – particularly at the glossy end of the market – comes across as much more relaxed and far less constrained than much newspaper design. Part of that is down to the positioning of headlines and captions, but it's also transmitted by the use of colour. While we see much more use of colour in newspapers now, an average features spread is still likely to be black and white, which gives it added gravitas.

CASE STUDY – PETER CARVOSSO, FEATURES EDITOR OF THE *IRISH INDEPENDENT*

Describe your newspaper

The *Irish Independent* is by far the most widely read daily paper in Ireland. It's a middle-market paper that is popular throughout the country. Following the success of the London *Independent*'s compact edition, the *Irish Independent* went down the same route with a dual compact/broadsheet.

What's the set-up of the *Irish Independent* features desk?

On my section (not the magazines) there are four staff writers and three to four production executives. The subbing and layout are outsourced. We also use a lot of freelance writers.

What is the day-to-day routine of the desk?

We have two broadsheet and four compact pages a day to fill. There's a health and living supplement on Monday, a listings/arts/rock magazine on Friday, a Saturday magazine and a twenty-eight-page tabloid news review on Saturdays. Each of the supplements has its own editor, but the executive features editor/deputy editor (Frank Coughlan) has overall responsibility for them. On Mondays I sit down with my deputy and work out the midweek pages, and also get a provisional list together for the Saturday review. On Tuesdays we have a conference review with the writers. Seven or eight stories in the review have to be related to the week's news, although it can be peripheral. I try to have a mix of light and solid stuff. The cover story is generally a serious issue, and the centre spread is light. The back of the book is arts-orientated.

What sort of stories catch your eye?

Exclusives that get us the front-page skyline on a Saturday.

What do you want (and not want) from writers?

- Get copy in on time, make it compelling reading, accurate and don't land us with a libel suit. Don't make me work on your story! Make it clean, clear and with killing quotes that we can write a headline from. If you can't write a headline from it in three minutes, it's a bad story!
- I can't tolerate sermonising. I don't want stuff that's someone's opinion with a few quotes. I want good yarns about people.
- I get annoyed by lack of nous. You need to be street-wise. People ideally should have been a reporter before they become a features writer.
- Save me from writers who think they can change the world with one story.

Biography?

I started on weekly papers in London – the *Middlesex County Times* and the *Ealing Gazette* – covering councils, courts and my own patch and earned five pounds a week! I then went to the *Hemel Hempstead Evening Echo* and learned layout there. I moved on to the *Evening Standard* as a features sub for four or five years and had a fantastic time. Charles Wintour was the editor, Simon Jenkins was the features editor and Max Hastings the chief features editor. It was a great learning experience working with all of those at the age of twenty-five. I moved to Ireland in 1979 because I was mad-keen on fishing. I was features editor on the *Evening Herald* in Dublin for two or three years, then became deputy editor for ten years. I moved to the *Irish Independent* as assistant day editor, then became features editor in 2000, which is what I'd always wanted to do. (And I still go fishing . . .)

Glossary

agency: organisation supplying news and pictures to newspapers and magazines

anchor: story placed at the bottom of the page to hold it up

B2B: business-to-business publications (*see* trade press)

backgrounder: a feature exploring the issues behind a big news story

bastard measure: any measure that isn't the normal setting

bleed: when a photo extends off the side of a page

blogs: short for web log: a personal, online diary which can be kept private or viewed by anyone

blurb: description of stories within the newspaper or magazine (used to entice people to read on)

box: copy enclosed by rules for emphasis and to separate it from the main text

broadsheet: large-sized newspaper (such as the *Daily Telegraph* and the *Sunday Times*)

byline: the reporter's name on a story

campaigning journalism: a related series of stories taking up a particular cause

caption: text accompanying a picture or graphic

centre spread: the middle two pages in a newspaper

colour piece: a descriptive feature which is likely to contain the journalist's impressions

column: a bylined article, usually appearing weekly or monthly in a publication; or a vertical section of copy on a page

comment piece: an article, generally analytical, where a journalist expresses their own opinions (also known as opinion piece and think piece)

compact: a 'quality' tabloid newspaper (such as the *Independent* and *The Times*)

contacts book: a portable address book containing names and contact details of a journalist's sources

copy: editorial material, such as stories and features

coverlines: the text on the front cover of a magazine drawing attention to the main features inside

cross-head: text (usually one word) placed within the body of a story for design purposes

cut-out: where part of a photograph is cut away for design reasons

cuttings: stories saved from newspapers and magazines; reporters will keep their own cuttings file; publications now have electronic cuttings libraries.

cuttings job: a story put together from the cuttings without first-hand interviews

deadline: time by which copy must be submitted

drop cap: the first letter of a word set larger than the rest which runs down several lines of text (used at the start or partway through a feature as part of the page design)

editorial: the column which expresses the newspaper's view on the day's big stories (*see* leader); or all non-advertising copy in a publication

exclusive: a big story carried first by a publication

fact box: boxed-in list of facts relating to a story

first person piece: a story told directly by the person affected by or involved with it, recounting their own experiences

freelance: a journalist not on the permanent staff of an organisation who contributes to a number of publications

heavies: the serious papers, such as the *Guardian, The Times* and the *Daily Telegraph*

human interest story: a story focusing on personal aspects of a person's life that may be deemed newsworthy

intro: short for introduction (the first paragraph of a story)

inverted pyramid: the traditional way to structure news stories, with the strongest material at the top and the weakest at the bottom

investigative journalism: stories setting out to reveal something (often what someone wants hidden)

leader: the editorial column (*see* editorial)

listings: lists of entertainment events, including venue, times and contact details

mid-market: tabloids such as the *Daily Express* and the *Daily Mail*, which lie in style and appearance between the 'heavies' and the 'red tops'

news feature: topical feature examining an issue in the news

off-beat: unusual story (maybe with a humorous angle)

op ed: short for opposite editorial (the page opposite the leader and usually containing columns and comment pieces)

opinion piece: *see* comment piece

panel: see box

personality piece: *see* profile

pic (plural: pix): abbreviation for picture (usually a photograph)

pitch: a story proposal sent to a newspaper or magazine

profile: a feature focusing on an individual (sometimes known as a personality piece)

pull quote: a short extract from a feature set in larger point size to break up the page as part of the design

Q&A feature: a feature where both the reporter's questions and the interviewee's answers are reproduced

red top: tabloid newspaper such as the *Sun* or the *Mirror*, so-called because the masthead (the paper's titlepiece) is red

reverse: white type printed on a black or tinted background

rule: a line separating or surrounding text

running story: a story that develops over several hours, days or weeks

sans serif: a typeface which has no serifs, such as Helvetica

serif: the strokes on letters in certain typefaces, such as Times Roman

sidebar: a shorter story printed alongside a feature and providing more information or another angle on it

silly season: supposedly the time of year (usually the summer holidays) when there is little hard news around, so stories and features may become trivial

sketch: a light article or column describing an event. Often used in reporting the House of Commons

spoiler: when someone gives away too much of the plot of a book or a film or a play and ruins the surprise for readers or the audience

standfirst: a paragraph at the top of the story (before the intro) that guides the reader into the piece; may contain the writer's byline

strapline: a smaller heading placed over the main headline on a story

sub-deck: a smaller headline underneath the main headline

sub-editor: responsible for editing reporters' copy and writing headlines and captions. Some publications now call them page editors

tabloid: popular newspapers whose size is about half that of a broadsheet, but note some of the 'heavy' papers are now in tabloid format

taster: a production journalist who selects the best stories; or a coverline; or a sample of a story sent as part of a pitch

teaser: a headline or intro that hints at the main angle of the story

think piece: *see* comment piece

thumbnail: a very small picture or extract of text

tip-off: information about a story given to a journalist by a member of the public

titlepiece: the newspaper's name and logo, used at the top of the front page

TOA: abbreviation of triumph over adversity that refers to human interest features where the subject has overcome difficult personal circumstances (also known as TOT – triumph over tragedy)

trade press: magazines aimed at businesses (*see* B2B)

USP: abbreviation of unique selling point, something that makes a new competitor stand out from the rest

Bibliography and further reading

Adams, Sally with Hicks, Wynford (2009) *Interviewing for Journalists*, London: Routledge
Barber, Lynn (1992) *Mostly Men*, London: Penguin
Barber, Lynn (1999) *Demon Barber*, London: Penguin
Davies, Nick (2008) *Flat Earth News*, London: Chatto & Windus
de Burgh, Hugo (ed.) (2008) *Investigative Journalism*, London: Routledge
Evans, Harold (1994) *Good Times, Bad Times*, London: Weidenfeld & Nicolson
Evans, Harold (2000) *Essential English*, London: Pimlico
Friedlander, Edward Jay and Lee, John (2008) *Feature Writing for Newspapers and Magazines*, Boston, MA: Pearson
Frost Chris (2003) *Designing for Newspapers and Magazines*, London: Routledge
Hale, Don (2002) *Town Without Pity*, London: Century
Harcup, Tony (2004) *Journalism Principles and Practice*, London: Sage
Hennessy, Brendan (2006) *Writing Feature Articles*, Oxford: Focal
Hennessy, Val (1990) *A Little Light Friction*, paperback edn, London: Futura
Hicks, Wynford (2006) *English for Journalists*, London: Routledge
Hicks, Wynford with Adams, Sally, Gilbert, Harriett and Holmes, Tom (2008) *Writing for Journalists*, London: Routledge
Hicks, Wynford and Holmes, Tim (2002) *Subediting for Journalists*, London: Routledge
Humphries, Tom (2003) *Laptop Dancing and the Nanny Goat Mambo*, London: Pocket Books
Keeble, Richard (2001) *Ethics for Journalists*, London: Routledge
Keeble, Richard (2005) *The Newspapers Handbook*, London: Routledge
Keeble, Richard (ed.) (2005) *Print Journalism: A Critical Introduction*, London: Routledge
McKay, Jenny (2005) *The Magazines Handbook*, London: Routledge
O'Connor, Joseph (1995) *The Secret Life of the Irish Male*, London: Minerva
Pape, Susan and Featherstone, Susan (2006) *Feature Writing: A Practical Introduction*, London: Sage
Pilger, John (ed.) (2005) *Tell Me No Lies*, London: Vintage
Randall, David (2007) *The Universal Journalist*, London: Pluto
Raphael, A. (1993) *Grotesque Libels*, London: Corgi
Sellers, Leslie (1985) *The Simple Subs Book*, Oxford: Pergamon
Whittaker, Jason (2008) *Magazine Production*, London: Routledge

Index